An Educator's Guide to
THE ROLE OF THE
PRINCIPAL

Eric M. Roher
B.A., M.A., LL.B.

Simon A. Wormwell
B.A., LL.B.

Aurora Professional Press
a division of Canada Law Book Inc.
240 Edward Street, Aurora, Ontario, L4G 3S9

© CANADA LAW BOOK INC., 2000
Printed in Canada

All rights reserved. No part of this book may be reproduced in any form by any photographic, electronic, mechanical or other means, or used in any information storage and retrieval system, without the written permission of the publisher.
The paper used in this publication meets the minimum requirements of American National Standards for Information Sciences — Permanence of Paper for Printed Library Materials, ANSI Z39.48-1992.

Cover Photograph:
Charles Thatcher/Tony Stone Images

Canadian Cataloguing in Publication Data

Roher, Eric M., 1954-
 An educator's guide to the role of the principal

Includes index.
ISBN 0-88804-342-2

1. School principals – Legal status, laws, etc. – Canada. 2. Educational law and legislation – Canada. I. Wormwell, Simon A., 1971-   . II. Title.

KE3850.R63 2000   344.71'07   C00-932288-4
KF4133.R63 2000

*This book is dedicated to our respective spouses
Beth Roher
and
Karen Edge.*

Foreword

The role of the school principal has become dramatically more complex over the past decade. This has occurred on all fronts: school-based management; accountability requirements at all levels; and various education statutes which have compounded the legal reality of what it means to be a principal.

Most legal advice to principals comes in the form of the dry cryptic reading of the education legislation itself, or the carefully crafted bureaucratic policy memoranda of school boards and the Ministry of Education.

Roher and Wormwell's *An Educator's Guide to the Role of the Principal* is the only book of its kind which the principal can turn to for comprehensive, accessible, interesting and helpful advice on virtually every legal matter he or she may face. The principal's role is first placed in its wider context which is to provide passionate, committed leadership for the well-being of all students being served by schools. Every major issue is addressed in both a factual and interpretive manner, including guidelines for action which enable principals to anticipate and therefore pre-empt problems.

Individual chapters focus on negligence and liability, student records, teacher performance, the problem parent, the non-custodial parent, school attendance, managing medication, suspensions and expulsions, and safe schools. The chapters are informative and interesting, no small feat in working through the legal terrain of today's schools.

In the absence of Roher and Wormwell's book, principals have had to learn the hard way. Nothing accelerates the learning curve like being faced with legal action. Unfortunately, the cost of learning this way in both legal and human terms is enormous. What is best about the *Educator's Guide to the Role of the Principal* is that legal learning becomes anticipatory. The principal can come to understand problematic issues in advance and learn to problem-solve at all stages as issues unfold.

In the final analysis, Roher and Wormwell make two major contributions. The first is direct in helping principals become better leaders in all of the domains covered in the book. The second, and more hidden contribution, is perhaps more important in the long run. The more sophisticated principals become about legal matters, the less they will become embroiled in exhausting cases. Thus, the more energy principals will have to do their core leadership work, which is to develop schools in which all students can learn.

Toronto, Ontario
September, 2000

Michael Fullan, Dean
Ontario Institute for Studies in Education,
University of Toronto

Preface

It seems only appropriate that two individuals who spent certain memorable moments in their youth visiting their respective principals' offices should write a book about the role of the principal.

The role of the principal is a tricky subject, given the fact that neither of us have ever worked or served in this capacity. However, over the years, we have provided considerable legal advice to school boards and schools on the statutory duties and responsibilities of principals and teachers, their common law obligations and the application of school board policies. The role of the principal is a subject which, in light of the dramatic changes in the education system across Canada, is critical to ensure leadership and effective management in our schools.

This book began life as an in-service presentation to principals in the Toronto area. It started as an attempt to outline and confirm the duties and responsibilities of both principals and teachers. But we found it evolving, in the process, into an examination of the changing role of the principal. In an Ontario context, the exclusion of principals and vice-principals from teachers' collective bargaining units under Bill 160, the new role and authority of school councils, fewer trustees in each district school board, new duties under the *Safe Schools Act, 2000*, and the new curriculum, among other things, have contributed to this new role.

Recent education reforms have created new relationships and responsibilities for both principals and vice-principals. They have taken on roles which are in the process of being defined and refined throughout Canada. Their new position requires an ability to manage and lead in turbulent times.

The process of writing this book has been a considerable challenge, as no sooner had a chapter been written than the Government of Ontario promptly amended the relevant legislation. As we completed our writing, new legislation was passed in the areas of safe schools and education accountability. It is essential in a book of this nature to draw a "line in the sand" with respect to legislation. At the time of writing, we have attempted to include the relevant legislative changes to date.

As readers will note, this book has a distinct Ontario focus. Given the fact that we are Ontario lawyers, the book reflects our practice. Some of the legislation and common law principles which apply in Ontario are applicable in other provinces. However, where possible, we have tried to set out general principles.

We have been very fortunate to have had the help of dedicated colleagues, friends and professionals who have assisted in the completion of this work. John Warren and Randy Echlin and our colleagues at Borden Ladner Gervais LLP have generously provided us with assistance and support. In addition, we appreciate the backing of our colleagues in the Education Law Group who have provided tremendous assistance with this project. In particular, Carole Hoglund, Michael Fitzgibbon, Robert Weir, Melanie Warner and Ted Murphy have contributed to different aspects of this book and provided extensive feedback. Also, John Morris of the Health Law Group has provided invaluable insight and expertise with respect to Chapter 8, "Managing Medication in Schools".

Further, the book could not have been completed without the assistance and guidance of the many educators with whom we work on a day-to-day basis. In particular, we are grateful to Walter Freel of the Toronto District School Board and Tom Donovan of the Toronto Catholic District School Board who were kind enough to read the manuscript and offer suggestions for improvement.

We sincerely appreciate the support of Michael Fullan, Dean of the Ontario Institute for Studies in Education, in agreeing to write the Foreword for this book. In addition, we wish to thank Rebecca Cutler, Brian Dingle, Debbie Ganesh, Kathryn Kirkpatrick, Danielle Lavallée, Karin MacArthur and Kim Motyl for their research assistance. We are also indebted to our assistants, Holly McWilliams and Ruth Glaysher, who have provided support "beyond the call of duty" throughout the course of this project.

We are grateful to Howard Davidson of Aurora Professional Press, a division of Canada Law Book Inc., who has guided the project for the past two years. We are also indebted to Anne Campbell for her meticulous and conscientious editing of the manuscript.

This book gave us a chance to reflect on a number of important questions. What types of schools are required to succeed in the new economy? How does one create a problem-solving school culture? What is the role of the principal in this changing environment? How do we foster leadership skills among principals and vice-principals? How do we develop a greater awareness of education law issues? We hope that the book which follows, the result of our inquiry, will help readers to answer these questions for themselves.

Toronto, Ontario
September 1, 2000

Eric M. Roher
Simon A. Wormwell

Table of Contents

Foreword v
Preface vii

1 Duties and Responsibilities of Principals 1

Introduction. 1
Life after Bill 160 3
Duties of Principals 15
Duties of Teachers. 20
Voluntary/Required Duties 25
School Councils 27
Labour Relations 30
Human Rights 36
Conclusion 37

2 Negligence and Liability 39

Introduction. 39
Duty of Care 41
Standard of Care 44
Duty to Provide Proper Supervision 52
Duty to Keep School Safe and in Good Repair. 68
Educational Malpractice 71
Reporting the Presence of Communicable Diseases 73
Suggested Measures 74

3 Student Records and Confidentiality 77

Introduction... 77
Ontario Student Record.................................... 78
The OSR in Legal Proceedings 82
Municipal Freedom of Information and Protection of Privacy Act 86
Confidentiality 90

4 Documenting Teacher Performance................. 97

Introduction... 97
A Duty to Evaluate and Document........................... 99
Implementing an Evaluation Policy.......................... 103

5 Dealing with the Problem Parent..................... 113

Introduction... 113
Parental Harassment 114
Developing an Appropriate Response 115
Civil Proceeding 120
Criminal Code... 127
A Parent Protocol 129

6 The Rights of Non-Custodial Parents................ 131

Introduction... 131
Relevant Legislation 132
Role of the School 132
Rights of Non-custodial Parents 134
Student Names 138
Managing School Relationships 140

7 School Attendance...................................... 143

Introduction... 143
Obligation to Attend School 144
Responsibility for Enforcing School Attendance............. 145
Dealing with the Problem of Non-attendance 146
Preventing Attendance Problems 150

Table of Contents xi

8 Managing Medication in Schools 153

Introduction 153
Duty and Standard of Care in Ordinary Circumstances 154
Duty and Standard of Care in an Emergency 160
Assignment to Administer Medication 162
Managing Students with Diabetes 164
Managing Students with Allergies 166
Conclusion 170

9 Suspensions and Expulsions 173

Introduction 173
The Suspension Process 175
The Expulsion Process 182
Procedural Fairness 185
Programs for Suspended and Expelled Students 187
Preventative Steps 187
Summary of Procedure Under Safe Schools Act, 2000 189

10 Safe Schools 193

Introduction 193
What is Violence? 194
Youth Gangs 196
Club Drugs 200
Police Investigations on School Premises 201
Search and Seizure in Schools 204
Dealing with Trespassers 209
Reporting Child Abuse 212
Ontario Safe Schools Act, 2000 214
Creating a Problem-solving School Culture 217

Index 223

1

Duties and Responsibilities of Principals

Mother (calling upstairs in the morning): "*It's time to get up for school.*"
Chris: "*I'm not going to school!*"
Mother: "*Why not?*"
Chris: "*Because everybody at the school hates me – the teachers, the kids, the janitor – they all hate me!*"
Mother: "*You have to go. You're the principal.*"

A recent job notice in the local newspaper reads as follows:
Wanted. A miracle worker who can do more with less, pacify rival groups, endure chronic second guessing, tolerate low levels of support, process large volumes of paper and work double shifts (75 nights a year out). He or she will have carte blanche to motivate, but cannot spend much money, replace any personnel or upset any constituency.[1]

INTRODUCTION

The job of principal has become increasingly complex. Principals are having to balance competing sets of demands. School boundaries have become more and more transparent. The new curriculum, parent and community demands, government policy, changing technology, and staff morale issues have all contributed to a complex school environment.

The role of principals in implementing innovations more often than not consists of being on the receiving end of externally initiated changes. The constant bombardment of new tasks and continual interruptions have kept principals off balance.

---

[1] R. Evans, "Getting Real About Leadership", 29:36 *Education Week* 14 (April 12, 1995).

1

Professor Farson, author of *Management of the Absurd*,[2] advises that there are no easy solutions. He says that "once you find a management technique that works, give it up". He points out that there is no external answer which will substitute for the complex work of changing one's own situation.

Michael Fullan, Dean of the Ontario Institute for Studies in Education, believes that effective teachers craft their own theories of change, consistently testing them against new situations. He says that, in turbulent times, the key test of leadership is not to arrive at early consensus, but to create opportunities for learning out of dissonance.[3] Fullan states that the "new leadership" requires principals to take their schools' accountability to the public: "Successful schools are not only collaborative internally, but they also have the confidence, capacity, and political wisdom to reach out, constantly forming new alliances."[4]

Principals have a critical role to play in leading change in the school as an organization. Researchers have made a distinction between leadership and management, and emphasize that both are essential. Leadership relates to mission, direction and inspiration. Management involves designing and carrying out plans, getting things done and working effectively with people.[5]

Important requirements for leadership involve: (i) articulating a vision; (ii) getting shared ownership; (iii) evolutionary planning; (iv) creating a collaborative school culture; and (v) fostering staff development. Management involves: (i) negotiating demands and resources; and (ii) co-ordinated and persistent problem-solving. It should be recognized that both sets of characteristics are essential and must be blended within the same person or team.[6]

Researchers have attempted to unravel the meaning of problem-solving by attempting to examine how "expert" principals go about solving actual problems. They found that successful principals took action to strengthen their schools' improvement culture. In addition, researchers concluded that effective principals fostered long-term staff development, engaged in direct and frequent communication about cultural norms and values, and shared power and responsibility with others.[7]

Professor Rosenholtz, an expert in education management and governance, points out that an effective principal is a collaborative teacher who makes continuous improvements in the school as an organization. She states:

> Great principals do not pluck their acumen and resourcefulness straight out of the air. In our data, successful schools weren't led by philosopher kings with supreme character and unerring method, but by a steady accumulation of common wisdom

---

[2] R. Farson, *Management of the Absurd* (New York: Simon and Schuster, 1997).
[3] M. Fullan, "Breaking the Bonds of Dependency", *Educational Leadership* (Association for Supervision and Curriculum Development, April, 1998), at p. 8.
[4] *Ibid.*, at p. 9.
[5] M. Fullan, *Successful School Improvement: The Implementation Perspective and Beyond* (Toronto: OISE Press, 1992), at p. 85.
[6] *Ibid.*
[7] *Ibid.*, at p. 86

and hope distilled from vibrant, shared experience both with teacher leaders in schools and colleagues district wide.[8]

The role of the principal is not solely one of implementing innovations in specific classrooms. There is a limit to how much time a principal can spend in individual classrooms. The larger goal is to transform the culture of the school. This points to the centrality of the role of the principal in working with teachers to shape the school as a workplace with shared goals, teacher learning opportunities and teacher commitment, focused on student learning.

As an important part of that role, an effective principal must understand his or her legal rights and responsibilities. It is recognized that principals are educators who uphold the highest standards and principles of the profession. However, in school boards across Canada, principals and vice-principals appear to be taking on new duties and responsibilities. This book has been written to provide guidance in responding to salient issues affecting our schools. The purpose of the book is to provide principals with a more complete understanding of their duties and responsibilities and to assist them in preparing for their changing role. It is intended to provide principals and vice-principals with a legal framework for making effective and prudent day-to-day decisions.

LIFE AFTER BILL 160

In 1997, the Ontario government introduced a comprehensive reform package intended to fundamentally alter the education system. These reforms are set out in the *Fewer School Boards Act, 1997*[9] (Bill 104) and the *Education Quality Improvement Act, 1997*[10] (Bill 160). Bill 104 was proclaimed in force on April 24, 1997. Among other initiatives, it provided for the amalgamation of existing school boards. Bill 160 received Royal Assent on December 8, 1997, though most of its provisions did not come into force until January 1, 1998. While Bill 104 described the framework for educational reform, Bill 160 attempted to introduce some detail into the implementation process. Essentially, Bill 160 gave district school boards the authority to address many of the uncertainties created by Bill 104.[11]

In June, 2000, the Ontario government introduced two new statutes which would change different aspects of the *Education Act*.[12] The *Education Accountability Act, 2000*[13] (Bill 74) contained four major components involving co-instructional activities, class size, instructional time and compliance mechanisms. In addition, the *Safe Schools Act, 2000*[14] (Bill 81) was intended to

---

[8] *Ibid.*
[9] S.O. 1997, c. 3.
[10] S.O. 1997, c. 31.
[11] B.W. Earle, "Restructuring in Education in Ontario" (paper presented at the Insight Conference, Toronto, October 21, 1997).
[12] R.S.O. 1990, c. E.2.
[13] S.O. 2000, c. 11.
[14] S.O. 2000, c. 12.

increase respect and responsibility and to set standards for safe learning and safe teaching in schools. Among other things, it provides that the Minister may establish a provincial Code of Conduct governing the behaviour of people in schools. Bill 81 has added significant new responsibilities to the principal's role and, in particular, has introduced a new statutory regime governing both the suspension and expulsion of students. While reviewing the reform package in detail is beyond the scope of this chapter, some key issues are highlighted to illustrate the intent of the legislation and the extent of its reach.

Overall, the amendments to the *Education Act* over the past three years have created a sea change in the education environment across the province. The changes to the Act involving, among other things, the new authority of school councils, the exclusion of principals and vice-principals from the teachers' collective bargaining units, the changing role of the trustee and new duties in school discipline have, and will continue to, transformed the role of the principal. In dramatically restructuring the education system across Ontario, the provincial government has significantly changed the duties and responsibilities of school principals.

Fewer School Boards Act, 1997

The primary objectives Bill 104 was enacted to accomplish include: a reduction in the number of school boards and trustees; the establishment of the Education Improvement Commission; and the creation of the Education Quality and Accountability Office. At the time Bill 104 came into force, 129 major school boards existed in Ontario. The effect of this legislation was to reduce the number of boards to 72 by January 1, 1998.[15] Notably, Bill 104 created the so-called "mega-board", which consists of "the urban area of the City of Toronto incorporated by the *City of Toronto Act, 1997*".[16] Comprised of the former North York, Scarborough, Etobicoke, Toronto, York and East York boards, the Toronto District School Board is now the largest school board in Canada.

Bill 104 amended the *Education Act* by providing for the establishment of the amalgamated district school boards. The Lieutenant Governor in Council enacted regulations which define each district school board[17] and provide for the number of members on each district school board.[18] In addition, Bill 160 provided a framework within which newly amalgamated district boards would negotiate with teachers' federations towards new collective agreements, replacing the pre-existing agreements.[19]

---

[15] *Establishment and Areas of Jurisdiction of District School Boards*, O. Reg. 185/97.
[16] *Establishment and Areas of Jurisdiction of District School Boards*, s. 3, para. 14.
[17] *Establishment and Areas of Jurisdiction of District School Boards*.
[18] *Representation on District School Boards – 1997 Regular Election*, O. Reg. 250/97.
[19] B. Smeenk, "Education Labour Relations: New Rules and New Players Under Bill 160" (paper presented at the Canadian Bar Association – Ontario 1998 Institute for Continuing Legal Education, Toronto, January 29, 1998).

Across Ontario, school trustees were reduced from 1900 to approximately 700, under Bill 104. Trustee representation ranges from five to twelve for each new district school board, with the exception of the Toronto District School Board, which has 22 trustees. Under the Bill 104 amendments, trustees are expected to provide policy direction and support, rather than participating in the daily management of district school boards. In return for their contributions, district school boards may provide trustees with an honorarium of up to a maximum of $5,000. By reducing the role of trustees, the legislation is intended to permit principals and supervising officers to assume greater responsibility for the direction and management of their schools.

The Education Improvement Commission (the "EIC") was created by Bill 104 for the purpose of overseeing and facilitating the transition period to the new education system. It was given broad powers to monitor the transfer of assets, liabilities and employees to the new school boards, and to ensure the new assets were not unduly diminished in the process. In addition, the EIC was empowered to oversee the actions of school boards in the pre-amalgamation phase.[20] In order to do so effectively, the EIC was given the authority to order school boards to provide reports and information, and to have those orders filed in the Ontario Court (General Division) [now the Ontario Superior Court] and enforced as if they were orders of a court. In addition, the EIC was empowered to appoint an auditor to audit the affairs of a board. While most of the EIC's powers to investigate the financial affairs of boards have been taken over by the Minister,[21] the EIC continues to exist in the capacity of performing research and advisory functions. A further initiative established by Bill 104 was the creation of the Education Quality and Accountability Office (the "EQAO").[22] The mandate of the EQAO includes improving the accountability of schools to parents with respect to their children's academic progress. In particular, the EQAO is committed to improving the evaluation and reporting of student academic achievement, in part, by conducting province-wide testing.

Education Quality Improvement Act, 1997

The primary issues addressed by Bill 160 can be broadly categorized as the funding of education, teacher employment, and collective bargaining and governance. Bill 160 introduced a new model for financing education in Ontario. Traditionally, education has been funded through a combination of property taxes and provincial government grants. Under Bill 160 the provincial government has replaced this method of funding with provincial government grants under a

---

[20] "Ontario Public School Boards' Ass'n et al. v. Ontario (A.G.)" (Borden & Elliot Memorandum to Clients and Other Interested Parties, September, 1997), at p. 1.
[21] This is accomplished through new forms of regulation (*Education Act*, s. 8(1), para. 27.1) and intervention (*Education Act*, Part IX, Division D – Supervision of Boards' Financial Affairs).
[22] The EQAO came into force under the *Education Quality and Accountability Office Act, 1996*, S.O. 1996, c. 11, which was proclaimed in force July 5, 1996.

"fair-funding" model. The government has indicated that such model would attempt to ensure that funding is fair and equitable, by equalizing discrepancies in board revenues through a grant system.[23]

Teachers' employment has been modified, in part, by the newly defined role of school councils, and statutory requirements governing such issues as class size, preparation time and instructional time. Bill 160 defined in more detail the role of school councils (formerly called "advisory school councils"). In particular, the Bill provided school councils with the authority to advise principals on matters related to school discipline, school safety and local initiatives.[24] Across Ontario, district school boards have established a school council for each school operated by the respective boards.

With respect to class size, beginning in the 1998-1999 school year, each district school board had to determine the average class size of the classes in the aggregate as of October 31st. Under Bill 160, maximum class sizes for all school boards in the aggregate was set at 25 for elementary schools and 22 for secondary schools, subject to Ministerial permission to exceed these maximums.[25] The Minister was to review these maximums every three years.

In addition, under Bill 160, classroom teachers, despite any applicable conditions or restrictions in a collective agreement, were assigned "minimum teaching time" during the instructional program for each period of five instructional days during the school year. "Classroom teacher" was defined as a teacher assigned in a regular timetable to provide instruction to pupils, but did not include a principal or vice-principal. It would include department heads.

Minimum teaching time was set at an average of at least 1300 minutes for elementary school teachers and 1250 minutes for secondary school teachers. The calculations for minimum teaching time were to be based on all of the school board's classroom teachers and their assignments (on a regular timetable) on every instructional day during the school year in the aggregate.

School boards were to allocate to each school a share of the school board's aggregate minimum time for the school year. The principal of a school was to then make teaching time allocations "in his or her sole discretion" to enable the principal to adjust teaching assignments (with the possibility of less teaching time for department heads and others with added responsibilities outside the classroom as a result).

Under Bill 160, the *School Boards and Teachers Collective Negotiations Act*[26] was repealed. As a result, collective bargaining between teachers and their

---

[23] Earle, *op. cit.*, footnote 11, at p. 7.
[24] "Bill 160: The Education Quality Improvement Act" (Borden & Elliot Memorandum to Clients and Other Interested Parties, September, 1997).
[25] Under s. 4 of the *Education Accountability Act, 2000*, which received Royal Assent on June 23, 2000, the Ontario Legislature has amended s. 170.1 of the *Education Act* to: set the maximum average size of classes in junior kindergarten, kindergarten and grades 1 to 3 at 24; lower the maximum average size of elementary school classes in the aggregate from 25 to 24.5; and lower the maximum average size of secondary school classes in the aggregate from 22 to 21.
[26] R.S.O. 1990, c. S.2.

respective school boards is now subject to Part X.1 of the *Education Act* and the *Labour Relations Act, 1995*.[27]

Each district school board is now comprised of four fixed bargaining units: elementary teachers (not including occasional teachers); elementary occasional teachers; secondary teachers (not including occasional teachers); and secondary occasional teachers. Of significant importance is the exclusion of principals and vice-principals from the teachers' collective bargaining units.

Principals and vice-principals are no longer subject to existing collective agreements or entitled to partake in collective bargaining. Principals and vice-principals are excluded from the teachers' collective bargaining units along with supervisory officers and instructors in teacher-training institutions by the definition of "Part X.1 teacher". Principals and vice-principals are excluded from the *Labour Relations Act, 1995* by section 3(f) of that Act, so they are unable to be organized by a trade union under that legislation. They are put in the same position as supervisory officers under that Act.

The exclusion of principals and vice-principals from a teachers' bargaining unit resolves any conflict that a principal or vice-principal might have had in fulfilling the statutory duties to direct and manage a school, including teachers within the school, and his or her position as a member of the bargaining unit. Principals and vice-principals must still be qualified teachers and members in good standing of the Ontario College of Teachers, and they are able to perform the duties of a teacher despite the provisions of a collective agreement.[28]

It should be noted that on June 7, 2000, the Ontario Court of Appeal rendered a decision upholding the validity of the portions of the *Education Quality Improvement Act, 1997* excluding principals and vice-principals from teacher bargaining units and statutory membership in the teachers' unions. In *Ontario Teachers' Federation v. Ontario (Attorney General)*,[29] the teachers' unions sought a declaration that the provisions removing principals and vice-principals from teacher bargaining units contravened the freedom of expression and association guaranteed under the *Canadian Charter of Rights and Freedoms*. They alleged that the amendments in Bill 160 were made as a "reprisal" as a result of principal and vice-principal participation in province-wide protests and that this participation was protected under the Charter. The teachers' unions also argued that the amendments infringed the freedom of association guaranteed by the Charter by denying principals and vice-principals statutory membership in the teachers' unions. These arguments initially came before Mr. Justice Southey of the Ontario Court (General Division) who dismissed the application and held that the amendments were not introduced for punitive purposes and that the amendments themselves did not infringe the Charter.

---

[27] S.O. 1995, c. 1, Sch. A.
[28] E.M. Roher and R.W. Weir, "Life Under the Labour Relations Act, 1995", *Education Law News* (Summer, 2000) (Toronto: Borden Ladner Gervais LLP).
[29] (2000), 97 A.C.W.S. (3d) 254 (Ont. C.A.), affg 37 C.C.E.L. (2d) 56 (Gen. Div.).

The Ontario Teachers' Federation and branch affiliates appealed to the Ontario Court of Appeal. Mr. Justice Stephen Goudge, who wrote the judgment of the unanimous court, commenced his reasons by observing that "the fall of 1997 was a time of turmoil for the public education system in Ontario".

The Court of Appeal accepted, without deciding, that the principals and vice-principals were engaging in a protected activity under the Charter when they protested Bill 160. The court then moved on to consider whether the amendments to Bill 160 were a "reprisal" against principals and vice-principals. The court considered the "legislative intent" in making the amendments excluding principals and vice-principals from collective bargaining. The Court of Appeal agreed with the following words of Mr. Justice Southey:[30]

> I accept the argument of the applicants that the participation of the principals and vice-principals was the proximate cause of the amendments to Bill 160. *But for that participation in the strike, the amendments would not have been made. I am satisfied, however, that they were not made for punitive purposes, but for legitimate corrective purposes. They were made, as explained by the Minister in the Legislature, to remove the principals and vice-principals from a position of conflict arising out of their duty to manage the schools and their loyalty to other members of the unions.*

(Emphasis added.) During the strike, principals and vice-principals were faced with the choice of staying to manage the schools or leaving to participate in the protest organized by their unions; most principals chose the latter. The amendments were made to deal with this new "context" which clearly arose during the protest against Bill 160. Accordingly, the "reprisal" argument failed.

The Court of Appeal also went on to dismiss, largely on the basis of earlier authority from the Supreme Court of Canada, the argument by the Ontario Teachers' Federation that the amendments to Bill 160 infringed the freedom of association of principals and vice-principals.

Education Accountability Act, 2000

The *Education Accountability Act, 2000*, which received Royal Assent on June 23, 2000, was designed to make school boards accountable for meeting province-wide standards. The amendments to the *Education Act* under Bill 74 are intended to clarify the standard for instructional time in secondary schools, set lower maximum average class sizes at both the elementary and secondary school levels and ensure that school boards meet province-wide quality standards in areas such as class size, curriculum and special education.

Secondary School Teaching Time

Bill 74 maintains the current standard for secondary school teaching time of an average of 1250 minutes of instructional time per teacher per five instructional days, but modifies the way it is measured and expressed to an average of at least

---

[30] *Supra*, at p. 65.

6.67 eligible courses in the day school program during the school year. Eligible courses are defined as a credit course or a credit-equivalent course.[31] The school board will allocate to each secondary school a share of the board's aggregate minimum eligible course obligations. The secondary school principal, in his or her sole discretion, will allocate the school's share of the board's obligations amongst the classroom teachers in the school.[32]

The principal is required to make the allocation in accordance with any policies that the school board may establish. Bill 74 provides that this plan applies regardless of any conditions or restrictions in a collective agreement.[33]

Under Bill 74, the Minister may require school boards to submit their plans for complying in respect of any school year and to report on any matter related to compliance.[34] Moreover, the Minister may give such directions as she or he considers appropriate respecting the form, content and deadline for submission of a plan or report and the board is required to comply with those directions.[35] Where the Minister has concerns that the plans submitted may not result in compliance with the requirements, the Minister may direct the board to alter the plans in the manner directed, and the board is required to make the alteration and implement the plan as altered.[36]

Class Size

The Bill 74 amendments also lower the average class sizes in both elementary and secondary schools. Each school board must now ensure that the average size of its elementary school classes in the primary division, in aggregate, will not exceed 24 students, and that the average class size of all elementary classes (junior kindergarten through grade 8), in aggregate, will not exceed 24.5 students.[37] In addition, the maximum average size of secondary school classes for a board, in aggregate, is reduced from 22 to 21 students.[38]

Co-instructional Activities

Under Bill 74, "co-instructional activities" are defined as those activities other than providing instruction which support the operation of schools, enrich students' school-related experience or advance students' education. This includes participation in school-related sports, arts and cultural activities, parent-teacher and student-teacher interviews, letters of support for pupils, staff meetings and school functions.

Under Bill 74, the school board would have the exclusive right to determine how co-instructional activities would be provided. No matter relating to

---

[31] *Education Act*, s. 170.2.1(1) and (2).
[32] *Education Act*, s. 170.2.1(4).
[33] *Education Act*, s. 170.2.1(5) and (6).
[34] *Education Act*, s. 170.2.1(12).
[35] *Education Act*, s. 170.2.1(14).
[36] *Education Act*, s. 170.2.1(15).
[37] *Education Act*, s. 170.1(1) and (2).
[38] *Education Act*, s. 170.1(3).

co-instructional activities would be the subject of collective bargaining or come within the jurisdiction of an arbitrator or arbitration board.

It should be noted that, due to concerns raised by the labour movement and others, the provincial government decided not to proclaim in force those sections of Bill 74 dealing with co-instructional activities. In June, 2000, the Minister of Education, Janet Ecker, indicated that the government would not proclaim these sections in force, unless teachers' unions used this as a bargaining chip and started to withdraw from these activities. The Minister indicated that the sections remain in the legislation as "an insurance policy for our students".[39]

Under the legislation, if proclaimed, school boards would be required to develop and implement a plan to provide for co-instructional activities in their schools each year. In the event the legislation is proclaimed, the plan for the provision of co-instructional activities would be required to include a framework within which principals will operate in assigning duties to teachers. The framework would address the assignment of duties on school days and non-school days, during parts of the school day when instruction is delivered and parts when it is not delivered, and on school premises and elsewhere.

Under the legislation, if proclaimed, the principal, in accordance with the board plan would be required to develop and implement a school plan to provide co-instructional activities. A plan and an assignment could be made despite any applicable conditions or restrictions in a collective agreement. A teacher would be required to participate in the provision of co-instructional activities, in such manner and at such time as the principal directs. The principal would be required to consult the school council at least once in each school year respecting the school plan providing for co-instructional activities.

Compliance

Under the Bill 74 amendments to the *Education Act*, the Minister is able to direct an investigation of the affairs of a school board if the Minister has concerns that the board may not be in compliance with:

- curriculum requirements;
- co-instructional activities requirements;
- class size requirements;
- teaching time requirements;
- trustee honorarium or trustee expense requirements; or
- the requirements set out for the application of funds under the grant regulations.[40]

Under Bill 74, a complaint alleging non-compliance could be made by the school council of a school governed by the board, or by supporters of the board on any of the grounds listed. Upon receipt of a complaint, the Minister may direct an

---

[39] "*Education Accountability Act* means better school experience for students", News Release (Ministry of Education, June 20, 2000).
[40] *Education Act*, s. 230.

Duties and Responsibilities of Principals 11

investigation or provide a written response to the complaint setting out the reasons for not directing an investigation.[41]

Where the Minister directs an investigation, she or he may appoint as an investigator an employee in the Ministry or any other person. In appointing the investigator, the Minister is to specify, in writing, the nature of the possible non-compliance. The investigator may then investigate any of the affairs of the board that in his or her opinion relate to the kind of non-compliance specified by the Minister.[42]

On completion of an investigation, the investigator will report in writing to the Minister who will transmit a copy of the report to the secretary of the board. If the Minister were to find that the report disclosed evidence of non-compliance or evidence that non-compliance would likely result, the Minister could give any directions to the board that she or he considered advisable to address the non-compliance.[43]

Under the Bill 74 amendments, if the Minister was of the opinion that the board had failed to comply with a direction, the Lieutenant Governor in Council could make any order she or he considered necessary or advisable to vest in the Ministry control and charge over the administration of the affairs of the board. Where an order was made, the Minister would have control and charge over the board generally with respect to any matter in any way affecting the board's affairs.[44] The Minister would have control and charge over the exercise and performance by the board of its powers, duties and obligations. This would continue until the school board was in compliance.

Safe Schools Act, 2000

The Ontario government's *Safe Schools Act, 2000*, which is intended to promote respect, responsibility and civility in Ontario schools, received Royal Assent on June 23, 2000.[45] Bill 81 introduces the provincial Code of Conduct, which sets out provincial standards of behaviour. It specifies mandatory consequences for students who do not comply with these standards.

The provincial standards of behaviour apply not only to students, but also to all individuals involved in the publicly funded school system, including parents or guardians, volunteers, teachers and other staff members, whether they are on school property, on school buses or at school-authorized events or activities.

---

[41] *Education Act*, s. 230.1(4) and (5).
[42] *Education Act*, s. 230.2(1) to (4).
[43] *Education Act*, s. 230.2(7) and 230.3(1).
[44] *Education Act*, s. 230.3(2).
[45] At the time of writing, ss. 306 to 311 of the *Education Act*, as enacted by Bill 81, were not in force but were expected to be proclaimed during the 2000-2001 and 2001-2002 school years.

Bill 81 introduces sweeping changes to student discipline in Ontario schools.[46] In addition to giving authority to the new Code of Conduct, Bill 81 contains a range of fundamental changes, including the following:

- Teachers are given the authority to suspend students for one day.
- School principals are given the authority to expel students from their school for up to one school year.
- Parents or guardians have the right to request a review and/or an appeal of an expulsion.
- Mandatory requirements may now be set for students who have been expelled to attend strict discipline or equivalent programs in order to re-enter the school system.
- School boards may be required to provide programs for suspended students.
- The board may establish policies and guidelines respecting appropriate dress for students in schools.
- The opening or closing exercises in schools must include the singing of *O Canada*, and may include the recitation of a pledge of citizenship.

Under the Bill 81 amendments, it is mandatory that a student be suspended from his or her school and from engaging in all school-related activities if the student commits any of certain listed infractions while he or she is at school or is engaged in a school-related activity, including: uttering a threat to inflict serious bodily harm on another person; being under the influence of alcohol; swearing at a teacher or at another person in a position of authority; or committing an act of vandalism which causes extensive damage to school property at the pupil's school.[47]

The minimum duration of a mandatory suspension is one school day and the maximum duration is 20 school days.[48] The minimum and maximum duration may be varied by regulation.

The Bill 81 amendments provide that, if a teacher observes a student committing an infraction which requires a mandatory suspension, the teacher will suspend the student or refer the matter to the principal.[49] The principal has a duty to suspend a student who commits an infraction requiring mandatory suspension, unless a teacher has already suspended the student for the infraction. Despite the requirements set out in Bill 81, there are mitigating factors which may be considered and suspension of a student is not mandatory in such circumstances as may be prescribed by regulation.[50]

A teacher cannot suspend a student for a period of longer than one day. In the event that a teacher who suspends a student is of the opinion that a longer suspension is warranted, the teacher may recommend to the principal that the

---

[46] "Legislature passes *Safe Schools Act*", News Release (Ministry of Education, June 14, 2000).
[47] *Education Act*, s. 306(1).
[48] *Education Act*, s. 306(2).
[49] *Education Act*, s. 306(3).
[50] *Education Act*, s. 306(4) and (5).

suspension be extended. Upon receiving a recommendation from a teacher, the principal may extend the suspension to up to 20 days.[51]

Decisions to suspend a student are subject to review and appeal. However, Bill 81 provides that a decision to suspend a student for one day or less cannot be reviewed or appealed.[52]

Under the Bill 81 amendments to the *Education Act*, expulsions will be mandatory for certain prescribed conduct, such as possessing a weapon, committing sexual assault or trafficking in weapons or illegal drugs.[53] For mandatory expulsions, a principal is required either to conduct an inquiry or refer the matter to the school board for an expulsion hearing. If the principal conducts an inquiry and is satisfied that the student committed the infraction, the principal may impose a "limited expulsion" or refer the matter to the school board for a hearing.[54] A limited expulsion is one in which the principal or the school board specifies a date on which the student may return to school (which cannot be more than one year after the date on which the principal suspended the student) or the student meets the requirements for readmission as established by a school board.

Two categories of expulsion are created: "limited expulsion" from a particular school; and "full expulsion" from all schools in the province.[55] When considering the type and duration of expulsion which may be appropriate in particular circumstances, the principal or school board is required to consider the student's history and such other factors as may be prescribed by regulation.[56]

The Bill 81 amendments also provide for discretionary expulsions. In this regard, a student may be expelled if the student engages in an activity which, under a policy of the school board, is one for which expulsion is discretionary.[57] It should also be noted that, under the provisions of Bill 81, decisions to expel a student are subject to appeal.[58]

Changing Role of the Principal

The recent amendments to the *Education Act* have significantly changed the duties and responsibilities of a number of key players in the education system. For example, teachers' employment has been modified, in part, by the statutory requirements governing such issues as class size, preparation time and instructional time. And the principal and vice-principal have emerged with relatively new roles under the revised Ontario regime.

---

[51] *Education Act*, s. 306(6) to (8).
[52] *Education Act*, s. 308.
[53] *Education Act*, s. 309(1).
[54] *Education Act*, s. 309(7).
[55] *Education Act*, s. 309(16).
[56] *Education Act*, s. 309(19).
[57] *Education Act*, s. 310(1).
[58] *Education Act*, s. 311.

The principal and vice-principal are taking on roles which are still in the process of being defined and refined throughout the province. Changes which have contributed to these new roles include:

- fewer trustees in each district school board;
- the new role and authority of school councils;
- exclusion from the teachers' collective bargaining units;
- new duties and responsibilities under the *Safe Schools Act, 2000*; and
- an enhanced role as member of the school board management team.

The new position of principal and vice-principal requires an ability to manage and lead in "turbulent times". It is a role with enhanced responsibilities as senior administrator, team leader and statesperson.[59]

Recent education reforms have created new relationships and demands on principals and vice-principals. Bill 160 has caused a fundamental change in the legal employment relationship between a school board and its administrators from one of management and union to one of master and servant. Principals and vice-principals are now clearly members of management and are no longer with their colleagues in the teachers' collective bargaining process.

In this regard, there has been a "cultural shift" in the education community.[60] It is essential that principals, vice-principals, teachers and senior administrators develop a new understanding of each other's roles.[61]

Across the province, in recent years, there has been conflict with teachers on a range of issues. Principals and vice-principals have become targets outside the collegial environment of their old bargaining units. They are on the front line in dealing with and responding to complaints and concerns from teachers, students and parents. Principals and vice-principals are the "critical link" between senior school board administration and teachers, students and parents.[62]

In his book, *Managing in Turbulent Times*,[63] management guru Peter Drucker states that, in turbulent times, an enterprise has to be managed to avail itself of unexpected opportunities. Drucker points out that both businesses and public service institutions should have strategies for tomorrow which anticipate the areas in which the greatest changes are likely to occur, and which enable them to take advantage of the unforeseen. Drucker says that "planning tries to optimize tomorrow the trends of today".[64]

---

[59] E.M. Roher, "Managing in Turbulent Times", *CAPSLE Comments* (September, 1998), Vol. 8, Issue 1, p. 2.

[60] J. Judson and K. Tranquilli, "The Changing Role of the Principal: Life After Bill 160", in W.F. Foster and W.J. Smith, eds., *Focusing on the Future: Seeking Legal and Policy Solutions in Education* (Georgetown: Canadian Association for the Practical Study of Law in Education, 2000), p. 257.

[61] *Ibid.*, at p. 258.

[62] *Ibid.*

[63] P. Drucker, *Managing in Turbulent Times* (New York: Harper & Row Publishers, 1980), at p. 61.

[64] *Ibid.*, at p. 61.

Drucker emphasizes that every institution needs to think strategically about what its business is doing and what it should be doing. In an education context, schools should think through what their students need. What is "value" for our students? What are our schools' strengths? Are they the right strengths given their specific objectives and goals? Are they the strengths which fit the opportunities of tomorrow, or are they strengths which fitted those of yesterday? Are we developing strengths where the opportunities are? And, finally, what additional strengths do we have to acquire? Are they deployed where they will produce results?[65]

To assist principals and vice-principals in their changing roles, they should be given the support and resources necessary to help them make the transition to being a team leader and manager. In particular, school boards should provide leadership training and management in-service programs. The fine line to be walked is that of making principals and vice-principals a part of the management team without unduly affecting collegiality in the schools.

Additional support may be provided to principals by professional associations, such as the Ontario Principals' Council, the Catholic Principals' Council of Ontario or the Association des directeurs franco-ontariens (the French-language association of principals and vice-principals). These associations were established to represent and assist principals and vice-principals regarding the terms and conditions of their employment. These organizations also provide professional and legal services to their members and from time to time they consult with the Ministry of Education to assist in the development of sound educational policies and reforms.

DUTIES OF PRINCIPALS

Principals are responsible for the organization and management of individual schools as well as the quality of instruction in those schools. While the principal is the chief administrator within a school, with responsibilities towards parents, students and staff, the principal is also an educator. Under the *Education Act*, the principal is imbued with all the duties of a teacher as well as the additional duties of a principal. The two roles complement each other.[66]

It is crucial that all principals have a sound understanding of their prescribed statutory duties. Not only is such an understanding necessary to fulfil these duties but it is vital in ensuring that the principal fulfils his or her role in maintaining proper order and discipline in the school. Principals should also be familiar with the statutory duties of teachers. A good understanding of these duties and feeling comfortable with them will provide the solid foundation necessary for the principal to effectively carry out his or her responsibilities and enhance the principal's leadership in the school.

---

[65] *Ibid.*, at p. 65.
[66] Toronto Catholic District School Board, "Duties and Responsibilities of Teachers and Principals" (Toronto: January, 2000), at p. 3.

Statutory Duties

The *Education Act* prescribes specific duties of a principal. Section 265(a) provides that it is the duty of a principal of a school, in addition to the principal's duties as a teacher, to maintain proper order and discipline in the school. Under section 265(b), the principal has a duty to develop co-operation and co-ordination of effort among the members of the staff at the school.

Regulation 298[67] creates additional duties and, to a certain extent, reinforces the duties found in the *Education Act*. Under section 11 of the regulation, the principal, subject to the authority of the appropriate supervisory officer, is in charge of the organization and management of the school. Under section 11(3)(a), a principal has a duty to supervise instruction in the school and advise and assist any teacher in co-operation with the teacher in charge of the organizational unit or program.

Staff Relations

The principal is prescribed specific duties with respect to the administration of staff and staff relations under the *Education Act*. These duties include the following:

- to allocate, in accordance with the policies of the board, among the classroom teachers in the school the school's share of the board's aggregate minimum instructional time for the school year;[68]
- to determine the work to be done by teachers during the five working days preceding the start of the school year;[69]
- to require teachers to maintain proper order and discipline in the classroom and while on duty in the school and on the school grounds;[70]
- to develop co-operation and co-ordination of effort among the members of the staff of the school;[71]
- to prepare a timetable, conduct the school according to such timetable and the school year calendar or calendars applicable thereto, make the calendar or calendars and the timetable accessible to the pupils, teachers and supervisory officers and assign classes and subjects to the teachers;[72]
- to supervise the instruction in the school and advise and assist any teacher in co-operation with the teacher in charge of the organizational unit or program;[73]
- to assign duties to vice-principals and teachers in charge of organizational units or programs;[74]

---

[67] *Operation of Schools – General*, R.R.O. 1990, Reg. 298.
[68] *Education Act*, s. 170.2(4) and (5).
[69] *Education Act*, s. 171(3).
[70] *Education Act*, s. 264(1)(e).
[71] *Education Act*, s. 265(b).
[72] *Education Act,* s. 265(e).
[73] Regulation 298, s. 11(3)(a).
[74] Regulation 298, s. 11(3)(b).

- to provide for the supervision of students for the period of time during each school day when the school buildings and playgrounds are open to students;[75]
- to provide for the supervision of and the conducting of any school activity authorized by the board;[76]
- where performance appraisals of members of the teaching staff are required under a collective agreement or policy of the board, despite anything to the contrary in such collective agreement or board policy, to conduct performance appraisals of members of the teaching staff;[77]
- subject to the provisions of the board's policy or the provisions of a collective agreement, as the case may be, in respect of reporting requirements for performance appraisals, to report thereon in writing to the board or the supervising officer on request and give to each teacher so appraised a copy of the teacher's performance appraisal;[78]
- to make recommendations to the board with respect to the appointment and promotion of teachers and the demotion or dismissal of teachers whose work or attitude is unsatisfactory;[79]
- to provide for the instruction of pupils in the care of the school premises;[80] and
- to warn a teacher in writing, giving the teacher assistance and allowing the teacher a reasonable time to improve before recommending demotion or dismissal.[81]

Because the principal is responsible for the organization and management of the school, the principal shall require teachers to perform their duties under the *Education Act* and the regulations.[82] Under section 20 of Regulation 298, a teacher shall:

- be responsible for the effective instruction, training and evaluation of the progress of students in the subjects assigned to the teacher and for the management of the class or classes, and report to the principal on the progress of pupils on request;
- carry out supervisory duties and the instructional program as assigned by the principal and supply information regarding supervisory duties or instructional programs;
- co-operate fully in all matters related to the instruction of students if appointed to be in charge of an organizational unit or as a co-ordinator;

---

[75] Regulation 298, s. 11(3)(e).
[76] Regulation 298, s. 11(3)(f).
[77] Regulation 298, s. 11(3)(g).
[78] Regulation 298, s. 11(3)(h).
[79] Regulation 298, s. 11(3)(j).
[80] Regulation 298, s. 11(3)(k).
[81] Regulation 298, s. 11(4).
[82] *Education Act*, s. 264; Regulation 298, s. 20.

- be present in the classroom and ensure that the classroom is ready at least 15 minutes before the commencement of classes in the morning, where applicable, and five minutes before the commencement of classes in the afternoon, unless otherwise assigned;
- assist the principal in maintaining close co-operation with the community;
- prepare for use in the teacher's class such teaching plans and outlines as are required by the principal and the appropriate supervisory officer, and submit the plans and outlines to the principal or the supervising officer, on request;
- ensure that all reasonable safety procedures are carried out in courses and activities for which the teacher is responsible; and
- co-operate with the principal and other teachers to establish and maintain consistent disciplinary practices in the school.

In fulfilling his or her statutory duties with respect to staff relations, a principal is supported by the fact that many duties of a principal have a direct corollary in the duties of a teacher. As discussed in greater detail below, a teacher must comply with his or her statutory duties. Moreover, the statutory duties of a teacher are paramount to any rights or responsibilities created by collective agreement. Section 277.13 of the *Education Act* provides that: "In case of conflict, this Act and regulations made under it prevail over the provisions of a collective agreement." Accordingly, in fulfilling their various organizational and administrative duties and responsibilities, principals must consider the *Education Act* and regulations a primary source of authority and direction.

Delegation of Duties to Vice-principal

In addition to assigning various prescribed duties to teachers, a principal is responsible for assigning duties to a vice-principal. Pursuant to section 12 of Regulation 298, a vice-principal shall perform such duties as are assigned by the principal. In the principal's absence, a vice-principal shall be in charge of the school and shall perform the duties of the principal.

Additional Duties under the Education Act

In addition to those duties already outlined, section 265 of the *Education Act* establishes the following duties of a principal:

- to maintain proper order and discipline;
- to register the pupils and ensure that the attendance of pupils for every school day is recorded either in the register supplied by the Minister in accordance with the instructions contained therein or in such other manner as is approved by the Minister;
- in accordance with the *Education Act*, the regulations and the guidelines issued by the Minister, to collect information for inclusion in a record in

respect of each pupil enrolled in the school and to establish, maintain, retain, transfer and dispose of the record;
- to hold, subject to the approval of the appropriate supervisory officer, such examinations as the principal considers necessary for the promotion of pupils or for any other purpose and report as required by the board the progress of the pupil to his or her parent or guardian where the pupil is a minor and otherwise to the pupil;
- subject to revision by the appropriate supervisory officer, to promote such pupils as the principal considers proper and issue to each such pupil a statement thereof;
- to ensure that all textbooks used by the pupils are those approved by the board and, in the case of subject areas for which the Minister approves textbooks, those approved by the Minister;
- to furnish the Ministry and the appropriate supervisory officer with any information that it may be in the principal's power to give respecting the condition of the school premises, the discipline of the school, the progress of pupils and any other matter affecting the interests of the school, and to prepare such reports for the board as are required by the board;
- to give assiduous attention to the health and comfort of pupils, the cleanliness, temperature and ventilation of the school, the care of all teaching materials and other school property, and the condition and appearance of the school buildings and grounds;
- to report promptly to the board and to the medical officer of health when the principal has reason to suspect the existence of any communicable disease in the school and any unsanitary condition in any part of the school building or the school grounds;
- to refuse admission to the school to any person whom the principal believes is infected with or exposed to communicable diseases requiring an order under section 22 of the *Health Protection and Promotion Act*[83] until furnished with a certificate of a medical officer of health or a legally qualified medical practitioner approved by the medical officer of health stating that all danger from exposure to contact with such person has passed;
- subject to an appeal to the board, to refuse to admit to the school or classroom a person whose presence would in the principal's judgment be detrimental to the physical or mental well-being of the pupils; and
- to maintain a visitor's book in the school when so determined by the board.

---

[83] R.S.O. 1990, c. H.7.

DUTIES OF TEACHERS

The various statutory duties of teachers reinforce the central role that teachers play in the development and education of students. Teaching deals with the instruction of students on behalf of society, requiring the services of those who have received specialized preparation both in the content of human knowledge and the ways in which learning takes place. Teachers are dedicated to engaging and supporting student learning. Teachers are consistently concerned with developing critical thinking on the part of their students and attitudes and ideas which will assist students in personal growth. They demonstrate care and commitment to students and assist them in becoming life-long learners.

The Education Act

Section 264 of the *Education Act* establishes statutory duties for teachers. In part, section 264 provides:

> 264(1) It is the duty of a teacher and a temporary teacher,
> (a) to teach diligently and faithfully the classes or subjects assigned to the teacher by the principal;
> (b) to encourage the pupils in the pursuit of learning;
> (c) to inculcate by precept and example respect for religion and the principles of Judaeo-Christian morality and the highest regard for truth, justice, loyalty, love of country, humanity, benevolence, sobriety, industry, frugality, purity, temperance and all other virtues;
> (d) to assist in developing co-operation and co-ordination of effort among the members of the staff of the school;
> (e) to maintain, under the direction of the principal, proper order and discipline in the teacher's classroom and while on duty in the school and on the school ground;
>
> . . . . .
>
> (g) to conduct the teacher's class in accordance with a timetable which shall be accessible to pupils and to the principal and supervisory officers;
> (h) to participate in professional activity days as designated by the board under the regulations;
> (i) to notify such person as is designated by the board if the teacher is to be absent from school and the reason therefor;
> (j) to deliver the register, the school key and other school property in the teacher's possession to the board on demand, or when the teacher's agreement with the board has expired, or when for any reason the teacher's employment has ceased;

Additional duties are found in Regulation 298. Section 20 of the regulation establishes duties which further reinforce the obligations and responsibilities that teachers have to create a positive and supportive learning environment and to co-operate with the principal in fulfilling this role. Section 20, in part, provides:

> 20. In addition to the duties assigned to the teacher under the Act and by the board, a teacher shall,

(a) be responsible for effective instruction, training and evaluation of the progress of pupils in the subjects assigned to the teacher and for the management of the class or classes, and report to the principal on the progress of pupils on request;

. . . . .

(e) assist the principal in maintaining close co-operation with the community;

. . . . .

(h) co-operate with the principal and other teachers to establish and maintain consistent disciplinary practices in the school.

The Teaching Profession Act

The *Teaching Profession Act*[84] establishes the Ontario Teachers' Federation. The objects of the Federation include the promotion and advancement of the cause of education, raising the status of the teaching profession, the promotion and advancement of the interests of teachers, securing conditions which will make possible the best professional service and increasing interest in educational affairs.[85] Every teacher is required to be a member of the Federation and to co-operate with the Federation to promote the welfare of the organization.[86]

All members have the general duty under the regulations to "strive at all times to achieve and maintain the highest degree of professional competence and to uphold the honour, dignity, and ethical standards of the teaching profession".[87]

A member is charged with specific duties to students, including:

- to effectively educate his or her students and maintain a high degree of professional competence in his or her teaching;
- to endeavour to develop in his or her students an appreciation of standards of excellence and the principles of democracy;
- to show consistent justice and consideration in all of his or her relations with pupils;
- to refuse to divulge beyond his or her proper duty confidential information about students; and
- to concern himself or herself with the welfare of his or her students while they are under his of her care.[88]

---

[84] R.S.O. 1990, c. T.2.
[85] *Teaching Profession Act*, s. 3.
[86] *Teaching Profession Act*, s. 4.
[87] Regulation made under the *Teaching Profession Act*, s. 13. (Section 1 of the *Regulations Act*, R.S.O. 1990, c. R.21, expressly excludes regulations made pursuant to the *Teaching Profession Act* from the application of the *Regulations Act* and, as such, they are not required to be published in *The Ontario Gazette*. Accordingly, the Regulation made under the *Teaching Profession Act* does not have a conventional numerical citation.)
[88] Regulation made under the *Teaching Profession Act*, s. 14.

Additionally, members are required to comply with the statutes and regulations administered by the Ministry of Education, including the *Education Act* and the *Ontario College of Teachers Act, 1996*.[89]

The Ontario College of Teachers Act, 1996

The *Ontario College of Teachers Act, 1996* establishes the Ontario College of Teachers.[90] The College has authority over the professional growth and responsibilities of teachers. Among other things, the College is responsible for regulating the profession of teaching and maintaining qualifications for membership in the College.[91] It is important to note that not only teachers but principals, vice principals and supervisory officers are subject to the provisions of this Act.

A teacher may be disciplined by the College for acts of professional misconduct. Failure to comply with the *Education Act* is expressly defined as an act of professional misconduct.

The College has established Standards of Practice for the teaching profession.[92] The Standards of Practice focus on the responsibility of the teaching profession to enhance student learning. The Standards of Practice are evidenced by five key elements:

- commitment to students and student learning;
- professional knowledge;
- teaching practice;
- leadership and community; and
- ongoing professional learning.

The Standards of Practice affirm that teachers demonstrate care for and commitment to students and are dedicated to engaging and supporting student learning.[93] The Standards of Practice recognize that teachers are educational and community leaders who, through collaboration with colleagues, parents and other members of the community, enhance school programs and student learning. The Standards of Practice require teachers to demonstrate care and commitment to students, to provide support for student learning, to cultivate respect for diversity and equitable treatment in their students, and to encourage their students to grow as individuals and to become contributing members of society and life-long learners.

The Standards of Practice also recognize that teachers must carry out their duties as outlined in the legislation. Failure to comply with the duties set out in the

---

[89] S.O. 1996, c. 12.
[90] *Ontario College of Teachers Act, 1996*, s. 2(1).
[91] *Ontario College of Teachers Act, 1996*, s. 3(1).
[92] "Standards of Practice for the Teaching Profession" (Toronto: Ontario College of Teachers, 2000), at p. 1.
[93] *Ibid.*, at p. 7.

Education Act or with the Standards of Practice may constitute professional misconduct.

Professional Responsibilities

A teacher is responsible for the effective instruction, training and evaluation of the progress of pupils in the subjects assigned to that teacher. The teacher is also responsible for the management of the class and for reporting to the principal on the progress of pupils on request.[94] It is also the duty of a teacher to assist in developing co-operation and co-ordination of effort among the members of the staff of the school.[95] In terms of carrying out these professional responsibilities the *Education Act* creates a minimum school year, establishes the parameters of the instructional day and sets out the minimum number of minutes of instruction in a school week. In this regard, there are no statutory limits on the hours of work for teachers or the length of the school day.

The School Year

Regulation 304 establishes the school year.[96] The school year must fall between September 1st and June 30th and must consist of a minimum of 194 school days. Of those 194 school days, four days may be designated as professional development days while the remainder are to be instructional days.[97]

Regulation 304 provides a general framework for the establishment of the school year. Above the statutory minimum of 194 school days, school boards and unions are free to negotiate a limitation on the number of days on which teachers can be assigned duties. Absent express limitations in a collective agreement, school boards have the power to assign duties within the school year in excess of 194 days.

Additionally, a school board is expressly empowered to require teachers to report to work prior to the commencement of the school year. Section 171(2) of the *Education Act* provides that: "A board may require teachers to work during some or all of the five working days preceding the start of the school year."

The School Day

As with the school year, there is no limit on the length of the working day under the *Education Act*. Regulation 298 provides some limits on the scheduling of the instructional program within a school day.[98] With respect to daily instruction, Regulation 298 specifically provides that:

- The instructional program, exclusive of scheduled breaks between classes, must be a minimum of five hours per school day.

---

[94] Regulation 298, s. 20(a).
[95] *Education Act*, s. 264(1)(d).
[96] *School Calendar Year*, R.R.O. 1990, Reg. 304.
[97] Regulation 304, s. 2(3.1).
[98] Regulation 298, s. 3.

- The school day must fall between 8:00 a.m. and 5:00 p.m.
- The school day must include a scheduled interval for lunch of not less than 40 minutes.

Regulation 298 also requires that teachers be present in the classroom and ensure that the classroom is ready for students at least 15 minutes before the commencement of classes in the school in the morning and, where applicable, five minutes before the commencement of classes in the afternoon.[99] This statutory requirement may only be opted out of where the principal has assigned the teacher to other duties during the designated periods. Under Regulation 304, teachers are required to be in the school during regular school hours on examination days unless a school board directs otherwise.[100]

The instruction of students must take place within the prescribed hours. However, additional duties may be assigned by the principal outside of the instructional period in the school day.

Hours of Instruction

Section 170.2 of the *Education Act* establishes the minimum teaching minutes for classroom teachers in elementary schools. A classroom teacher is one who is assigned in a regular timetable to provide instruction to students and includes a temporary teacher who is assigned in a regular timetable to provide instruction, but does not include a principal or a vice-principal.

Section 170.2(2) mandates that every school board is to ensure that, in the aggregate, its classroom teachers in elementary schools are assigned to provide instruction to students for an average of at least 1300 minutes (during the instructional program) for each period of five instructional days during the school year. As with the 194-day school year, this represents a minimum amount of instructional time.

The allocation of instructional time within an elementary school is also prescribed by the *Education Act*. Section 170.2(4) and (5) sets out the method by which school boards and principals are to assign time during which teachers must provide instruction.

In this regard, a school board will allocate to each elementary school a share of the board's aggregate minimum time for a school year for all of its classroom teachers (during which they must be assigned to provide instruction to students). The principal of an elementary school, in his or her sole discretion, will allocate, among the classroom teachers in the school, the school's share of the board's aggregate minimum time for the school year.

In a secondary school context, minimum teaching time is calculated differently. Section 170.2.1(1) of the *Education Act* provides that, in a secondary school setting, a classroom teacher is one who is assigned in a regular timetable to provide instruction in an "eligible course" to students and includes a temporary teacher

---

[99] Regulation 298, s. 20(d).
[100] Regulation 304, s. 3(4).

who is assigned in a regular timetable to provide instruction in an eligible course to students, but does not include a principal or a vice-principal. "Eligible course" is defined as a credit course or a credit-equivalent course.

Section 170.2.1(2) of the Act mandates that every school board is to ensure that, in the aggregate, its classroom teachers in secondary schools are assigned to provide instruction to students in an average of at least 6.67 eligible courses in a day school program during the school year.

The allocation of instructional time within a secondary school is also prescribed by the *Education Act*. Section 170.2.1(3) provides that a school board will allocate to each secondary school a share of the board's aggregate minimum eligible course obligations for a school year for all its classroom teachers. Under section 170.2.1(4), the principal of the secondary school, in his or her sole discretion, will allocate, among the classroom teachers in the school, the school's share of the board's aggregate minimum obligations for the school year.

The *Education Act* specifically provides that the allocation of minimum eligible course obligations both to the schools and by the principal may be made despite any conditions or restrictions in a collective agreement. In this regard, the Act confirms that the requirements set out in the statute are paramount to any rights or responsibilities created by a collective agreement.

In addition, the Act provides that the school board may establish policies with respect to the allocation of the board's aggregate minimum obligations. Where such policies are established, the principal is required to make the allocation to classroom teachers accordingly.

VOLUNTARY/REQUIRED DUTIES

Teachers play a central and critical role in the education and personal development of students. The teacher's role is not limited to instructional time within the classroom but extends to encouraging students in athletic, musical or other pursuits. As previously mentioned, the *Education Act* does not limit hours of work for teachers. Duties may be assigned outside the instructional school day. Where such duties are not expressly prescribed by a collective agreement, a school board may nonetheless assign such duties where they are established by a course of conduct or where the assignment is reasonable within the context of the school.

The question of whether a specific activity engaged in by a teacher is voluntary or whether a teacher may be required to perform non-instructional services has been considered by the Supreme Court of Canada.[101] With respect to voluntary services, Chief Justice Laskin stated that services voluntarily performed could not become a term of a teacher's contract or a required duty. With respect to the distinction to be drawn between voluntary and required services, the Chief Justice

---

[101] *Winnipeg Teachers' Assn. No. 1 v. Winnipeg School Division No. 1* (1975), 59 D.L.R. (3d) 228, [1976] 2 S.C.R. 695.

took the view that voluntary services could evolve over a period of time into mandatory duties:

> It is, however, a different matter if services, originally voluntary, become, by course of conduct and of renewal of relationships over a period of time, recognized as part of the obligations of service upon which the relationship has developed.[102]

Additionally, Chief Justice Laskin adopted the view that not all duties had to be express under the collective agreement before they could be considered mandatory. In all cases, reasonableness must oversee the analysis:

> Contract relations of the kind in existence here must surely be governed by standards of reasonableness in assessing the degree to which an employer or a supervisor may call for the performance of duties which are not expressly spelled out. They must be related to the enterprise and be seen as fair to the employee and in furtherance of the principal duties to which he is expressly committed.[103]

According to Chief Justice Laskin, there are two situations in which teachers might find themselves obliged to perform additional or ancillary duties, outside of instruction and supervision, for which there is no contractual or statutory obligation:

- where teachers have performed the duties voluntarily over a period of time; and
- where the duties are related to the employer's enterprise, they are fair to the teacher and the request is reasonable.

The decision of Chief Justice Laskin has been relied upon, in various circumstances, by arbitrators in determining that participation in evening parent-teacher interviews and lunch-time supervision of students may be assigned to teachers as required duties.

Co-curricular activities may also be mandatory where they have been engaged in by teachers over a course of time or where the requirement to participate in the activity is fair and reasonable. Similarly, attendance on field trips or other excursions may become a required duty either because it is an activity that teachers have regularly engaged in or one that is related to the educational program as part of their teaching duties.

Many co-curricular activities contribute directly to the growth and development of students. The personal and pedagogical benefits to students participating in such activities cannot be separated from the instructional program provided by the board. As such, and depending on the activity in question, it may be reasonable for a principal to require a teacher to perform such a duty.

Ultimately, the issue of whether an activity is voluntary or not may vary from school board to school board and, in some circumstances, even from school to school. It is dangerous to be too categoric about characterizing activities as

---

[102] *Supra*, at p. 235.
[103] *Supra*.

voluntary or contractual.[104] However, certain generalizations can be made. Field trips, such as an excursion to see a play in Stratford, which relate to the school curriculum are recognized as part of one's teaching duties. In addition, participation in staff meetings organized by the principal during the school day is considered part of the body of duties required of teachers. Furthermore, coaching and teaching students involved in sports teams which form part of the physical education program would be required activities.

As indicated earlier in this chapter, on June 23, 2000, the *Education Accountability Act, 2000* received Royal Assent in the Ontario Legislature. However, the Minister of Education, Janet Ecker, confirmed the government's intention not to proclaim in force sections of that Act dealing with co-instructional activities, such as sports, arts and special school activities, unless teachers' unions used this as a bargaining chip and started to withdraw from these activities.[105] This new legislation, if proclaimed in force, would require teachers to participate in co-instructional activities (non-classroom student activities). To that end, principals would be required to develop and implement school plans for co-instructional activities and to assign duties relating to those activities to teachers.

SCHOOL COUNCILS

School boards are required to establish school councils for each school operated by the school board. The requirement to establish school councils is found in the *Education Act*. The *Education Act* also requires that principals fulfil certain obligations with respect to school councils. However, more specific objectives for school councils are found in "Policy/Program Memorandum No. 122",[106] issued by the Ministry of Education and Training in 1995 (the "Policy"). The Policy emphasizes the Ministry's commitment to encouraging partnerships between school, students, their families and members of the community and to permitting each of these parties to participate and advise on educational matters.

The Policy establishes that school councils are advisory groups made up of parents whose children attend the school and other interested parties.[107] It is important to remember that school councils cannot usurp the role of the principal. Principals and vice-principals must always manage the affairs of the school with reference to their duties under the *Education Act*. These duties cannot be delegated or removed except by express statutory authority. Any decision of a school council which usurps the statutory role of the principal would ultimately be of no force or

---

[104] E.J. Shilton, *Education Labour and Employment Law in Ontario* (Aurora: Canada Law Book Inc., 1998), paras. 5.1010 to 5.1030.
[105] News Release, *op. cit.*, footnote 39.
[106] Ontario Ministry of Education and Training, "Policy/Program Memorandum No. 122: School Board Policies on School Councils" (issued April 12, 1995).
[107] *Ibid.*, section 2.

effect since school councils have no authority to take on anything beyond an advisory role.

Members of the School Council

The principal of a school is a designated member of the school council. In secondary schools, a student must also be a member of the school council whereas, in elementary schools, the principal has the discretion to decide whether or not a student representative will participate. The remainder of the school council consists of the following:

- parents and guardians of students enrolled in the school;
- community representatives;
- a teacher; and
- a non-teaching staff member.[108]

Parent, student, teacher and non-teaching staff members are elected by their respective peer groups. Community representatives are appointed by the school council. The Policy specifically provides that parents and guardians will form a majority of the school council. The chair of the school council must also be a parent elected by the school council.

Role of the School Council

The Policy provides that school councils will provide advice to the school principal and, where appropriate, the school board on any of the following matters that the school council has identified as a priority:

- the local school-year calendar;
- the school code of behaviour;
- the curriculum and program goals and priorities;
- the responses of the school and the school board to achievement in provincial and board assessment programs;
- the preparation of the school profile;
- the selection of principals;
- school budget priorities, including local-capital improvement plans;
- school-community communication strategies;
- methods of reporting to parents and the community;
- extra-curricular activities in the school;
- school-based services and community partnerships related to social, health, recreational and nutrition programs;
- community use of school facilities;
- the local co-ordination of services for children and youth; and
- the development, implementation and review of board policies at the local level.[109]

---

[108] *Ibid.*, section 1.
[109] *Ibid.*, section 2.

The Policy also establishes that the school council shall:

- establish its goals, priorities and procedures;
- organize information and training sessions to enable members of the council to develop their skills as council members;
- hold a minimum of four meetings per year which are open to members of the school community;
- communicate regularly with members of the school community and parents to seek their views and preferences with regard to matters being addressed by the school council; and
- promote the best interest of the school community.[110]

The Role of the Principal

In addition to his or her role as a member of the school council, the Policy assigns specific responsibilities to the principal. A principal must:

- facilitate the establishment of the school council;
- support the school council's activity;
- seek input from the school council in areas for which it has been assigned responsibility and provide information to the council;
- communicate with the chair;
- ensure that copies of the minutes of the council's meetings are kept at the school;
- assist the school council in communicating with the school community; and
- encourage the participation of parents from all groups or people within the school community.[111]

Regulations under the *Education Act* also prescribe specific responsibilities to the principal respecting school councils. Section 11 of Regulation 298, in part, requires a principal to:

- provide for the prompt distribution to the members of the school council of any materials received by the principal from the Ministry which are identified as being relevant to the functions of the school council and for distribution to the members of the school council;
- make the names of the members known to the parents of students enrolled in the school in each school year; and
- promptly provide the names of the members of the school council to a supporter of the board or to a parent of a student in the school on request.

The principal may publish the names of members of the school council in a newsletter or by any other means which is likely to make the names known to the relevant parents. Such publication must be made by the earliest of the end of

---

[110] *Ibid.*
[111] *Ibid.*, section 3(c).

September or 30 days following the determination of the membership of the school council.[112]

Any conflict between the role of the school council as set out in the Policy and the statutory duties of the principal must be resolved in favour of the principal's statutory duties. The role of the school council is advisory and designed to assist the principal. However, the principal is ultimately responsible for the management and administration of the school. Although the school council is clearly to provide advice on certain aspects of school management, the ultimate authority to make particular decisions rests with the principal. The principal's statutory duties cannot be assumed by or delegated to the school council. As with staff, it is always advisable that the principal cultivate a co-operative approach with the school council regarding issues which concern the school and the broader community.

LABOUR RELATIONS

Principals are responsible for the organization and management of individual schools as well as the quality of instruction in those schools. While the principal is the chief administrator within the school, with responsibilities towards parents, students and staff, the principal is also an educator.

As indicated earlier in this chapter, under Bill 160, the *School Boards and Teachers Collective Negotiations Act* was repealed. As a result, collective bargaining between teachers and their respective school boards is now subject to Part X.1 of the *Education Act* and the *Labour Relations Act, 1995*. Given the principal's essential management and leadership role within a school, it is more important than ever that principals possess a good understanding of the salient provisions of the *Labour Relations Act, 1995*.

In this section, we will examine the impact of the *Labour Relations Act, 1995* in the education setting, including unfair labour practice provisions of the Act, the duty of fair representation, expedited grievance procedure and the duty not to strike. An understanding of these provisions will provide principals with the foundation to effectively carry out their responsibilities and enhance their leadership role in the school.[113]

The Ontario Labour Relations Board

Perhaps one of the more fundamental changes is the introduction of the Ontario Labour Relations Board (the "OLRB") into education-related collective bargaining. Under the old *School Boards and Teachers Collective Negotiations Act*, the Education Relations Commission played a much greater role in monitoring collective negotiations between school boards and teachers' unions.

---

[112] Regulation 298, s. 11(14).
[113] Roher and Weir, *op. cit.*, footnote 28, at p. 1.

The OLRB now has jurisdiction to consider all complaints involving a violation of the *Labour Relations Act, 1995*, including all unfair labour practice complaints as well as all complaints alleging a failure of either party to bargain in good faith. The OLRB has wide-ranging remedial powers in the event it determines that there has been a violation.

Unfair Labour Practices

The unfair labour practices provisions of the *Labour Relations Act, 1995* apply to relations between school boards and teachers' unions. Section 70 makes it an unfair labour practice for an employer to participate or interfere in the formation, selection or administration of a trade union. Employers are expressly not deprived of the freedom to express their views regarding labour relations, so long as they do not use coercion, intimidation, threats, promises or undue influence. The purpose of the section is to insulate employees from employer pressure and influences while exercising rights established by the *Labour Relations Act, 1995*. The OLRB will make a declaration of an unfair labour practice in situations where there is evidence that the employer's actions were motivated by anti-union animus.

The OLRB has said that, apart from the employer's right to express its views, the Act imposes a simple rule for the employer: "Do not interfere."[114] The OLRB has found a wide variety of employer conduct to constitute a violation of section 70, including where the employer gave an employee the use of company premises to hold an anti-union meeting,[115] conferred benefits and solicited grievances in order to undermine the union,[116] and supported an employee's committee against the union and reduced hours of work following the filing of a grievance.[117] The OLRB also found a contravention of the Act where an employer disciplined employees to prevent them from coming together on coffee breaks to discuss union business.[118]

Although the protection is broad, it does not limit the principal in his or her duty to manage the school. Many decisions made by principals will necessarily have an impact on teachers. Provided the decisions are made as part of the day-to-day management of a school and in good faith to further that end, principals will not likely face an unfair labour practice complaint. In the interests of healthy labour relations, it is always best to cultivate a practical and co-operative approach to labour relations issues. Principals should work co-operatively with teachers and

---

[114] *Appleman and BSOIW, Local 834 (Re)*, [1982] O.L.R.B. Rep. Aug. 1162, [1982] 3 Can. L.R.B.R. 275.

[115] *Canadian Chemical Workers Union and Somerville Belkin Industries Ltd. (Re)*, [1980] O.L.R.B. Rep. May 791, [1981] 1 Can. L.R.B.R. 100.

[116] *UFCW and Primo Importing & Distributing Co. (Re)*, [1983] O.L.R.B. Rep. June 959.

[117] *International Brotherhood of Teamsters, Chauffeurs, Warehousemen and Helpers of America and K-Mart Canada Ltd. (Re)*, [1983] O.L.R.B. Rep. May 649, 83 C.L.L.C. ¶16,037.

[118] *UE and R.C.A. Ltd. (Re)*, [1980] O.L.RB. Rep. May 764.

union representatives and make an effort to appreciate all reasonable concerns which might arise in the day-to-day management of a school.

Duty of Fair Representation

The *Labour Relations Act, 1995* also imposes a duty of fair representation on teachers' unions and other bargaining agents. Section 74 provides that a trade union shall not act in a manner which is arbitrary, discriminatory or in bad faith in the representation of any of the employees in the bargaining unit. Section 74 requires that a union act honestly and consider all relevant matters when representing its members.

A union may not make distinctions between members for any reason or on grounds which are not relevant to a matter. An employee who feels that the union has breached its duty of fair representation may apply to the OLRB to determine the issue.

The duty of fair representation applies both to the processing of grievances and to the conduct of negotiations. However, the OLRB will not lightly interfere with the wide discretion granted to the bargaining agent in negotiating in the best interests of the employees.

During a hearing regarding a failure to represent, the OLRB follows a non-technical procedure because the complainant is often not represented by counsel. The onus of proof on the complainant is to establish on a balance of probabilities that the union acted in a manner which was arbitrary, discriminatory or in bad faith. It should be noted that, where the OLRB cannot determine whose evidence to prefer, the complainant will fail.

Expedited Grievance Procedure

Section 49 of the *Labour Relations Act, 1995* sets out a process by which grievances under a collective agreement can be referred to a single arbitrator on an expedited basis. The Act mandates that a party to a collective agreement may request that the Minister of Labour refer to a single arbitrator any difference between the parties to the collective agreement arising from the interpretation, application, administration or alleged violation of the agreement.

An arbitrator appointed by the province must commence to hear the matter referred to him or her within 21 days after the receipt of the request by the Minister. The arbitrator is then required to deliver an oral decision forthwith or as soon as practicable without giving his or her reasons in writing.

Where a request is received under section 49(1) to refer a grievance to a single arbitrator, the Minister must appoint an arbitrator who will have exclusive jurisdiction to hear and determine the matter, including any question as to whether a matter is arbitrable and any question as to whether the request was timely.

From a school administrator's perspective, given the expeditious nature of this process, once an arbitration date is set by the Ministry of Labour, it cannot be adjourned without the consent and approval of both the teachers' union and the school board. In this regard, the section 49 process can be extremely inconvenient as it foists the first day of hearing on the parties, whether they have conflicts with the specified date or not. In the event that there is a need for future hearing dates, the process is more accommodating and all future dates are agreed to by the parties involved.

No Strikes or Lock-outs During the Life of the Collective Agreement

Fundamental to the collective bargaining relationship and healthy labour relations is the requirement that there will be no strikes or lock-outs during the operation of a collective agreement. In addition to the no strike or lock-out provisions, employees and employers cannot make threats during the operation of a collective agreement. The *Labour Relations Act, 1995* provides that no employee shall threaten an unlawful strike and no employer shall threaten an unlawful lock-out of an employee.[119] Similarly, no trade union or officer, official or agent of a trade union shall procure, counsel, support or encourage an unlawful strike or threaten an unlawful strike.[120]

Where no collective agreement is in operation, the parties must seek conciliation prior to the commencement of a legal strike or lock-out. Strikes may not occur immediately after the expiration of a collective agreement unless a strike vote is taken 30 days or less before the collective agreement expires or any time after the collective agreement expires. More than 50% of those voting must vote in favour of a strike to put employees in a lawful strike position.[121]

The exact point at which collective activity becomes a strike may not always be easy to grasp. Under section 1(1) of the *Labour Relations Act, 1995*, strikes are broadly defined:[122]

> "strike" includes a cessation of work, a refusal to work or to continue to work by employees in combination or in concert or in accordance with a common understanding, or a slow-down or other concerted activity on the part of employees designed to restrict or limit output;

Given this expansive definition, it is helpful to consider some specific examples of where concerted activity has been held to be a strike. In *Grand Erie District*

---

[119] *Labour Relations Act, 1995*, s. 79(6).
[120] *Labour Relations Act, 1995*, s. 81.
[121] *Labour Relations Act, 1995*, s. 79(3).
[122] Section 20 of the *Education Accountability Act, 2000* redefines "strike" for the purposes of the application of the *Labour Relations Act, 1995* to boards and teachers. Under the revised definition, a strike now includes:

> ... any action or activity by teachers in combination or in concert or in accordance with a common understanding that is designed to curtail, restrict, limit or interfere with the operation or functioning of one or more school programs, including but not limited to programs involving co-instructional activities, or of one or more schools including, without limiting the foregoing,
> (i) withdrawal of services,
> (ii) work to rule,
> (iii) the giving of notice to terminate contracts of employment.

School Board and OSSTF, District 23 (Re),[123] a 1999 decision of the OLRB, teachers engaged in a work-to-rule campaign while in a legal strike position. As part of that campaign, teachers engaged in the following activities:

- They entered school 15 minutes before the school day began.
- They left school 15 minutes after the school day ended.
- They attended no meetings during the day, including staff, department, heads or curriculum meetings.
- They undertook to provide a class list indicating a percentage mark for each student only upon the request of the principal.
- They provided no tutorials for students.
- They worked on marking only during the school day.
- They refused to attend parent-teacher interview nights.

During the campaign, the school board sent a letter to the union district president indicating that it considered the teachers' actions to be a violation of school board policy and threatening legal action if this activity continued. The union filed an unfair labour practice complaint, alleging that the teachers were engaging in lawful strike activity and were, therefore, protected by the *Labour Relations Act, 1995*.

The OLRB supported the school board. The OLRB found that the school board had not engaged in an unfair labour practice. In writing the letter, the school board had merely conveyed to the union executive its view that the teachers' actions were illegal. Far from an unfair labour practice, the OLRB recognized that parties are entitled to have a view on the legality of each other's actions and found that the school board had acted responsibly in advising the union of its views. The school board had not disciplined or threatened to discipline teachers but had, in its letter, merely accused the union of engaging in unlawful strike activity.

With respect to the issue of whether the teachers' activities constituted a strike within the meaning of the *Labour Relations Act, 1995*, the OLRB noted that section 19(2) of the *Education Act* permits school boards to close specific schools if a strike by teachers makes it dangerous for the students to attend that school or for the facility to remain open. The union argued that this provision of the *Education Act* contemplates that a partial withdrawal of services will be a strike or there would be no need to give a school board the power to close schools.

The OLRB confirmed that, in this case, the teachers were engaged in a strike. It noted that the right to strike is specifically included in the *Education Act*. (While not precisely accurate, the *Education Act* certainly does contemplate such a right.) The teachers' statutory duties, which they had to some extent refused to perform, in the view of the OLRB, could not be read as limiting this right. The OLRB determined that the teachers, acting in combination, were refusing to perform some of their work. Under the *Labour Relations Act, 1995*, this was quintessential strike activity and, provided the teachers' actions occurred within the statutory time frame, perfectly legal.

---

[123] [1999] O.L.R.B. Rep. Jan./Feb. 44, 50 C.L.R.B.R. (2d) 183.

The *Grand Erie District School Board* case illustrates two important principles. First, it is not an unfair labour practice for a school board to express honestly held views regarding the legality or, more accurately, the illegality of union activity. Secondly, work-to-rule campaigns and other concerted refusals to perform duties are strikes. When in a legal strike position, such activity is protected by the *Labour Relations Act, 1995*. When teachers are not in a legal strike position, such activity is not protected by the Act and teachers can be compelled to perform their regular duties.

Outside of the education context, the following activity by employees has also been deemed, by the OLRB, to be a strike:

- a concerted effort to refuse to accept supervisory assignments;
- a concerted refusal to perform some or all of the required duties of one's employment; and
- a concerted refusal to cross pickets lines by employees not on strike themselves.

Where this or similar activity takes place during the life of a collective agreement, such activity may be deemed an unlawful strike. The question of which services are voluntary and which services are required will be central to determining what is and what is not lawful strike activity. Since voluntary services may generally be withdrawn in a true work-to-rule campaign without teachers engaging in a strike, the question will have to be carefully considered in each particular instance.[124]

It is also illegal for an employer to lock out employees during the life of a collective agreement. Lock-outs are broadly defined by section 1(1) of the *Labour Relations Act, 1995*:

> "lock-out" includes the closing of a place of employment, a suspension of work or a refusal by an employer to continue to employ a number of employees, with a view to compel or induce the employees, or to aid another employer to compel or induce that employer's employees, to refrain from exercising any rights or privileges under this Act or to agree to provisions or changes in provisions respecting terms or conditions of employment or the rights, privileges or duties of the employer, an employers' organization, the trade union, or the employees;

The *Labour Relations Act, 1995* expressly forbids an employer from counselling, procuring, supporting or encouraging an unlawful lock-out.[125]

As previously discussed, principals and vice-principals should be aware that, as part of management, and as leaders in their respective schools, they have obligations towards teachers. Principals and vice-principals must not engage in or encourage any unfair labour practice and must respect teachers' rights to negotiate collectively. It is also recognized that principals and vice-principals will not partake in the management or administration of the relevant teachers' unions. In

---

[124] Roher and Weir, *op. cit.*, footnote 28.
[125] *Labour Relations Act, 1995*, s. 82.

this regard, principals and vice-principals should not attend union meetings, unless they are specifically requested to participate.

At the same time, principals and vice-principals are required to manage the day-to-day operation of their schools. Principals must ensure that students are taught and adequately supervised. They must also take reasonable steps to ensure the safety of the school community. Conflict in the school is obviously not conducive to fulfilling these responsibilities.

Overall, principals and vice-principals should be cautious regarding any form of coercion, intimidation, threats or undue influence which could be regarded as anti-union. In the interests of healthy labour relations, it is advised that principals and vice-principals cultivate a practical and co-operative approach to labour relations. Principals and vice-principals should work with teachers and their union representatives in an effort to achieve a positive and collegial working and learning environment.

HUMAN RIGHTS

The Ontario Human Rights Commission has described the purpose and the policy underlying the Ontario *Human Rights Code*[126] as follows:

> The *Code* states that it is public policy in Ontario to recognize the inherent dignity and worth of every person and to provide for equal rights and opportunity without discrimination. The provisions of the *Code* are aimed at creating a climate of understanding and mutual respect so that each person feels a part of the community and feels able to contribute to the community.
>
> Human rights law is based on the principle that employment decisions should be based on the applicant's ability to do the job rather than on factors that are unrelated to job requirements, qualifications or performance.[127]

Section 1 of the Ontario *Human Rights Code* establishes that every person has a right to equal treatment with respect to services, goods and facilities without discrimination because of a prohibited ground of discrimination. Section 5 of the Code provides for equal treatment of all persons in employment. For the purposes of the *Human Rights Code*, the prohibited grounds of discrimination in employment are race, ancestry, place of origin, colour, ethnic origin, citizenship, creed, sex, sexual orientation, age, record of offences, marital status, same-sex partnership status, family status and handicap.

Employment interviews also require sensitivity to human rights concerns on the part of the persons conducting the interview. For example, questions which may even incidentally illicit a response about an individual's family status must be avoided. The Ontario Human Rights Commission considers that there are no permissible questions which may be asked of applicants about race, colour, sex,

---

[126] R.S.O. 1990, c. H.19.
[127] Ontario Human Rights Commission, *Employment Application Forms and Interviews* (Toronto: 1997).

sexual orientation, family status, marital status or handicap.[128] In addition, questions regarding creed are generally not considered permissible by the Commission.[129]

With respect to citizenship, place of origin and ethnic origin, the Commission considers that it is permissible to ask an applicant whether he or she is legally entitled to work in Canada. The Commission also considers that it is permissible to ask an individual whether he or she is 18 years of age or older and less than 65 years of age.[130] In a school setting, a concern may arise as to whether an individual has been convicted of an offence for which a pardon has not been granted. Principals should be aware that the Ontario College of Teachers requires criminal background checks on all new members.

In the provision of services, principals must also be aware of human rights issues which may arise with respect to students in the school. Not only does the school have a clear obligation under the *Human Rights Code* to provide an educational environment which is free from discrimination and an obligation to accommodate individual differences, it is one of the fundamental goals of educators to foster and promote mutual understanding and a respect for human rights. By setting positive examples for their students, principals and teachers imbue those students with values and attitudes which permit them to grow and exert a positive influence on the entire community.

CONCLUSION

In describing his basic philosophy, the French writer Emile Zola said: "If you ask me what I have come to do in this world... I will reply: I'm here to live my life out loud."

To be effective in whatever pursuit one chooses, an individual must have a degree of passion. Passion involves both engagement and involvement. The best teachers are ones who extend and push their respective students and develop an enthusiasm, spirit and commitment for a particular subject-matter.

Benjamin Zander, the conductor of the Boston Philharmonic, once said: "I have no pride. I'll do anything that's necessary to get people involved. I am a dispenser of enthusiasm." Zander said that what makes a great symphony is each member of

---

[128] *Ibid.*

[129] Separate school boards have greater flexibility under the *Human Rights Code* in achieving and pursuing inherent religious or denominational questions. The *Human Rights Code* expressly recognizes the rights and privileges of separate school boards. Section 19(1) of the Code provides:

> 19(1) This Act shall not be construed to adversely affect any right or privilege respecting separate schools enjoyed by separate school boards or their supporters under the *Constitution Act, 1867* and the *Education Act*.

The *Canadian Charter of Rights and Freedoms* also provides that it does not affect any rights or privileges guaranteed to separate schools under the Constitution.

[130] Ontario Human Rights Commission, *op. cit.*, footnote 127.

the orchestra soaring to unimaginable heights. This means that members don't just play their part by rote or memory, but have a passion and spirit for their music. Similarly, it is the authors' view that, to be effective, principals and vice-principals must bring a degree of passion and enthusiasm to their duties and responsibilities.

In this digital, high-tech era, work is changing, competition is changing and business is changing. Therefore, education will also invariably change. There are new models of education being developed across Canada with the kind of thinking needed to succeed in the new economy. These models emphasize the social dimensions of learning, the teamwork that it involves, that it is participatory and the creation of collaborative and consultative cultures.[131]

Increasingly, schools across Canada are encouraging creativity and responsibility, as well as academic achievement, in the performance of their students. They are driven by educators who share an understanding of and a passion for the essence of education. They are daring to ask some difficult questions: What is learning all about? What is the larger purpose of education? What kind of school do we have the ability to create? Increasingly their work is done in partnership – principals, teachers, students and parents – all of them helping to shape a new vision of learning.[132]

As we have indicated, government policy, parent and community demands, changing technology and staff morale issues have contributed to the complex school environment. Recent education reforms have created new relationships and responsibilities for both principals and vice-principals. They have taken on new roles which are in the process of being defined and refined throughout Canada.

It is our view that an understanding and awareness of education law issues is more important than ever. Principals and vice-principals should be mindful of their duties and obligations under relevant statutes and at common law. They play an absolutely critical role in inspiring, motivating and providing direction to the staff in their schools. They set the tone, articulate the vision and provide the leadership. Effective principals and vice-principals are those who inculcate a passion for learning as they reculture their school and work together with staff, students and parents to create and shape a supportive and co-operative school environment.

---

[131] S. Terry, "Schools That Think", *Fast Company* (April, 2000), p. 306.
[132] *Ibid.*

2

Negligence and Liability

INTRODUCTION

References to the legal concepts of "negligence" and "liability" can turn the task of planning for a school year into a nerve-racking exercise for many educators. Nevertheless, educators must concern themselves with the potential for liability associated with operating a school. There are many reasons for lawsuits against schools and school authorities. There is an inherent risk of liability any time hundreds of students and staff come together on school grounds. In addition to the common risks associated with a heavily used property such as a school, active learning on and off school grounds can involve more risky activities for the benefit of students.

This chapter is designed to assist school principals and administrators in making the necessary preparations to reduce the risk of injury or loss associated with the activities of a school and, in turn, to lower the risk of legal liability. The objective is to strive to achieve a safer and more productive school. By implementing some or all of the suggestions in this chapter, principals and vice-principals may better address the level of anxiety that can come with school supervision.

In recent years, there has been increased litigation against schools and school authorities. In more and more cases where students have been injured in a school environment, lawsuits have resulted against educators and their respective school boards.

One explanation for the recent increase in litigation is that the target of a lawsuit is no longer the local community school but rather large incorporated school boards and insurance companies which are perceived to have "deep pockets". It is also argued that the introduction of the *Canadian Charter of Rights and Freedoms* in the early 1980s and a number of highly publicized Charter cases since that time have generated an increased awareness of legal rights among both students and parents.[1]

---

[1] E.M. Roher, "Negligence and Liability in Schools", *Education Law News* (Summer, 1998) (Toronto: Borden & Elliot), p. 1.

At the same time there has been a greater focus on legal themes in the context of popular culture. Television shows such as *Ally McBeal* and movies such as *Philadelphia* emphasize litigation as an attractive option for resolving disputes. Finally, well-publicized American cases, such as the O.J. Simpson civil trial, have demonstrated that the judicial system can be used to obtain significant levels of compensation.

As the nature and scope of school activity expands, so does the potential liability of school authorities. Outdoor education and school trips to remote, often adventurous, places invite greater risk than education in a traditional classroom. "Learning-through-doing" with potentially dangerous chemicals and advanced equipment also creates greater risk than textbook learning. Young athletes, with increasingly sophisticated skills, often use dangerous apparatus in the performance of difficult manoeuvres.

In Canada, most school authorities consider these to be acceptable risks naturally associated with providing meaningful educational experiences for students. However, these risks force an ongoing assessment of the standard of care owed to students in different circumstances.

The duty of care imposed on school authorities is also expanding as a result of the fact that schools are assuming, voluntarily or otherwise, more parental and community roles. For example, many schools have assumed a duty to care for students long before school begins in the morning or long after school ends in the afternoon. Some schools provide recreation and outdoor education on weekends. And many schools have assumed a duty to provide nutrition, medication and highly specialized physical and psychological care to students with special needs who are being mainstreamed into "regular" classes.

There is no simple answer as to when schools or school authorities can be sued for breach of duty leading to liability for damages. The range of litigious issues is as varied as the human experience itself. In general, Canadian courts have been supportive of school personnel. However, depending upon the particular circumstances, a court may also apply rigorous standards when evaluating an individual's conduct. Liability cases are usually specific in that no two cases are the same. Nonetheless, educators may benefit from an understanding of the basic legal principles of tort law as applied in the school context. In addition, this chapter will examine the analytic process used by the courts to determine negligence and liability.[2]

Liability for Negligence

Common law courts have developed a set of legal principles which, taken together, permit the courts to make findings of liability against persons determined to be legally responsible for another's loss or injury. These principles are collectively known as the law of "tort". A tort is a legal concept used to describe a

---

[2] *Ibid.*

wrong that the law will redress by an award of damages.[3] The aim of the court, once liability has been found, is to award an amount in damages which would place the plaintiff in substantially the same position as he or she would have enjoyed but for the actions of the defendant. There are various forms of torts, including torts for a person's intentional acts. However, in this section, we will be concerned with unintentional acts or omissions which may cause a loss or injury to another. In the realm of tort law, this involves the concept of "negligence".

Most commonly, lawsuits to recover damages to compensate for injuries or losses sustained in the school setting contain allegations of negligence on the part of school board employees. As with many areas of the law, just what actions or omissions will lead to a finding of negligence are impossible to predict with certainty. Rather, a determination of negligence will be based on the application of certain legal principles to each unique set of facts and circumstances. The allegations contained in a negligence suit can be frighteningly broad. However, generally speaking, the plaintiff in a negligence suit must prove certain elements to be successful. These are:

- The defendant owed a *duty of care* to the plaintiff.
- The defendant *breached* the *standard of care* owed to the plaintiff.
- The defendant's breach was the *proximate cause* of the plaintiff's injury.
- The plaintiff suffered actual *damage* or *loss* as a result of the injury.[4]

A case of negligence will only be made out if the plaintiff introduces evidence to prove each of these criteria on a balance of probabilities.

DUTY OF CARE

If there is no duty, in law, to ensure the safety or well-being of another person, then there cannot be a finding of liability in negligence if that person has been injured or has suffered a loss. A duty of care can have its basis in either statute or common law. With respect to the duty of a school board, principal or teacher to ensure the safety and well-being of students, that duty has been well established by both statute and common law.[5] Where government policy requires parents to have their children attend school to a specified age, it comes as no surprise that the institution in whose care children are placed is under a corresponding duty. As a result, where a student suffers an injury in school or during a school-sponsored activity, there is often little debate as to whether that student was owed a duty of care by the applicable school staff and authorities.

---

[3] E.M. Roher, *Violence in the Workplace* (Toronto: Carswell, 1999), at p. 6; L.N. Klar, *Tort Law*, 2nd ed. (Toronto: Carswell, 1996), at p. 1.

[4] E.M. Roher, *An Educator's Guide to Violence in Schools* (Aurora: Aurora Professional Press, 1997), at p. 27.

[5] A.F. Brown and M.A. Zuker, *Education Law,* 2nd ed. (Toronto: Carswell, 1997), at p. 59.

Statutory Duty of Care

Provincial statutes dealing with education create statutory duties of care for persons at various levels of the education system. These duties are in addition to duties which exist at common law. These duties can be general in scope or quite specific. Statutory duties regarding education are largely the result of a desire by legislators to clearly identify their expectations for the conduct of educators.

In Ontario, these duties are set out in the *Education Act*[6] (the "Act") and its regulations. As was indicated in Chapter 1, "Duties and Responsibilities of Principals", section 265 of the Act describes duties specific to a school principal. Parts of this section contain duties relevant to maintaining the safety and well-being of students:

> 265. It is the duty of a principal of a school, in addition to the principal's duties as a teacher,
>
> (a) to maintain proper order and discipline in the school;
>
> . . . . .
>
> (j) to give assiduous attention to the health and comfort of the pupils, to the cleanliness, temperature and ventilation of the school, to the care of all teaching materials and other school property, and to the condition and appearance of the school buildings and grounds;
>
> . . . . .
>
> (m) subject to an appeal to the board, to refuse to admit to the school or classroom a person whose presence in the school or classroom would in the principal's judgment be detrimental to the physical or mental well-being of the pupils;

The principal's responsibility for maintaining order in a school is also made clear in section 264 of the Act which lists a teacher's duties. Section 264(e) requires a teacher to maintain, under the principal's direction, "proper order and discipline in the teacher's classroom and while on duty in the school and on the school ground".

In Ontario, attention should also be paid to Regulation 298.[7] It places additional, specific duties on a school principal. Section 11 of the regulations provides, in part:

> 11(1) The principal of a school, subject to the authority of the appropriate supervisory officer, is in charge of,
>
> (a) the instruction and the discipline of pupils in the school; and
>
> (b) the organization and management of the school.
>
> . . . . .
>
> (3) In addition to the duties under the Act and those assigned by the board, the principal of a school shall, except where the principal has arranged otherwise under subsection 26(3),

---

[6] R.S.O. 1990, c. E.2.
[7] *Operation of Schools – General*, R.R.O. 1990, Reg. 298.

(a) supervise the instruction in the school and advise and assist any teacher in co-operation with the teacher in charge of an organizational unit or program;

. . . . .

(e) provide for the supervision of pupils during the period of time during each school day when the school buildings and playgrounds are open to pupils;
(f) provide for the supervision of and the conducting of any school activity authorized by the board;

. . . . .

(l) inspect the school premises at least weekly and report forthwith to the board,
    (i) any repairs to the school that are required, in the opinion of the principal,
    (ii) any lack of attention on the part of the building maintenance staff of the school, and

. . . . .

(n) report promptly any neglect of duty or infraction of the school rules by a pupil to the parent or guardian of the pupil;

Though education legislation in other provinces may not provide an extensive list of specific duties, reference to the maintenance of "order and discipline" in schools may be sufficient to impose a statutory duty of care on educators.[8]

It is important to note that the breach of a statutory duty of care is not proof of negligence. However, it may be used as evidence by a court to determine whether a defendant's actions have fallen below the appropriate standard of care, thus making the defendant liable. As a result, educators may breach their statutory duties, but not be found liable in negligence. Conversely, an educator need not breach a statutory duty to be found negligent.[9] However, principals should be aware of these duties in education legislation and strive to fulfil them consistently. They serve to affirm and supplement the duties which exist at common law and are a useful guidepost in judging the actions of educators.

Common Law Duty of Care

School authorities acting *in loco parentis* owe a common law duty of care to students on or off school premises during official school hours and at times when they voluntarily assume responsibility for students. A school board is vicariously liable for all acts of negligence by its employees and volunteers acting within the scope of their employment or authority. It should be noted that, in most cases, liability "flows" from the teacher to the principal to the corporate board.

---

[8] Brown and Zuker, *op. cit.*, footnote 5, at p. 60.
[9] Roher, *op. cit.*, footnote 4, at p. 30.

Canadian common law has clearly established that educators owe their pupils a duty of care. Teachers and principals have a unique and special relationship with the students who attend their schools. Since students are required to attend school or take home schooling, parents who send their children to a school are entitled to expect that educators will take reasonable precautions to protect students from foreseeable risks of harm.[10]

STANDARD OF CARE

The Careful or Prudent Parent

A standard of care is essentially the standard of behaviour against which the actions or omissions of the defendant in a negligence claim will be judged. If the defendant's actions or omissions fall below the standard of care in a particular case, there will have been a breach of the duty of care owed to the plaintiff. While this seems conceptually simple, it is more difficult in application. Judging a defendant's behaviour against a standard which is usually stated in general terms is not an easy task. The result in a given case can be hard to predict. When deciding a case, the court will examine individual facts and circumstances surrounding the relevant events in the context of the appropriate standard of care.

Canadian courts have held that the standard of care owed to a pupil by a school board and its principals and teachers is that of a *reasonably careful or prudent parent* in the circumstances.[11] This standard has long been applied to the actions of educators in relation to their students.[12] Obviously, the standard of a reasonably careful or prudent parent in the circumstances is a heightened duty of care. In a normal negligence case involving an adult defendant, the standard of care would be that of a reasonable *person* in the circumstances. The application of a parental standard of care to educators in their work with pupils is reflective of the special relationship they share with their students. As indicated earlier, teachers and principals are required to care for their pupils in law. Thus, where school authorities stand in place of a parent in the operation of a school (referred to as acting *in loco parentis*), they will be held to this higher standard.

This is not to say that the standard of a careful or prudent parent has not been criticized. Though the careful or prudent parent standard may often be applied in the context of a prudent parent of a large family, commentators have noted that this standard is inappropriate where the "family" consists of upwards of 30 children of various backgrounds and abilities. For the school principal who is responsible for the entire student body, this standard of care seems particularly onerous. The

---

[10] *Ibid.*, at pp. 30-31.
[11] *Myers v. Peel County Board of Education* (1981), 123 D.L.R. (3d) 1, [1981] 2 S.C.R. 21.
[12] See *Williams v. Eady* (1893), 10 T.L.R. 41 at p. 42 (C.A.), which discussed the definition of the duty of a schoolmaster as being "bound to take care of his boys as a careful father would take of his boys".

standard can seem even more arbitrary where school authorities take on programs which are not directly educative, such as nutrition programs.[13]

The standard of a careful or prudent parent is also a flexible one which permits courts great latitude in its application. This can lead to unpredictable results, though courts are often reluctant to find educators to be in breach of their duties. Some commentators would prefer the standard of a "reasonable and competent instructor"[14] and argue that, in some cases, this is in fact the standard a judge may tacitly apply.[15] However, principals must assume that, in the determination of a negligence claim, they will be judged on the standard of a careful or prudent parent and act diligently on that basis.

As noted, the standard of care will be applied in the context of the particular circumstances of each case. In the leading Canadian decision regarding the standard of care in the school setting, the Supreme Court of Canada acknowledged that this standard of care must be applied flexibly in more modern times where larger groups of students participate in a wider variety of more complicated activities.[16] This 1981 case involved serious injuries suffered by a 15-year-old boy in attempting to dismount from rings in a gymnastics class at high school. The court had to determine whether the school board was negligent in its choice of matting and whether the teacher was negligent in allowing a boy with only a "spotter" to perform gymnastic manoeuvres otherwise unsupervised in the exercise room. The student attempted a difficult manoeuvre without his spotter. He fell off the rings, broke his neck and was rendered a quadriplegic.

The court recognized that the careful or prudent parent standard had been somewhat qualified in light of the greater variety of activities conducted in schools, with larger groups of students using more complicated and dangerous equipment. Mr. Justice McIntyre held that this standard cannot be applied in the same manner and to the same extent in every case. He listed several factors which affect the application of this standard, including:

- the number of students being supervised at any given time;
- the nature of the exercise or activity in progress;
- the age of the students;
- the degree of skill and training which the students may have received in connection with the activity;
- the nature and condition of the equipment in use at the time; and
- the competence and capacity of the students involved.

---

[13] E. Doctor, "The In Loco Parentis Doctrine: A Valid Standard for Teachers?" (May, 1992), 9 *Edulaw School Newsletter* 66 at pp. 66-7.

[14] A.W. MacKay and G.M. Dickinson, *Beyond the "Careful Parent": Tort Liability in Education* (Toronto: Emond Montgomery Publications, 1998), at pp. 10-17.

[15] A.W. MacKay, "Liabilities: The Nightmare That Won't Go Away But Can be Effectively Managed" (address to the Canada Law Book Symposium, "The New ABCs of Learning", Toronto, November 26, 1999) [unpublished].

[16] *Myers v. Peel County Board of Education, supra,* footnote 11.

Another factor that the court said should have been recognized was the "proclivity of young boys of high school age to act recklessly in disregard, if not in actual defiance, of authority".[17] The court held that the foreseeability of an accident or injury depends on an accurate appreciation and assessment of these risk factors.

The Supreme Court of Canada concluded that, given the facts of this case, the standard of care to be exercised in providing for the supervision and protection of students – that of a careful and prudent parent – was not met. Mr. Justice McIntyre ruled that a prudent parent would not be content to provide the protective matting used when other, more protective mats were available. He also stated that a prudent parent would not permit his or her son to leave the gymnasium to practise potentially dangerous manoeuvres in a room without adult supervision.[18]

Breach of the Standard of Care

To be successful in a negligence suit, the plaintiff must also demonstrate that the defendant's behaviour breached the standard of care applied by the court. A breach of a duty of care can occur by means of a positive act where a principal or teacher commits an act contrary to his or her duty, or by means of an omission where the individual does not appreciate the nature and extent of the duty of care and fails to do what should be done. As was previously discussed, failure to carry out an action required by statute, regulation or board policy will not necessarily lead to a finding of negligence, but it may be convincing evidence of the same. In addition, the plaintiff must demonstrate that he or she suffered a loss or injury which was in fact caused by the defendant's breach.

Causation

In order to prove that a principal or teacher was negligent, a plaintiff must also demonstrate that there was a proximate causal connection between the defendant's conduct and the plaintiff's injury. The requirement of a causal connection has often been generalized as the "but for" test. If the student's injury would not have occurred "but for" the conduct of the defendant, then, generally speaking, the required causal connection between the actions of the defendant and the injury to the student will have been established. However, for a finding of liability to ensue, the plaintiff must also show that the harmful consequences of the defendant's behaviour were *reasonably foreseeable*. In other words, were the actions of the defendant a proximate cause of the injury? A defendant may not be held liable for a freakish type of injury.[19]

The test of foreseeability is whether the type of injury (not the exact injury) is reasonably possible. For example, in one case a student suffered a significant eye

---

[17] *Supra*, at p. 13.
[18] See Roher, *op. cit.*, footnote 1, at p. 2.
[19] See A.M. Linden, *Canadian Tort Law*, 6th ed. (Toronto: Butterworths, 1997), at pp. 104-106.

injury during a sewing class.[20] The student was in a grade 8 cooking and sewing class comprised of 13 students, five of whom were sewing at the time of the accident. The material the student was sewing by machine "bunched", causing the needle to break into three pieces. One piece of the needle became embedded in the student's eye. Though there was no evidence of any knowledge of previous eye injuries from similar events, there was evidence of previous injuries to the hands and arms of others from needle breakages, as well as needle breakages from bunching of material. As a result, the court determined that a careful or prudent parent with this teacher's background and knowledge of sewing should have warned her students that the bunching of material could occur with dangerous consequences. The court concluded: "In the end, I find that a *reasonably prudent sewing teacher owed* the students the duty of care to have warned them of the particular dangers involved in sewing on the spot".[21] (Emphasis added.) It held that the school board and the teacher were equally liable for the student's injuries.[22]

Hypothetical examples, one extreme and one common, may assist. If a student is struck by lightning on a field trip which is supervised by the principal, the principal could be found negligent if he or she caused the accident in some way, perhaps by ordering the student to stand beneath a solitary tree in an electrical storm or by failing to warn of the dangers involved in standing beneath that solitary tree. In circumstances where only one teacher is assigned by the principal to yard duty during recess, and a student is struck and injured by another student, the court may find liability where it is satisfied that proper supervision would have prevented the harm. By requiring precautions to prevent reasonably foreseeable injuries to students to whom a duty of care is owed, the law of negligence approximates a standard of common sense. It requires reasonable precautions to protect a pupil from reasonably foreseeable risks of harm, but not all possible precautions to prevent any conceivable risk of harm.

Damages

The final element to be demonstrated in a negligence claim is that of damage or loss suffered by the plaintiff. Recognized losses can take a number of forms, including physical injury, pain and suffering, emotional distress, loss of enjoyment of life, loss of income and so on. Allegations of loss should be more than trivial or a court may consider dismissing the lawsuit. Practically speaking, a lawsuit is unlikely to be commenced or continued where the possible award of compensation may be outweighed by the legal fees and other costs of the case. This reality can protect educators from numerous lawsuits based on trivial matters or minimal damage claims.[23]

---

[20] *Brown v. Essex County Roman Catholic Separate School Board* (1990), 22 A.C.W.S. (3d) 500 (Ont. H.C.J.).
[21] *Supra*, at p. 9 of the judgment.
[22] "Negligence and Liability: Injury During Sewing Lessons", *Edulaw School Newsletter*, Vol. 2, No. 5 (Calgary: Edulaw, January, 1991), p. 35.
[23] Roher, *op. cit.*, footnote 4, at p. 45.

Though a court can direct negligent defendants to take certain actions through an injunction,[24] the vast majority of negligence claims are remedied through an award of monetary damages. The aim of the court is to place the injured person back in the position that he or she would have been in had the negligence not occurred. Some cases may involve many different types of losses leading to considerable damage awards. Obviously, where injuries are more severe or have serious consequences to a student's future, damage awards may be higher.

In a British Columbia case, a nine-year-old girl suffered severe burns to her face and neck in an accident on a school field trip.[25] She won a negligence suit against the relevant school board and others. On an appeal regarding damages, the damages for her economic losses were increased from $26,000 to $165,000. This was due to her substantially diminished earning capacity because of her low self-esteem, poor body image, lack of confidence and low-risk lifestyle, all directly linked to her injuries. Also included in this amount was a sum for the loss of an economically advantageous permanent interdependent relationship. Her total damages were well over $300,000. High damage awards such as this are rare in Canadian cases. However, they warn of the serious risk involved in many school activities and the importance of taking adequate precautions.

Vicarious Liability

Though it is usually the actions of principals, teachers and staff which are scrutinized in a negligence claim, it is often the school board as employer which is responsible for paying for relevant damages. This occurs through the legal concept of "vicarious liability" which imputes liability to a person for the acts of others.[26] In the employment context, this means an employer will, in certain circumstances, be held liable for the conduct of its employees. Though a school board is a corporate entity which has legal duties and may be liable for its own negligence, a school board need not be negligent itself to be vicariously liable for the acts of its employees. As a result, where an injured pupil brings a negligence action, allegations are usually made against the teacher, principal and school board together (even where the principal was not directly involved) since it is uncertain as to how liability may be divided among these parties.[27]

For the principles of vicarious liability to apply, it must generally be shown that the conduct of the employee was within the scope or course of his or her employment. For this to be the case, the acts of the employee must have been acts

---

[24] *Ibid.*
[25] *Anderson v. Miner* (1999), 44 C.C.L.T. (2d) 152, 191 W.A.C. 39 (B.C.C.A.), varg 69 A.C.W.S. (3d) 665 (S.C.). See E. Doctor, "Damages for Field Trip Accident Increased", *Education Law Reporter*, Vol. 10, No. 7 (Calgary: Edulaw, March, 1999).
[26] S.R. Ball, *Canadian Employment Law* (Aurora: Canada Law Book Inc., 2000), section 20:10.1.
[27] A.F. Brown, *Legal Handbook for Educators*, 4th ed. (Toronto: Carswell, 1998), at p. 106.

authorized by the employer or acts which can be considered a means of carrying out an authorized act.

Generally speaking, the scope of employment is broadly interpreted to include a wide range of activities. This is so for a number of reasons. The employee is unlikely to be adequately insured and may not be able to adequately compensate the plaintiff for his or her injuries.[28] In this way, the party who is most able to pay may be held liable. Other rationales for imposing vicarious liability on employers include the element of control that an employer may have over its employees, and the reasoning that an employer should be responsible for the acts of its authorized representatives.[29] However, principals and their staff may still be personally liable for their actions. A principal or teacher may be found liable for negligence in supervision for allowing acts to occur if the standard of the reasonably diligent parent has not been met. In addition, should a principal or teacher involve students in activities which have nothing to do with school activities or extra-curricular activities, the principal or teacher may be found to be personally liable. It should also be noted that an employer's vicarious liability does not displace the personal liability of an employee.[30]

Defences

Limitation Periods

To ensure that persons do not continually face the risk of lawsuits originating from dated events, limitation periods for the bringing of actions have been created. These prevent the bringing of an action once a certain amount of time has passed since the events giving rise to the allegations. Generally speaking, the time period will not begin to run until the "date of discoverability of damage" by the plaintiff.[31] The relevant limitation periods vary from province to province and can be established by more than one statute in each province. In Ontario, there is specific legislation providing a shorter limitation period for actions against public authorities, such as schools boards. Section 7(1) of the *Public Authorities Protection Act*[32] imposes a six-month limitation period for all actions against public authorities for the alleged neglect or default of their *statutory or public duties*. This can include actions against school authorities.

Though this limitation period is broad in its effect, it will not apply to all activities of a board, its schools and its staff. This six-month limitation period can be narrowly construed, reducing the protection principals or teachers may find under the *Public Authorities Protection Act*. For example, in one case the catcher

---

[28] Brown and Zuker, *op. cit.*, footnote 5, at p. 57.
[29] Ball, *op. cit.*, footnote 26, sections 20:10.1 and 20:10.2.
[30] J.C. Batzel, "Negligence and the Liability of School Boards and Teachers Towards Students", in W.F. Foster and W.J. Smith, eds., *Reaching for Reasonableness: The Educator as Lawful Decision-Maker* (Chateauguay: Lisbro, 1999), p. 113, at p. 115.
[31] Linden, *op. cit.*, footnote 19, at pp. 101-102.
[32] R.S.O. 1990, c. P.38.

in a school three-pitch game suffered a broken leg during a collision at home plate.[33] The catcher claimed that the injury was caused by a large hole in the left side of the batter's box in which he caught his leg during the collision. The catcher sued the school board and the coach, alleging that the injury was caused by the unsafe condition of the playing field. Ultimately, no negligence was found on the part of the defendants. However, the court permitted the lawsuit to continue, despite the fact that it was brought three years after the injury occurred. The court restrictively interpreted the statute, distinguishing between school authorities exercising purely public duties which are protected by a shorter limitation period, and their exercise of private duties which are not so protected. Since the duty to maintain property in good order had a private aspect, this activity did not enjoy the protection of the *Public Authorities Protection Act*. The court noted that where the actions of a public authority are similar to those of a private body, and affect members of the public in a similar manner, the public authority is not deserving of special protection. Thus, in Ontario, in certain cases where the distinction between public and private acts is blurred, school authorities may face lawsuits years after a mishap.

In a case where the plaintiff is a minor or suffers from a disability, the six-month limitation period provided for by the *Public Authorities Protection Act* must be read in conjunction with section 47 of the *Limitations Act*,[34] which provides:

> 47. Where a person entitled to bring an action mentioned in section 45 or 46 is at the time the cause of action accrues a minor, mental defective, mental incompetent or of unsound mind, the period within which the action may be brought shall be reckoned from the date when such person became of full age or of sound mind.

The leading case in this regard is *Papamonolopoulos v. Toronto (City) Board of Education*.[35] In that case, the Ontario Court of Appeal was asked to consider whether section 47 of the *Limitations Act* is restricted to limitation periods set out in that statute or whether it is a general provision applicable to all limitation periods, including the one set out in section 11 [now section 7] of the *Public Authorities Protection Act*.

In *Papamonolopoulos*, the 16-year-old plaintiff suffered a permanent disability while playing a supervised game of touch football at her school as part of her daily scheduled activities. At first, her injuries appeared to be trifling but, in due course, her condition worsened and she eventually had to undergo surgery. Unfortunately, the nature of the disability made her unsuitable for her vocation of choice. The plaintiff subsequently brought an action against the school board some 13 days after she attained the age of majority but some 15 months after the date of her

---

[33] *Phelps v. Scarborough Board of Education* (1993), 40 A.C.W.S. (3d) 1078 (Ont. Ct. (Gen. Div.)). See "No Negligence in Baseball Game", *Edulaw for Canadian Schools*, Vol. 5, No. 5 (Calgary: Edulaw, January, 1994), p. 35.
[34] R.S.O. 1990, c. L.15.
[35] (1986), 30 D.L.R. (4th) 269, 56 O.R. (2d) 1 (C.A.), leave to appeal to S.C.C. refused 35 D.L.R. (4th) 767*n*, 58 O.R. (2d) 528*n*.

injury. Although the trial judge assessed her damages at $94,643.32, he dismissed the action as being out of time under the *Public Authorities Protection Act*, rejecting the notion that the limitation under section 11 did not begin to run until she had attained the age of majority under section 47 of the *Limitations Act*.

On appeal, Brooke J.A. of the Ontario Court of Appeal ruled that the provisions of a statute of limitations should be liberally construed in favour of the individual whose right to sue for compensation is in question. He held that section 47 applied generally to limitation periods prescribed by the *Limitations Act* and, in the absence of clear wording to the contrary, by *other statutes* which provided for the limitation of an action. Thus, in a case where the plaintiff is a minor, the limitation period does not begin to run until he or she reaches the age of majority. Similarly, where the plaintiff has a mental defect, is mentally incompetent or of unsound mind, the period during which the action may be brought is suspended until he or she becomes of sound mind. In the result, Brooke J.A. allowed the appeal and granted judgment in favour of the plaintiff in the sum of $94,643.23 together with prejudgment interest and costs.

Statutory Limitation

In some provinces, legislators have specifically provided educators with additional limitations on their degree of liability. For example, section 232 of the Saskatchewan *Education Act, 1995*[36] indicates that, where a school board, principal or teacher approves or sponsors a school activity, no teacher, principal or other person responsible for the conduct of the pupils is liable for damage caused by pupils during those activities or for personal injuries suffered by pupils during those activities. Though this section offers some protections for school board employees such as principals, it offers no protection for the school board itself.[37] In addition, education statutes in British Columbia, Manitoba and Prince Edward Island contain certain exemptions from liability for school boards and their employees, depending upon the specific circumstances involved.[38]

Contributory Negligence

Students themselves have a duty to act with reasonable care for their own safety. Therefore, a principal or school board may attempt to prove, in defending a negligence suit, that the student breached this duty and thereby contributed to or caused his or her own loss. While a finding of contributory negligence will not prevent a plaintiff from recovering entirely, it will reduce the claim for damages in the same proportion that the plaintiff is found to be responsible for the injury. Where it is impossible to determine the respective degrees of fault of the student and the principal or school board, the Ontario *Negligence Act*[39] prescribes that the parties will be deemed to be equally negligent.

---

[36] S.S. 1995, c. E-02.
[37] Batzel, *op. cit.*, footnote 30, at p. 116.
[38] See *School Act*, R.S.B.C. 1996, c. 412, ss. 94 and 95; *Public Schools Act*, R.S.M. 1987, c. P250, ss. 86 to 89; *School Act,* S.P.E.I. 1993, c. 35 (c. S-2.1), ss. 119 and 120.
[39] R.S.O. 1990, c. N.1, s. 4.

There are many cases where students have been found to be contributorily negligent. The student's conduct will be judged according to a variety of considerations. Generally speaking, the student will be held to the standard of a reasonably prudent and intelligent student of the same age and in the same circumstances. For instance, in the case discussed earlier of the student who sustained eye injuries from a broken sewing-machine needle, the student was found to be 10% negligent. He attempted to continue to sew after the material had bunched up, despite having received instructions to stop and call for help if he experienced any difficulties.[40]

Voluntary Assumption of Risk

Though the voluntary assumption of risk is a complete defence to a negligence claim, it will rarely apply in the education setting. To successfully assert this defence, a defendant must demonstrate that the plaintiff not only accepted the risk involved in the particular activity, but also that the plaintiff accepted legal liability for the loss. Acceptance may take the form of an express agreement or be implied from the actions of the plaintiff. Since it is difficult for most young students to fully comprehend all of the actual *and* legal risks of an activity, this defence may be of limited application.[41]

One area where this defence may apply is to participation in sports. It is a well-established rule that a person who participates in a game or sport voluntarily assumes the normal, inherent risks of participation. As a result, school boards and principals will be protected against lawsuits for damages if the student is injured in the normal course of the activity. For example, in *Thomas (Next Friend of) v. Hamilton (City) Board of Education*,[42] a case involving a student who sustained serious neck injuries while making a football tackle, the student's lawsuit was dismissed largely on the basis of his voluntary assumption of the game's risks. It was determined that his injury, though devastating, came within the ambit of those risks inherent in a contact sport such as football. These were risks of which the student was well aware. It is important to note, however, that the voluntary assumption of risk only extends to the usual risks of the activity in question and not to unreasonable risks such as the intentional infliction of harm or the negligent acts of supervisory authorities.

DUTY TO PROVIDE PROPER SUPERVISION

Many negligence lawsuits against teachers, principals and school boards are based on allegations that the supervision of the student(s) involved was insufficient. For principals, such allegations are directly linked to their regulatory

---

[40] *Brown v. Essex County Roman Catholic Separate School Board* (1990), 22 A.C.W.S. (3d) 500 (Ont. H.C.J.).
[41] MacKay and Dickinson, *op. cit.*, footnote 14, at pp. 87-9.
[42] (1994), 20 O.R. (3d) 598, 85 O.A.C. 161 (C.A.).

duties towards students. Specifically, section 11(3)(e) and (f) of Regulation 298 under the *Education Act* requires a principal to "provide for the supervision of pupils during the period of time during each school day when the school buildings and playgrounds are open to pupils" and to "provide for the supervision of and the conducting of any school activity authorized by the board". These statutory duties reinforce a principal's duty of supervision at common law.

Allegations of improper supervision permeate many actions involving negligence in the school setting. Before considering the supervision of students participating in specific activities, it may be useful to look at the supervision of students in a more general context. One case which illustrates a principal's duty of supervision is *Brost v. Board of Trustees of Eastern Irrigation School Division No. 44*.[43] In this Alberta case, a six-year-old girl was injured during school recess when she fell off a swing. Although there was a teacher in charge of the playground during recess, there was no supervision of the children in their use of the swings at the time. The court held both the school board and the principal responsible in negligence for their failure to provide proper supervision of the playground during recess. With regard to the defendants' negligence, the court stated:

> [T]he facts of the present case indicate that there was no method or systematic plan of supervision, and what supervision there was does not indicate that the authorities or master (the superintendent) felt under any duty to exercise the care of a prudent parent in supervising the pupils in their use of the swings.
>
> . . . . .
>
> [T]he Board of Trustees and the principal of the school failed to exercise the degree of care to safeguard the small pupils of the school in the use of the swings that the law requires, and that what happened to the plaintiff . . . resulted therefrom. It was quite foreseeable that this or some accident would sooner or later happen.[44]

Here the duty to provide for proper supervision rested on the principal and the board. Specifically, the court stated that the risk of injury from swinging too high was foreseeable such that supervision of the play area and instruction to young students were necessary. It is clear that the principal's duty to establish and maintain a proper supervision system is of great importance; students must be supervised and protected from all injuries which are reasonably foreseeable in the circumstances.

However, the duty to provide supervision is not without limits. For instance, where the lack of supervision was not the cause of the injury, or where proper supervision would not have prevented the injury, there will not be liability for school authorities despite their actions. Nevertheless, a comprehensive program of supervision should be in place to prevent student injury and liability. In setting up such a program, a balance must clearly be struck between the supervision of

---

[43] [1955] 3 D.L.R. 159, 15 W.W.R. (N.S.) 241 (Alta. C.A.).
[44] *Supra*, at pp. 169-70.

students and the need for students to develop independence and a sense of personal responsibility in their activities.[45]

In a 1996 British Columbia case, a 16-year-old student suffered a broken wrist after he fell from a tree that he had climbed while waiting to bat during a school baseball game.[46] The supervising teachers participated in the game. The student sued the school board and the teachers involved and the allegations included negligent supervision. The court found that the student was owed a duty of care during this school activity. The standard of care was that of a careful and prudent parent of a large family, taking into account factors such as the student's age, intelligence, behavioural propensities, degree of skill and training, competency and capacity, and any inherently dangerous conditions.

The court held that there was no breach of the duty to properly supervise the game. It found that the teachers participated to serve as role models and to ensure the safety of students under their care. Other students who saw the student climbing the tree did not report it and the tree was too dense to see the student in it. Also, the injury was not reasonably foreseeable since the student, though lacking focus in school, was mature and showed no propensity to climb trees. Nor were there incidents of other students climbing trees on school property. No negligence was found in the case. This decision is useful in illustrating that, depending on the circumstances of the case, the level of supervision required of school staff will have reasonable limits.

A number of factors can be gleaned from the applicable case law, which will help a school principal in developing a reasonable supervision policy. Factors that a court may consider, in determining whether an appropriate level of supervision was met in a particular case, include:

- the circumstances of the injury;
- any applicable school board regulations and policies;
- the school's schedule or policy for supervision of the particular activity or area, and whether it was in place on the given day;
- instructions to staff or students about the conduct expected of them;
- the ratio of supervisors to students for the particular activity;
- the activity in which the students were engaged, and any inherent danger associated with it;
- the age and maturity of the students involved;
- any special circumstances concerning the individual student(s) involved;
- weather conditions for outdoor activities; and
- the geography of the area to be supervised.[47]

---

[45] Batzel, *op. cit.*, footnote 30, at pp. 120-21.
[46] *Catherwood (Guardian ad Litem of) v. Heinrichs* (1996), 63 A.C.W.S. (3d) 1291, [1996] B.C.J. No. 1373 (Q.L.) (S.C.). See "Negligent Supervision of Students", *Edulaw for Canadian Schools*, Vol. 8, No. 1 (Calgary: Edulaw, September, 1996).
[47] Batzel, *op. cit.*, footnote 30, at p. 122; *Dyer v. Board of School Commissioners of Halifax*, [1956] 2 D.L.R. (2d) 394 (N.S.S.C.).

In the Classroom

From time to time, Canadian courts have had the opportunity to consider the nature of proper classroom supervision, including when absence from the classroom would be considered reasonable. For example, in a 1989 Ontario case, a teacher left his special education class unattended for approximately three minutes.[48] While he was assisting a student in removing her jacket and hanging it in the hallway, one young boy grabbed and twisted the arm of another young boy, causing his arm to fracture. The student who caused the injury had not exhibited any such conduct in the past. The court noted that the teacher had left the class for only a short period of time for the sole purpose of assisting another student. It concluded that to find that the teacher was in breach of his standard of care in this situation would be "absurd".

In a second case, a high-school student, while seated in a classroom before the teacher was present, was struck in the eye by a paper clip propelled by means of an elastic band by a classmate.[49] This act was apparently the last in a series of incidents involving the two students. The plaintiff commenced legal proceedings against: the classmate who had propelled the paper clip; the classroom teacher; and the school board, on the basis that it had failed to maintain a proper system of supervision.

While evidence was introduced to illustrate that the student in question had engaged in similar conduct in the past, the court found that this conduct had not been observed by, or reported to, the teacher or any other member of the school board. As a result, neither the teacher, nor the principal, nor the school board had reason to anticipate that the student would cause injury to another person. The court ruled that the responsibility and liability for the incident were confined to the two students.

In analyzing the potential liability of school authorities for occurrences in the classroom during a teacher's absence, factors which may be considered in a Canadian court include:

- the reasons for the teacher's absence;
- the duration of the absence;
- the time of the accident;
- the nature and makeup of the class; and
- whether previous incidents had demonstrated the need for a higher level of supervision.[50]

---

[48] *Misir v. Children's Rehabilitation Centre of Essex County*, [1989] O.J. No. 1653 (Q.L.) (Dist. Ct.).
[49] *McCue v. Board of Education for Borough of Etobicoke* (1982), 18 A.C.W.S. (2d) 127 (Ont. H.C.J.).
[50] Roher, *op. cit.*, footnote 1, at p. 3.

Physical Education and Sports

Athletic activity is one setting in which there is clearly an inherent risk of injury. Accidents can occur due to faulty equipment, inadequate training of students in an activity or improper supervision. However, accidents and injuries can occur here, as in other areas, even when no one has been negligent.

A school cannot be an insurer of the safety of all students under its care. In particular, there is an inherent risk of injury in most athletic activities. However, only if the student is exposed to unreasonable risks will a teacher be considered negligent.

In a 1976 British Columbia case, a 15-year-old student became a quadriplegic as a result of attempting a somersault from a gymnastics springboard.[51] The physical education teacher was found negligent for not realizing that the addition of a box for jumping created a dangerous situation. The teacher had been working on school reports rather than supervising the several athletic activities which were taking place in the gymnasium.

The court considered the liability of school authorities for injuries sustained by their pupils and held that it is not negligent on the part of school authorities to permit a pupil to undertake a particular physical manoeuvre if:

- the activity is suitable to the pupil's age and mental and physical condition;
- the student is progressively trained and coached to do the activity properly and avoid the danger;
- the equipment is adequate and suitably arranged; and
- the performance of the activity is properly supervised, having regard to its inherently dangerous nature.[52]

The British Columbia Court of Appeal held that the teacher had a duty to meet the standard of care of a reasonably skilled physical education instructor rather than that of a careful parent. However, more recent decisions have suggested that in fact the general "prudent parent" standard continues to apply in the context of physical education.

In 1994, the Ontario Court of Appeal considered a case where a 16-year-old high-school student had been rendered a quadriplegic as a result of a neck injury suffered during a school football game.[53] The student sued, among others, his coaches and the board of education, which ran the curricular and extra-curricular football programs. At trial, the action was dismissed. The Ontario Court of Appeal held that the trial judge made no error in applying the standard of care of the careful or prudent parent.

---

[51] *Thornton v. School District No. 57* (1976), 73 D.L.R. (3d) 35, [1976] 5 W.W.R. 240 (B.C.C.A.), vard with respect to damages 83 D.L.R. (3d) 480, [1978] 2 S.C.R. 267.
[52] *Supra*, at p. 58.
[53] *Thomas (Next Friend of) v. Hamilton (City) Board of Education* (1994), 20 O.R. (3d) 598, 85 O.A.C. 161 (C.A.).

The student alleged that the defendants should have warned him and his parents of the risks of playing football. The student also stated that the coaches failed to recognize that he was not in condition to play and was not properly trained as to how to tackle. In addition, it was alleged that the defendants should have known that the student's "long, lean, swan neck" rendered him more susceptible to injury.

The Ontario Court of Appeal ruled that football is commonly known to be a dangerous sport which results in many injuries. It held that the trial judge was correct in concluding that neither the school board nor the coaches were negligent and that the student and his mother had consented to the normal risks of the game. The court concluded that the injury was sustained during a routine play and, although the consequences of the injury were devastating, the injury came within the ambit of those risks inherent in a contact sport such as football.

In the School Yard

The school yard is likely the most challenging location for a school's staff to supervise. Inevitably, when a child is injured in a school yard, the issues of whether a supervision system was in place, its adequacy, and whether the teachers responsible for supervision performed their task properly will arise. If the system of supervision itself was the cause of the accident, then the principal responsible for the supervision of school premises could be held liable. There is some legal authority indicating that the careful or prudent parent standard of care may be inappropriately stringent when a principal is designing and implementing a supervision procedure for an entire school population.

In *Board of Education for City of Toronto v. Higgs*,[54] the principal's policy of using four supervisors to supervise a playground was judged against the standard of a prudent principal. In this case, the policy was designed for all of the principal's 750 students, all of whom could not be under the principal's immediate care. Though this system was found to be reasonably safe, the court also stated that the degree of care to be exercised depends on the particular circumstances of each case.[55]

In a 1988 British Columbia case, a high-school student playing rugby in the snow attempted a dive, imitating the head-first slide of a baseball player.[56] The student's neck was broken and he was rendered a quadriplegic. The British Columbia Court of Appeal held that the physical education teacher was not to blame for such an unforeseeable act. Thus, the court ruled that the teacher did not expose students, who were playing rugby in the snow, to an undue risk of harm.

Similarly, in a 1993 case, the British Columbia Court of Appeal considered a school-yard incident in which an errant throw during a game of catch bounced in the grass and struck a student who was sitting in the yard, damaging his

---

[54] (1959), 22 D.L.R. (2d) 49, [1960] S.C.R. 174.
[55] See Brown and Zuker, *op. cit.*, footnote 5, at pp. 70-74.
[56] *Fraser v. Campbell River School District No. 72* (1988), 54 D.L.R. (4th) 563 (B.C.C.A.), leave to appeal to S.C.C. refused 56 D.L.R. (4th) vii, [1989] 1 S.C.R. viii.

eye.[57] There was no evidence that the boys playing catch had been "goofing around", and the victim himself testified that he had believed he was seated a safe distance from the game. The Court of Appeal held that the game of catch was not inherently dangerous, that the boys playing the game were sensible, and that a careful parent would have allowed his or her child to sit on the grass nearby. Thus, the court held that the teacher who was supervising the yard had not breached the standard of care required of him.

The size of school properties, the nature of equipment or apparatus on school property and the large number of students involved in various activities all lead to unique problems in devising a system of school-yard supervision. Most school boards have specific policies for the supervision of school property and principals should refer to these policies when planning supervision. In developing a system of school-yard supervision, educators should consider the following obligations:

- the duty to inquire into and warn students about the inherent dangers of the activity;
- the duty to oversee the progress of the activity;
- the duty to furnish secure and adequate equipment and facilities; and
- the duty to obtain prior parental consent to participation in any recreational or sports activity which is not part of the regular school program.[58]

Outside School Hours

Generally speaking, where there is an accident on school property outside of normal school hours, school authorities will not be responsible for the injuries. For example, in a 1991 case, a school was found not to have breached its duty of care when a student was injured, having fallen off the hood of a car driven by another student.[59] In this case, the student suffered serious head injuries when he fell off the hood of the car (on which he had been seated) which was being moved by another student in the school parking lot. The Ontario Court (General Division) found that this injury occurred after school hours and outside the scope of school activities. There was no evidence of prior accidents or misbehaviour in the parking lot and therefore no need to appoint a supervisor for this area. Thus, the court concluded that the school had not breached the duty of care that it owed to the student.

However, as with most generalizations of the law, there are a number of exceptions. In a different case, a student was injured by a paper clip shot by another student using an elastic band before classes commenced. The court noted that the students were expected to arrive early and the principal's duty towards them arose

---

[57] *Plumb (Guardian ad Litem of) v. Cowichan School District No. 65* (1993), 83 B.C.L.R. (2d) 161, 54 W.A.C. 300 (C.A.).

[58] *Gagnon v. Alma (Comm. Scolaire)* (1989), 50 C.C.L.T. 250 (Que. C.A.). See "Intentional and Unintentional Torts", *Edulaw School Newsletter,* Vol. 2, No. 1 (Calgary: Edulaw, September, 1990).

[59] *Sked (litigation guardian) v. Henry* (1991), 28 M.V.R. (2d) 234 (Ont. Ct. (Gen. Div.)).

before classes began. The court found that the principal was negligent for not providing adequate supervision and setting rules for the students.[60] In certain circumstances, the duty of care owed by educators to students during the school day may also extend to before or after school. This may occur in the following circumstances:

- where there are "school sponsored" or extra-curricular activities during off-hours, including activities off school property;
- where students remain on school property for a reasonable time before and after school;
- where the school provides supervision for students on school property before or after school which parents have come to rely on;
- where a teacher performs work within the scope of his or her employment, such as after-hours study classes or sports activities; and
- where there is liability as an occupier of lands for injuries to students or members of the public occurring on school property due to negligent maintenance of that property.[61]

Obviously, schools must deal with the reality of working parents whose children arrive at school early and leave late. Parents' expectations with respect to the supervision of their children, unreasonable or not, often extend beyond class hours. While schools and their teachers cannot provide the equivalent of day-care services, there are a number of steps which can be taken to reduce a school's potential risk for liability outside school hours while remaining realistic about the presence of students for reasonable periods before and after school.

Parents should not be able to extend a principal's duty of care beyond normal hours by simply dropping their children off at school early or picking them up late. However, the task of balancing the needs of parents against the resources and responsibilities of the school rests mainly with the principal. To place reasonable limits on a school's duties, clear hours of supervision should be established for both before and after school. These policies must be communicated to parents at the outset of each school year with regular reminders as required. The hours of supervision should also remain as consistent as possible. If a particular student repeatedly arrives at school early or remains late, then the principal should consider contacting the student's parents and reminding them of the policy.[62] The expectations of students and parents regarding safety measures, in addition to the activity involved, will determine the extent of any liability.[63] Where students and

---

[60] *Titus v. Lindberg*, 38 A.L.R. (3d) 818 (N.J.S.C. 1967).
[61] "Liability: Planning a Safe School Year", *Edulaw for Canadian Schools*, Vol. 6, No. 2 (Calgary: Edulaw, October, 1994); "Duty of Care After School Dismissal", *Edulaw School Newsletter*, Vol. 2, No. 8 (Calgary: Edulaw, April, 1991). Occupiers' liability will be discussed later in this chapter.
[62] A.W. MacKay and L.I. Sutherland, *Teachers and the Law: A Practical Guide for Educators* (Toronto: Emond Montgomery, 1992), at p. 12.
[63] Roher, *op. cit.*, footnote 1, at p. 5.

parents are properly informed of these policies, a principal will not normally be liable for injuries to persons from non-school events outside those hours.

Where there is a particular risk to students on or in close proximity to school property, it may be incumbent on school authorities to bring this risk to the attention of students and parents. This may help to avoid injuries to students after school dismissal. In one case, a six-year-old student was struck by a motorist at an uncontrolled intersection near his school.[64] The student was returning home during the lunch hour. The student commenced a lawsuit against the driver of the car. The driver then sued the school board, among others, alleging its responsibility for the accident for failing to provide a school patrol program, safety instruction or supervision for students crossing at the intersection. The particular school was an inner-city school with a high student turnover rate. It was assumed to have a duty of care to students following dismissal within the proximity of the school.

The question arose as to whether the requisite standard of care had been met by the school in the circumstances. The trial judge ruled that neither the motorist nor the school had been negligent in the circumstances. The trial judge found that the school had taken a range of precautionary measures including: continuing traffic safety education for students and parents; newsletters containing traffic safety rules which were sent to parents; the posting of traffic rules around the school; an hour of traffic instruction annually for grade 1 students on their first day which included instructions to use the controlled intersection; traffic safety reviews; outdoor demonstrations on the third day of school; and a "safety week" program. The school also decided, in consultation with a police officer, not to patrol the intersection in order to discourage its use.[65]

It should be noted that on appeal the court found that the motorist was not proceeding with sufficient caution. The British Columbia Court of Appeal ruled that the motorist should have expected pedestrians and should have kept a lookout for them. It held that the student's act of running into the motorist's lane was also an important cause of the mishap. The court concluded that fault should be attributed equally between the motorist and the student.

In many instances, students and teachers may use school facilities or property for activities not sanctioned by the school or its board. This may occur for the sake of convenience. For example, in one British Columbia case, a high-school student playing rugby became a quadriplegic when a scrum collapsed during a game played for the British Columbia Rugby Union.[66] The game took place, with the approval of the school board, at the school where the student attended and played on the rugby team. In fact, one of the coaches of this match was a teacher and rugby

---

[64] *Dao (Guardian ad Litem of) v. Sabatino* (1993), 16 C.C.L.T. (2d) 235 (B.C.S.C.), revd on other grounds 123 W.A.C. 185, 24 B.C.L.R. (3d) 29 (C.A.).

[65] "Court Assumes Duty of Care After School Dismissal", *Edulaw for Canadian Schools*, Vol. 5, No. 8 (Calgary: Edulaw, April, 1994).

[66] *Hamstra (Guardian ad Litem of) v. British Columbia Rugby Union* (1989), 1 C.C.L.T. (2d) 78 (B.C.S.C.), revd on other grounds 123 D.L.R. (4th) 693, 94 W.A.C. 202, supplementary reasons 124 D.L.R. (4th) 607, 99 W.A.C. 156 (C.A.), revd 145 D.L.R. (4th) 193, [1997] 1 S.C.R. 1092.

coach at the school, who had encouraged the student to play in this fateful game. As a result of his injuries, the student sued the British Columbia Rugby Union, the teacher and the school board. In this case, the trial judge ruled that the school board was not liable for the student's injuries as it had no involvement in organizing the match. The trial judge also found that the school board was not vicariously liable for the actions of the teacher since he was acting as an agent of the rugby union and not as a representative of the school or school board. In this situation, the teacher was acting in a voluntary capacity such that the standard of care expected of him was that of an ordinary coach in the circumstances. In other cases, there may not be such a clear line separating school activities from those of a purely voluntary nature. Students and parents should be made aware of the voluntary nature of certain activities outside of school hours. Where such an activity before or after school does not form part of a teacher's supervisory responsibilities, that fact should also be communicated to students and parents.[67]

It should be noted that this case was reversed on other grounds by the British Columbia Court of Appeal. It held that the trial judge had erred in discharging the jury on the basis that certain evidence had inadvertently come out during the rugby union's case, after the student's case had been concluded. As a result, the Court of Appeal ordered a new trial.

Conduct off School Property

As a general rule, school authorities are not responsible for injuries suffered off school property, or occurring as students travel to and from school. However, there are circumstances in which the duty of principals and their staff to supervise students extends beyond the boundaries of school property. Common examples include the proximity of a school to known hazards, the transportation of students in certain circumstances and school excursions. In these situations, the role of the principal will be to ensure that a proper supervisory system is in place.

School principals should make themselves aware of hazards near school property, especially those hazards where it would be reasonably foreseeable that students might face danger.[68] Obvious hazards include a busy or uncontrolled roadway, natural features such as ravines, cliffs or bodies of water, infrastructure such as hydro-electric installations and hazards on adjoining properties. As school principals are aware, it is impossible to guarantee that students will not gain access to such hazards despite the best of precautions. As a result, boards, principals and staff will not be liable for injuries suffered by students where the injuries occurred

---

[67] "Sports Activities and Provincial Sports Organizations: Who is Liable", *Edulaw School Newsletter*, Vol. 2, No. 2 (Calgary: Edulaw, October, 1990). It should be noted that school grounds used with authorization by other organizations should be properly maintained in order to prevent injuries to participants, in accordance with occupiers' liability legislation: see *Pelletier v. Young Men's Christian Assn.*, [1999] B.C.J. No. 1868 (Q.L.) (Prov. Ct.), where a baseball player was cut by an object concealed in uncut grass on school property.

[68] Batzel, *op. cit.*, footnote 30, at p. 125.

as a result of the students' negligence, or despite the reasonable precautions of a careful and prudent parent having been taken in the circumstances.

The Saskatchewan case of *Magnusson v. Board of the Nipawin School Unit No. 61 of Saskatchewan*[69] involved eye injuries suffered by a 14-year-old pupil in fairgrounds immediately adjacent to his school. The injury was caused by a piece of broken glass found on the fairgrounds by another student and swung towards a wasps' nest the children were disturbing. The injured pupil stepped in front of the student wielding the glass. The boys had left school premises to enter the fairgrounds during a recess and there were no fences preventing their access. On appeal of the trial judge's dismissal of the action, the injured student claimed that the school's supervision system was inadequate. The student alleged that the presence of glass on the fairgrounds was reasonably foreseeable such that a fence should have been erected or a teacher posted on the boundary between the properties. The school had assigned two teachers to supervise students during the recess period. The Saskatchewan Court of Appeal ruled that this supervision was adequate. It concluded that broken glass was potentially dangerous, but not inherently dangerous requiring additional precautions by the school.[70]

Transportation of Students

In the past decade, the rapid growth of the suburbs outside of Canadian cities has resulted in an increased demand for school transportation. Thousands of students across Canada ride buses to school due to the fact that they do not have a school in their own neighbourhood, they attend special classes or they would have to cross dangerous intersections.

The transportation facilities may be owned and operated by a particular school board or may be provided by an independent company not affiliated with the board. The question then arises as to the legal liability of a school board or board employees arising from student transportation.

As a general principle, Canadian courts have held that a board will be vicariously liable for any negligence occurring with respect to transportation facilities owned and operated by it. Where transportation is provided by a company *not* affiliated with the board, but the board retains a substantial degree of control over the bus company and over the discipline of the students while they are on the bus, the board's duty to these students will likely continue until they arrive home.

The issue in determining liability is whether the bus company is truly an independent contractor or, in reality, a servant of the board. The answer to that question depends on the degree of control exercised by the board over the bus company regarding both the method and the manner in which it operates.

In a 1975 Ontario case, a five-year-old child, who was to be let off a bus at a certain location, got off the bus without the driver noticing at an earlier location

---

[69] (1975), 60 D.L.R. (3d) 572 (Sask. C.A.).
[70] *Supra*, at p. 574.

and was hit by a car.[71] In this case, the board exercised considerable control over the bus company and had issued a policy statement to the company respecting transportation, with instructions that it was to be followed. The policy statement included provisions regarding discipline for students who did not exhibit safe riding habits on the bus. It also included regulations which indicated that the board's manager of transportation services was responsible for scheduling all transportation requirements for each school. On these facts, the court concluded that the bus company was a servant of the board and not an independent contractor. The board was held vicariously liable.

In a 1961 Ontario case, several students were injured when their school bus was struck by a train as they were being transported home.[72] In this case, there was a written agreement which specified that the bus company was an independent contractor. The bus company serviced and maintained its own buses at its own expense and hired, paid and discharged its drivers without consulting the board. Far from controlling the manner of driving, the court found that the board merely designated the route and instructed the driver to be careful and not to allow misbehaviour. The court ruled that it would require cogent and unequivocal evidence to demonstrate that the parties had, in fact, changed their relationship to one of master and servant. It held that the bus company was an independent contractor, not an employee. Therefore, the court concluded that the school board was not liable for the injuries suffered by the students.

In a 1987 British Columbia case, a school yard served as a pick-up point for area students using school buses for transport to other schools.[73] The school's principal had informed the board that he was encountering difficulty in controlling the lineups of students and that he would not be responsible for supervising students as they boarded their buses. However, the principal did supervise students in this context from time to time, which may have created an expectation of such supervision. A 16-year-old student was injured when the bus he was attempting to board backed over his foot. The principal was not supervising the lineup at the time but was only monitoring the number of students using the buses. The court ruled that the school board, the bus driver and the principal were all jointly liable for the student's injury. The court found that the school board was negligent for failing to respond to the principal's notices and for failing to arrange for an orderly boarding of buses. The court also concluded that the principal was negligent for failing to supervise the students on the day in question.

As indicated earlier, the courts have held that a school board may be vicariously liable for acts of negligence by its employees and volunteers acting within the scope of their employment or authority. In most cases, liability flows from the teacher and/or the principal to the corporate board.

---

[71] *Mattinson v. Wonnacott* (1975), 59 D.L.R. (3d) 18, 8 O.R. (2d) 654 (H.C.J.).
[72] *Baldwin v. Erin District High School Board* (1961), 29 D.L.R. (2d) 290, [1961] O.R. 687 (C.A.), affd 36 D.L.R. (2d) 244, [1962] S.C.R. vii.
[73] *Germschied v. Richardson* (1987), 7 A.C.W.S. (3d) 162, [1987] B.C.J. No. 2250 (Q.L.) (S.C.).

In the context of bus transportation, if a school's system of school-yard supervision commences at 8:30 a.m. and the board arranges for buses to drop off students on school premises at 8:10 a.m., a strong argument could be made that the board has a responsibility to supervise these students until the formal system of supervision commences.

Teachers will sometimes offer students transport to and from sporting events or other activities in their own vehicles. So long as this transport is related to a school activity, the educator's duty of care will extend to these activities. Since this transport may often occur in the course of employment, it could lead to a school board's vicarious liability in the event that injuries occur. The student's parents should be informed as to the mode of transportation being used regarding the school event. In addition, the school board should be properly insured in these circumstances.

Where students are dropped off at the school after a sports event or other activity and are waiting to be picked up by their respective parents, it is advised that the principal or another staff member remain at the school to supervise these students. In this regard, common sense precautions should be taken to ensure that the students are properly picked up by their parents or are able to return home safely.

School Excursions

Where field trips or excursions off school property are school-related activities, the standard of care of a careful or prudent parent will apply to educators.[74] Again, the role of the principal is to implement an adequate system of supervision or to properly supervise the students in the event that the principal participates in the trip.

The 1972 Ontario case of *Moddejonge v. Huron County Board of Education*[75] concerned two young girls who tragically drowned on a school field trip. The supervising teacher as well as one of the girls who drowned were unable to swim. No life-saving equipment was available. The teacher permitted the children to swim in an area which was close to a dangerous drop-off point. When the children drifted into the dangerous area, the teacher did nothing. The court held that the duty owed by a teacher or supervisor towards children in his or her charge on such a trip is to take such care of them as a prudent parent would of his or her own children. Since the teacher was acting within the scope of his employment, both the school board and the teacher were found liable.

In the 1993 Alberta case of *Bain v. Calgary Board of Education*,[76] a 19-year-old grade 11 vocational student sustained severe brain injuries while on an outdoor

---

[74] Brown and Zuker, *op. cit.*, footnote 5, at p. 62.
[75] (1972), 25 D.L.R. (3d) 661, [1972] 2 O.R. 437 (H.C.J.).
[76] [1994] 2 W.W.R. 468, 14 Alta. L.R. (3d) 319 (Q.B.). See also Brown and Zuker, *op. cit.*, footnote 5, at pp. 69-70; "Liability for Outdoor Education Accident", *Edulaw for Canadian Schools*, Vol. 5, No. 6 (Calgary: Edulaw, February, 1994).

education tour sponsored by the school and supervised by a teacher. Rather than watch a video on the approved outdoor education agenda, the student and some other boys wanted to climb a nearby mountain. After some hesitation, the teacher complied and dropped the students off at the base of the mountain, promising to return to pick them up in three hours. There was no marked trail so the students attempted a direct ascent of the mountain. The student fell from a steep rock face and struck his head, resulting in his injuries.

As an extension of the classroom, the supervising teacher was found to have owed the student a duty of care and at least the same standard of care as he would have in the school. Given the inherent dangers associated with the climbing, the expected standard of care may have been higher. The court ruled that the teacher was negligent for allowing the hike, for not properly preparing the students for it and for failing to properly supervise the hike. The court noted that the whole incident could have been avoided if the agenda for the evening activities, authorized by the school board and approved by the parents, had been followed.

In devising a system of supervision for students on excursions, familiar factors must be considered regarding the foreseeability of an accident and the precautions to be taken in order to meet the requisite standard of care. These factors include: the age and maturity of the students; the level of danger associated with the activities; the students' propensity for reckless behaviour; the intelligence and experience of the students; and any training required. In the *Bain* case, the student required supervision in this dangerous activity despite his age. Although, in general, a school principal does not attend on school excursions, he or she should ensure that adequate supervisory precautions have been taken and that the accompanying staff have the required training and experience to supervise the activities involved. In addition, a principal should always take steps to inform parents of the nature and details of any excursion and to have all necessary permission forms completed by students and/or their parents.

Parental Permission Forms

As discussed earlier, to minimize any possible liability, it is important for an educator to take preventative measures in advance of the school excursion or extra-curricular activity. Part of this preventative process involves the use of parental "permission" or "consent" forms. These forms have been in use for many years but they are by no means standardized and, even within individual schools, different forms may be in use. There is no single form which is ideal for all circumstances, but there are certain characteristics which every permission or consent form should have.[77]

There are several reasons why a parental permission form should be obtained. First, the permission form represents evidence that the teacher has informed the parent as to what the child is doing in school. Secondly, the form is an

---

[77] C. Hoglund, "Parental Permission Forms: Minimizing Liability During School Excursions", *Education Law News* (Fall, 1996) (Toronto: Borden & Elliot), p. 1.

acknowledgement from the parent that the planned activity is "acceptable". If something goes wrong, it is reassuring to be able to confirm that the parent had no objections to the activity itself.[78] This is especially true if there are particular risks involved in the activity. Thirdly, the parent may be discouraged from commencing a lawsuit on behalf of the child who has suffered a loss or injury if the parent has consented to the activity. What the permission form will not do, however, is prevent a child from bringing a legal action (through an adult) should some loss or injury occur. This right cannot be surrendered by the parent.

The permission form should be obtained from the person who has legal custody of the non-adult student. Normally, this would be a parent, but it could be a legal guardian or an agency appointed as ward, such as a children's aid society. Where feasible, it is preferable to have both parents sign the form.

The form is generally used when the proposed activity is outside the normal or expected classroom situation. Parents have a set of expectations as to what their children will be doing while in the care of a teacher. When the activity is inherently dangerous (*e.g.*, floor hockey or gymnastics), outside normal school hours, outside the school grounds or simply out of the ordinary, the parent's consent should not be implied. Instead, the consent should be expressly obtained, in writing.

To reduce the school's and the individual teacher's exposure to a lawsuit, it is important that teachers obtain permission or consent from the students' parents or legal guardians in advance of the event. The simplest way of ensuring that this is done is to insist that all teachers follow a standard procedure. The teachers should be made aware that, if they do not follow this procedure, they not only expose the school to potential liability, but they also expose themselves to such a claim.[79]

It is suggested that a school consider the following guidelines in preparing permission forms:

- The form must be signed and dated by the parent(s) or legal guardian(s).
- The form should contain the printed name of the child and the parent or guardian who signs the form.
- "Blanket" consents are not appropriate. The precise activity or activities to be covered by the consent should be named so that the parent will know exactly what is involved. For example, permission for the child to participate in extra-curricular athletic activities is insufficient, unless the sports are specified.
- Permission forms should be kept separate from other material being sent home from the school, such as newsletters.
- If especially rigorous activity is involved, a medical certificate should be obtained in order to verify that the student is fit for the activity.[80]

If the school would like the parent to indicate his or her willingness to help with supervision or transportation regarding the school excursion, the school should

---

[78] A. Brown, "Parental Permission Forms", *Ontario Public School Teachers' Federation News*, Vol. 5, No. 5 (June, 1991), p. 20.
[79] Hoglund, *op. cit.*, footnote 77.
[80] *Ibid.*

obtain this consent separately from the permission for the child to participate. Otherwise, the parent may contend that the signature was only an indication of willingness to help and not a consent to the activity for the child.

For a consent to be valid, it must be an informed consent. In other words, the parent's decision to sign the form must be based on full and accurate information. Therefore, considerable attention should be given to the communication which goes home. The information which accompanies the actual form must provide sufficient detail about the specific activity being proposed.

Permission forms may include the following items:

- the nature and purpose of the activity or trip;
- any unusual factors, such as rigorous exercise, water sports, flying, etc. (special risks must be clearly brought to the attention of the student and the parent);
- where the activity will be held and relevant times and/or dates;
- the supervision which will be provided and by whom (this should be in accordance with the school's guidelines);
- transportation arrangements, including mode of transport, whose vehicle will be used and who will be driving (*e.g.*, a teacher, volunteer or student);
- a reminder that student injury insurance coverage may be purchased;
- the cost of the activity and the need for lunches, special clothing, etc.;
- a reminder that parents should let the school know of any relevant medical conditions, just in case there has been a change which is not reflected in the student record (depending on the activity, the school may require a parental consent for medical assistance to be rendered in the event of an emergency involving significant injury); and
- any other information which could have some bearing on whether the parent would give or withhold permission (*e.g.*, some parents may not want their children to see plays or films on certain subjects).[81]

The form which is sent back to the school with the parent's signature should either contain the information about the activity or have the information attached. The parent's signature should confirm acceptance of the student's participation in a specific activity or excursion. For instance, a one-page form with a "tear-off and return" section at the bottom is not advised. Although it may not always be practical, it is suggested that the school send the information and the permission form home in duplicate, with one set to be returned. This ensures that both the school and the parent have the same information and documentation.

The parental permission form should be distinguished from a form signed by a parent which is intended to release the school and its employees from liability for negligence affecting a child, or which waives the right to bring a legal action. This form may be combined with the parent's promise to indemnify the school if the

---

[81] *Ibid.*

school is forced to pay damages to the child. A release or waiver form signed by a parent will not prevent the child from bringing a legal action. It is not binding on the child and, as a minor, the child cannot personally enter into such a contract. In particular, the courts have held that where, in the context of a school excursion, there is evidence of negligence, carelessness or recklessness on the part of the school teacher, a release or waiver form signed by a parent may not be enforceable.

Post-injury Advice

When a student is injured at school, parents obviously desire as much information as possible regarding what has occurred. Principals will naturally express their sympathy for the student and their concern for the student's well-being, and doing so is clearly appropriate. However, while communicating these feelings to parents, principals and other school authorities must not make statements which jeopardize the proper investigation of the matter by the school board's insurer, or the potential defence to a lawsuit. Some practical tips regarding the steps to be taken after a significant injury at school include:

- Immediately inform senior administration and the board's insurer using the procedure approved by the board.
- Co-operate with the insurance adjuster and lawyer who represent the school board.
- Keep *detailed* notes on any incident resulting in suspected or actual personal injury.
- Do not admit liability for any accident or other incident which occurs on school property.
- Do not give statements to parents, opposing lawyers or insurance adjusters.
- Do not share any insurance reports or personal notes with parents unless permitted to do so by the school board's insurer and/or relevant freedom of information legislation.[82]

While this advice requires a school principal to maintain a delicate balance between relaying genuine concern and protecting the interests of the school and its board, it is necessary to exercise forethought and care in these circumstances.

DUTY TO KEEP SCHOOL SAFE AND IN GOOD REPAIR

The principal's duty to keep school premises safe and in good repair is reinforced by specific statutory duties. For instance, section 265(j) of the Ontario *Education Act* requires principals to give "assiduous attention to . . . the cleanliness, temperature and ventilation of the school" as well as the "condition and appearance of the school buildings and grounds". Section 11 of Regulation 298 under the *Education Act* also requires the principal to undertake regular

---

[82] Brown, *op. cit.*, footnote 27, at pp. 121-2.

inspections of school premises and to report any required repairs or lack of attention by building staff to the school board. As a result of this legislation, and the principles of occupiers' liability, principals may face liability for reasonably foreseeable injuries occurring as a result of unsafe conditions, equipment or apparatus on school premises.

Occupiers' liability legislation imposes a duty on those in possession or control of premises to keep their premises safe for those who may reasonably be expected to enter. This legislation does not change the educator's standard of care of a "careful or prudent parent" for students during school activities. Rather, it provides a duty of care towards visitors and trespassers on relevant premises, including school property. The statutory duty of care will also apply to employees and other people, including students, who are on school property for reasons other than school-authorized activities. The legislation generally mirrors the common law principles of negligence to establish a duty of care for the occupiers of premises.[83]

In Ontario, the *Occupiers' Liability Act*[84] describes an occupier's duty of care as follows:

> 3(1) An occupier of premises owes a duty to take such care as in all the circumstances of the case is reasonable to see that persons entering on the premises, and the property brought on the premises by those persons are reasonably safe while on the premises.
> (2) The duty of care provided for in subsection (1) applies whether the danger is caused by the *condition of the premises* or by an *activity carried on on the premises*.

(Emphasis added.) An "occupier" includes a person who has responsibility for and control over the condition of the premises, or control over the persons allowed to enter the premises or the activities carried out on the premises.[85] Both school boards and school principals can be considered "occupiers" for the purposes of the legislation, though a school board may face liability for the acts of the principal.[86]

---

[83] Roher, *op. cit.*, footnote 4, at pp. 35-6.

[84] R.S.O. 1990, c. O.2. Similar to a negligence claim, for an action in occupiers' liability to be successful, the plaintiff must show that the defendant was an occupier of the premises at the time of the accident, that the defendant owed the duty of care of an occupier to the plaintiff (including that the plaintiff had not accepted the risk), that the defendant breached that duty of care by failing to take reasonable steps to eliminate the danger provided the particular danger was foreseeable, that the breach of the duty of care was a cause of the plaintiff's injury and that the plaintiff suffered damage as a result: see L.N. Klar et al., *Occupier's Liability* (Toronto: Carswell, 1995), at pp. 18-24 and 18-78. In some other provinces such as British Columbia and Manitoba, occupiers' liability legislation includes clauses creating duties of care with respect to the actions of third parties on the premises.

[85] *Occupiers' Liability Act*, s. 1.

[86] Roher, *op. cit.*, footnote 4, at pp. 35-6. See J.P. Bell, "Education Law in Ontario – Liability Issues Affecting Boards of Education, Its Trustees, Servants, Agents and Employees" (paper presented at the Canadian Bar Association – Ontario, May 30, 1986).

With respect to school principals, any liability they might incur would likely be related to their statutory duties regarding the provision of education in their schools. In Ontario, these duties include holding examinations necessary for the promotion of pupils, proper promotion of students,[97] the instruction of pupils in the school and performance appraisals of teaching staff.[98] The duty that a principal may owe with respect to the content of classes taught under his or her supervision is less clear. However, to the extent that principals are involved in placement decisions regarding student or teacher evaluations, a duty of care regarding the provision of education could be established. Professor Wayne MacKay of Dalhousie University has observed that recent actions challenging the provision of education have focused on the classification and measurement of student performance.[99] Such a trend may place the role of the principal under greater scrutiny.

Students and their parents have attempted to assert claims of educational malpractice in the United States and Canada but have failed to establish an accepted cause of action in the courts. There are a number of reasons why the courts have been reluctant to accept the cause of action. For example, allegations of "malpractice" have usually been brought against members of traditional professions which have a greater level of autonomy than teachers who are subject to an employer-employee relationship. In Ontario at least, the recent establishment of the Ontario College of Teachers has brought a greater level of professionalism to teaching.[100] The standard of care has also been difficult to describe with respect to the actions of teachers, since teaching does not involve a quantifiable level of precision, as with surgical procedures or standardized accounting. In addition, proving that poor instruction caused a particular injury is extremely difficult given the myriad of variables which can affect a pupil's learning. Given the years of instruction most pupils receive, it is extremely difficult to isolate the particular actions of certain educators as being responsible for a student's loss.[101]

In general, courts have been reluctant to accept educational malpractice suits due to public policy considerations. These considerations include the following:

- The courts are an inappropriate forum to test the efficacy of educational theories, policy, programs and pedagogical methods.
- The courts are not a proper forum to set and supervise standards of conduct for teachers.
- Recognition of educational malpractice as an actionable wrong would require the courts to oversee and supervise the administration of the public school system, something which they are not equipped to do.

---

[97] *Education Act*, s. 265; Regulation 298, s. 11.
[98] Regulation 298, ss. 11(1) and (3).
[99] MacKay, *op. cit.*, footnote 15.
[100] *Ontario College of Teachers Act, 1996*, S.O. 1996, c. 12.
[101] "Does the Failure to Learn Bespeak the Failure to Teach?", *Edulaw School Newsletter*, Vol. 2, No. 8 (Calgary: Edulaw, April, 1991).

- Recognition of educational malpractice as an actionable wrong would expose school boards to countless numbers of tort claims, real or imagined, by disaffected students and parents.[102]

In Ontario, the District Court dismissed an educational malpractice action in *Hicks v. Etobicoke (City) Board of Education*,[103] indicating that it was not open to the plaintiffs to challenge the board's procedures and decisions before the courts. In that case, the student in question progressed from grade 2 to grade 5 despite a lack of scholastic progress. The student commenced an action in negligence and alleged that the school board had failed to provide proper evaluation and corrective instruction. This case marked the first clear action based on educational malpractice in Canada. The court did not accept the claim against the school board due to policy considerations.[104]

More recently, Canadian courts have continued to apply these policy considerations. In British Columbia, the Provincial Court determined that allegations that a teacher had omitted a component of a prescribed French immersion program were not actionable in light of public policy considerations.[105] The court stated that other mechanisms, such as an appeal to the school board or parent councils, might be a more appropriate forum for seeking a resolution of education disputes. The court concluded by quoting Mr. Justice La Forest in *R. v. Jones*[106] as follows: "The courtroom is simply not the best arena for the debate of issues of educational policy and the measurement of educational quality".

REPORTING THE PRESENCE OF COMMUNICABLE DISEASES

A school principal also has very specific responsibilities with respect to reporting the presence of communicable diseases in the school. In Ontario, the *Health Protection and Promotion Act*[107] places such a duty on principals. Section 28 of that Act provides:

> 28. The principal of a school who is of the opinion that a pupil in the school has or may have a communicable disease shall, as soon as possible after forming the

---

[102] "Education Malpractice Action Disallowed", *Education Law Reporter*, Vol. 8, No. 7 (Calgary: Edulaw, March, 1997).
[103] [1988] O.J. No. 1900 (Q.L.) (Dist. Ct.).
[104] M.A. Hines, "Malpractice in Education", in W.F. Foster and F. Peters, eds., *Education & Law: Strengthening the Partnership* (Welland: Editions Soleil Publishing, 1993), p. 154.
[105] *Haynes (Guardian ad litem of) v. Lleres*, [1997] B.C.J. No. 1202 (Q.L.) (Prov. Ct.), discussed in "Educational Malpractice Not Actionable", *Education Law Reporter* (Calgary: Edulaw, March, 1998), p. 52.
[106] (1986), 31 D.L.R. (4th) 569 at p. 598, [1986] 2 S.C.R. 284, quoting from *State v. Shaver*, 294 N.W. 2d 883 (1980), at p. 900.
[107] R.S.O. 1990, c. H.7.

opinion, report thereon to the medical officer of health of the health unit in which the school is located.

The regulations under the *Health Protection and Promotion Act* include a list of diseases designated as communicable for the purposes of the legislation[108] and the information required in the report which generally includes the name and address of the student in question, the student's date of birth, the student's sex, and the name and address of the school the student attends.[109] The list of communicable diseases should be referred to as it contains common conditions such as food poisoning, chicken pox and various sexually transmitted diseases. The Ontario *Education Act* also provides that it is a principal's duty to report promptly to the board and to the medical officer of health when the principal has reason to suspect the existence of any communicable disease in the school, as well as "the unsanitary condition of any part of the school building or the school grounds".[110] In addition, where a school principal believes a person is infected with or has been exposed to communicable diseases requiring an order under section 22 of the *Health Protection and Promotion Act*, that person should be refused admission to the school until the principal has been provided with a certificate from the medical officer of health or an appropriate medical authority stating that all danger from exposure to contact with the person has passed.[111]

SUGGESTED MEASURES

Most school boards, in conjunction with their legal advisors, have developed policies, procedures or guidelines to address the risk of injuries and liability through the operation of their schools. Though these policies may not always be exhaustive, they should be referred to in preparation for each school year and in response to events as required. As general advice in managing risk in a school setting and meeting the required standard of care, we suggest the following measures which can be undertaken by principals at the school level:

- Be open and collaborative in the development and implementation of school policies. This may include input from staff and parents.
- Develop a consistent level of documentation of events at the school. This documentation should include a clear, chronological, factual outline of the relevant events, as well as possible witness statements.
- Review previous incidents of injury which have occurred in the school, including the number of incidents, the nature of the injuries and the circumstances giving rise to the incidents.

---

[108] *Specification of Communicable Diseases*, O. Reg. 558/91.
[109] *Reports*, R.R.O. 1990, Reg. 569.
[110] *Education Act*, s. 265(k).
[111] *Education Act*, s. 265(l).

- Consider such information as how the incident was handled by the administration and what measures could have been undertaken to eliminate or reduce the risk of injury.
- Continually re-evaluate existing safety procedures to ensure that they cover all foreseeable risks of harm.
- Follow any school guidelines which specify appropriate standards of care and supervision of students.
- Monitor and discuss the policy and practice concerning school excursions and outdoor events with other professionals.
- Keep abreast of what other schools are doing with respect to sports activities and supervision of students, such as proper equipment, safe premises and appropriate training.
- Follow developments in the law through education law periodicals.
- Implement a regular policy and procedure review of the appropriate standards of care and supervision of students for teaching and support staff. New staff should be provided with an initiation meeting or in-service program to review these policies.[112]

---

[112] Roher, *op. cit.*, footnote 1, at p. 6; S. Bate, "The Changing Role of the Principal" (address to the Canada Law Book Symposium, "The New ABCs of Learning", Toronto, November 26, 1999) [unpublished]; MacKay, *op. cit.*, footnote 15.

3

Student Records and Confidentiality

INTRODUCTION

In the course of operating a school, a principal and his or her staff gather, generate and retain a great deal of information regarding their students. Much of this information is of a very personal nature, and may include facts regarding a student's performance, conduct, health, family status and residence. In Ontario, the *Education Act*[1] requires a principal to establish and maintain this type of information in a student's official "record", commonly called an Ontario Student Record ("OSR"). The OSR is the record of a student's educational progress through schools in Ontario. The *Education Act* requires that the principal of a school collect information "for inclusion in a record in respect of each pupil enrolled in the school and to establish, maintain, retain, transfer and dispose of the record".[2]

School authorities may also collect information regarding students which is not maintained in their OSR. In either case, the law places restrictions on what information can be collected or stored and under what conditions it may be used or disclosed to students, their parents or third parties. As would be expected with personal information, there are expectations of privacy, that is, the right of an individual to control his or her personal information.[3] In addition, students may confide in professional staff in situations where they expressly or impliedly expect their communications will remain confidential. The law of confidentiality protects this expectation and relates to whether, and under what conditions, persons holding information which was communicated in confidence, or obtained with the expectation of confidence, may voluntarily disclose such information to third parties. Also, there may be circumstances where the law will compel the disclosure of confidential information in the course of legal proceedings.

---

[1] R.S.O. 1990, c. E.2.
[2] *Education Act*, s. 265(d).
[3] E.M. Roher, "Privacy, Confidentiality and Privilege in a School Context" (paper presented to the Conference of the Canadian Association for the Practical Study of Law in Education, Saskatoon, May 1 to 3, 1994), in W.F. Foster, ed., *Rights, Responsibilities & Reasonableness: Striking the Balance in Education* (Chateauguay: Lisbro, 1995).

ONTARIO STUDENT RECORD

The *Ontario Student Record (OSR) Guideline, 2000*,[4] which was updated in March, 2000 (the "Guideline"), sets out the policies of the Ministry of Education with regard to the establishment, maintenance, use, retention, transfer and disposal of the OSR. It replaces the *Ontario Student Record (OSR) Guideline, 1989*.[5]

An OSR is to be established for each student who enrols in a school operated by a school board or the Ministry of Education. The Guideline provides that each student and the parent(s) of a student who is not an adult must be informed of the purpose and content of the OSR at the time of enrolment. The OSR is an ongoing record and will be transferred, under the terms set out in the Guideline, in circumstances where a student transfers to another school in Ontario.

The contents of the OSR are outlined in the Guideline. Each OSR should consist of several components, including biographical information, transcripts, report cards, health information, photographs, standardized or specialized testing results, court documentation on custody and access arrangements, and suspension letters regarding incidents of violence. A principal may also place in the OSR any information which may be beneficial to teachers in the instruction of the pupil.

Section 2 of the Guideline elaborates on the specific duties of a school principal with respect to the OSR. It provides, in part:

> It is the duty of the principal of a school to:
> - establish, maintain, retain, transfer and dispose of a record for each student enrolled in the school in compliance with this guideline and the policies established by the board;
> - ensure that the materials in the OSR are collected and stored in accordance with the policies in this guideline and the policies established by the board;
> - ensure the security of the OSR;
> - ensure that all persons specified by a board to perform clerical functions with respect to the establishment and maintenance of the OSR are aware of the confidentiality provisions in the *Education Act* and the relevant freedom of information and protection of privacy legislation.[6]

Therefore, the responsibilities of a principal extend beyond the inclusion of appropriate information in the OSR. The principal is ultimately responsible for its security and ensuring that the information is properly managed by school staff.

Contents of an OSR

The Guideline provides a detailed description of the required contents of an OSR. An OSR will consist of the following components:

---

[4] Ontario Ministry of Education, *The Ontario Student Record (OSR) Guideline, 2000* (March, 2000), at p. 3.

[5] Ontario Ministry of Education, *Ontario Student Record (OSR) Guideline, 1989* (December, 1989).

[6] Guideline, *op. cit.*, footnote 4, at pp. 5 and 6.

Student Records and Confidentiality 79

- an OSR folder;
- report cards;
- a student transcript, where applicable;
- a documentation file, where applicable;
- an office index card; and
- additional information identified as being conducive to the improvement of the instruction of the student.[7]

With respect to information pertaining to schools that a student attended, the Guideline indicates that the following will be provided:

- the name of each school that the student attended;
- the name of the board or the name of the person who operated the private or federal school;
- the date of entry and the date of last attendance in each grade; and
- the name of a teacher contact.

Secrecy of the OSR

Principals and teachers have an additional duty under the *Education Act* to maintain the private nature of the information contained in the OSR. Section 266(10) of the Act requires that an educator "preserve secrecy in respect of the content of a record that comes to the person's knowledge in the course of his or her duties". No person may communicate such knowledge to any other person except as may be required by his or her duties, or with the written consent of the parent or guardian where the student is a minor, or with the written consent of the student where the student is an adult. For the purposes of the Act, a student is considered a minor where he or she is under the age of 18.[8]

Access to the OSR

Section 4 of the Guideline states:

> Access to an OSR means the right of those persons authorized by the *Education Act* or other legislation to examine the contents of the OSR. In addition, municipal and provincial freedom of information legislation permits persons who have the right to have access to personal information to receive copies of the information.[9]

Under the provisions of section 266(3) of the *Education Act*, every student has the right to have access to his or her OSR. The Act provides that parents of a student have the right to have access to the student's OSR, until the student becomes an adult.[10] Under both the *Children's Law Reform Act*[11] and the *Divorce*

---

[7] *Ibid.*, section 3, at p. 7.
[8] *Age of Majority and Accountability Act*, R.S.O. 1990, c. A.7.
[9] Guideline, *op. cit.*, footnote 4, section 4, at p. 14.
[10] *Ibid.*
[11] R.S.O. 1990, c. C.12.

Act,[12] the legal right of a non-custodial parent to have access to a child includes the right to make inquiries and be given information concerning the child's health, education and welfare.[13]

In addition, section 266(2) of the *Education Act* provides that only supervisory officers, the principal and teachers at the school have access to the OSR for the purpose of improving the instruction of the student. For practical purposes in a school, this restriction also means that persons such as parent volunteers and elected school council members are prevented from accessing information in an OSR without proper written consent.[14] As will be discussed later in this chapter, additional access may be permitted under the municipal freedom of information legislation, under specified and limited circumstances.

It should also be noted that information from an OSR may be used to assist in the preparation of a report required under the *Education Act* or its regulations. Information from an OSR may be used in the preparation of a report for an application for further education or an application for employment, if a written request for such a report is made by an adult student, a former student or the parent(s) of a student.[15]

Transfer of the OSR

Under the Guideline, the transfer of the OSR means the transfer of all parts of the OSR other than the office index card. Subject to certain conditions, the original OSR is transferable only to schools in the Province of Ontario.[16]

When a student transfers to another school in Ontario, the receiving school must be sent written notification of the student's transfer indicating that the student's OSR will be sent upon receipt of an official written request. When a student transfers to a school outside of Ontario, only a copy of the student's OSR may be sent upon receipt of an official written request. The Guideline provides that, in the event the original OSR is being transferred between schools operated by the same school board, it may be transferred by a delivery service provided by the board.[17]

Under the Guideline, a student retires from school when he or she ceases to be enrolled in school. In circumstances where a student retires from the school which maintained an OSR for the student, the principal will provide the following to the parents of the student, if he or she is not an adult, or to an adult student:

- an up-to-date copy of the student's Ontario Student Transcript; and

---

[12] R.S.C. 1985, c. 3 (2nd Supp.).
[13] See Chapter 6, "The Rights of Non-Custodial Parents".
[14] B. Stokes Verworn, "Privacy and School Records: Fair Ground Rules", in W.F. Foster and W.J. Smith, eds., *Reaching for Reasonableness: The Educator as Lawful Decision-Maker* (Chateauguay: Lisbro, 1999), p. 89, at p. 93.
[15] *Education Act*, s. 266(6)(b). See also the Guideline, *op. cit.*, footnote 4, section 5, at p. 17.
[16] Guideline, *op. cit.*, footnote 4, section 6, at p. 18.
[17] *Ibid.*

- the information and materials stored in the OSR folder which are not required to be retained under the retention schedule.[18]

The retention schedule set out in section 8 of the Guideline provides that the following components of the OSR must be retained for five years after a student retires from school:

- report cards;
- the documentation file; and
- additional information identified by the school board as appropriate for retention.

The following components of the OSR must be retained for 55 years after a student retires from school:

- the OSR folder;
- the Ontario Student Transcript; and
- the office index card.[19]

Correction and Removal of Information in the OSR

Section 266(4) of the *Education Act* also permits students and their parents to take steps towards correcting or removing information in the OSR. If, in the opinion of the adult pupil, or the parent or guardian of a pupil under the age of 18, the OSR contains information which is inaccurately recorded or is not conducive to the improvement of instruction of the pupil, the pupil or parent may make a written request to the principal to correct the alleged inaccuracy or remove the information from the record. If the principal agrees with the request, the material will be corrected or will be removed from the file and destroyed or returned to the adult student or the parent or guardian of a student who is not an adult. No record of the request is to be kept in the OSR.

If the principal refuses to comply with the request, the Act provides additional procedures for the parent(s) or adult student. The parent(s) or the adult student may request in writing that the principal refer the request to the appropriate supervisory officer. The supervisory officer will either: require that the principal comply with the request; or submit the OSR and the request to a person designated by the Minister of Education.[20] In the event the supervisory officer requires that the principal comply with the request, no record of the request will be retained in the OSR.

Under the provisions of the Guideline, where the supervisory officer submits the request to a person designated by the Minister, that person will hold a hearing, which the principal and the person(s) who made the request will attend. Subsequent to the hearing, the person designated by the Minister will make a

---

[18] *Ibid.*, section 7, at p. 20.
[19] *Ibid.*, section 8, at p. 21.
[20] *Ibid.*, section 9, at p. 22.

decision on the matter. The decision will be final and binding.[21] If the person designated by the Minister requires that the principal comply with the request, no record of the request will be retained in the OSR. If the person designated by the Minister denies the request, the original request, including the date on which it was made, and the statement of final decision will be retained in the documentation file.[22]

The OSR and the Principal's Role

It is important to note that none of the restrictions regarding access to and use of a student's OSR prevent a school principal from performing the essential duties of his or her job. Section 266(7) of the *Education Act* specifically states that nothing in the provisions regarding student records prevents the compilation and delivery of information in an OSR as may be required by the Minister of Education or by the school board. This means that a school principal can disclose information in an OSR when completing a required report. Additionally, the principal may use the OSR of a pupil enrolled in his or her school for the purposes of discipline in respect of conduct which may contravene school rules or its code of behaviour.[23] A principal may also have to release information regarding a student to the local medical officer of health upon request. However, that information must be limited to the pupil's name, address, telephone number and birthdate, and the parent or guardian's name, address and telephone number.[24]

THE OSR IN LEGAL PROCEEDINGS

The *Education Act* creates a legal privilege in the information contained in an OSR. This restricts its use in legal proceedings, except under certain conditions. Section 266(2)(b) of the Act provides that, except for certain purposes, the OSR is "not admissible in evidence for any purpose in any trial, inquest, inquiry, examination, hearing or other proceeding, except to prove the establishment, maintenance, retention or transfer of the record", without the written permission of the pupil's parent or guardian or, where the pupil is an adult, the written permission of the pupil. The Act specifically provides that, except where the record has been introduced in evidence pursuant to section 266 of the *Education Act*, no one is required to testify in relation to the content of the record.[25]

Notwithstanding these provisions, there may be occasions where access to the OSR of a current student or former student will be sought. In such cases, boards should obtain legal advice from their counsel in order to respond to such questions as:

---

[21] *Ibid.*
[22] *Ibid.*
[23] *Education Act*, s. 266(13). See A.F. Brown, *Legal Handbook for Educators*, 4th. ed. (Toronto: Carswell, 1998), at p. 115.
[24] *Education Act*, s. 266(2.1).
[25] *Education Act*, s. 266(9).

- Does the *Education Act* prevent the production of the OSR?
- Is the OSR relevant to the proceedings?
- If the OSR is relevant to the proceedings, should a copy, rather than the original, be submitted to the court?[26]

Civil Proceedings

Typically, a summons to witness will be initiated by counsel in a personal injury suit, divorce or custody dispute requiring a principal or supervisory officer to attend court at a specified time and place with a student's OSR. The OSR may be requested by a parent or guardian of the student or by the solicitor for the student. In addition, the OSR may be subpoenaed by an adverse party in a legal action.[27]

In any of these situations, the adult student, or parent or guardian (where the student is under the age of 18), may provide written permission to make the record available. Where a subpoena to produce the record is received but the adult student or the parent or guardian does not consent to its release, the school should refrain from releasing the OSR until a court order is obtained. Such action will protect the school against any allegations that it has violated the provisions of the *Education Act* regarding the privileged nature of pupil records. Where a principal is subpoenaed to give evidence, he or she may be asked to testify as to the fact that the record is what it purports to be.

Where a principal is subpoenaed to produce the OSR, he or she should make a copy of the record and take both the original and copy to court. Most judges will permit the copy to be entered into evidence, allowing the principal to retain the original. The principal should inform the judge that the subpoena is inconsistent with section 266(2) of the *Education Act*. The principal must then relinquish the documents if ordered to do so by the judge.[28]

Criminal Proceedings

In criminal matters, the provisions of the *Education Act* are less effective in protecting the privacy of student records. This is due to the fact that the *Criminal Code*[29] and the *Canada Evidence Act*,[30] which govern criminal matters and are both federal statutes, take precedence over the *Education Act*, which is provincial legislation. The federally legislated summons provisions prevail over the provisions of the *Education Act* dealing with access to student records.[31]

Valid search warrants requiring the surrender of an OSR to the police or subpoenas requiring the testimony of a principal or supervisory officer should be

---

[26] Guideline, *op. cit.*, footnote 4, para. 4.5, at p. 15.
[27] E.M. Roher, "The Truth and Nothing But the Truth About Going to Court", *Education Law News* (Winter, 1992) (Toronto: Borden & Elliot), p. 2.
[28] Guideline, *op. cit.*, footnote 4, para. 4.5.1, at p. 15.
[29] R.S.C. 1985, c. C-46.
[30] R.S.C. 1985, c. C-5.
[31] Guideline, *op. cit.*, footnote 4, para. 4.5.2, at p. 16.

obeyed. Again, the principal should inform the relevant authority (*i.e.*, the police or the judge) that use of any parts of the OSR as evidence in court proceedings is inconsistent with section 266(2) of the *Education Act*. The principal should present the police or the judge with both the original OSR and a complete and exact photocopy of it and suggest that the copy be submitted instead of the original.[32]

Overall, the following are guidelines you should consider if you are served with a summons or subpoena:

- Under section 266 of the *Education Act*, the documents contained in a student's OSR are privileged for the information and use of teachers, principals and supervisory officers of the school.
- Where an adult student or his or her parent or guardian (where the pupil is under the age of 18) provides written consent to make a record contained in the OSR available, it may be released to such student, parent or guardian.
- A normal summons or subpoena requires you to come to court (and, if so specified, to bring documents with you). It does not authorize or compel you to give information or hand documents to defence counsel, the Crown or a third party out of court.
- You should be prepared to attend court (or have a representative attend in court) on the date and time set out in the subpoena.
- When asked to bring an OSR to court, you should make a copy of the record and take both the original and the copy to court. You should then propose that the photocopy be submitted to the court instead of the original.
- The school board lawyer should be contacted with respect to disclosure requirements and court procedure. Solicitor-client privilege protects the information and advice exchanged between you and the board lawyer.

Preparation of Witnesses

If you are required to give evidence in court, a lawyer may want to meet with you to review the facts that you and any relevant exhibits will provide. If you have been subpoenaed by counsel for a parent, student or other third party, you have no obligation to agree to meet with counsel or to provide them with information prior to the specified court date. A normal subpoena does not authorize or compel you to give information or provide documents to a third party out of court.

On the other hand, if you are a witness for the school board or you are a party in the proceedings, the board lawyer or your lawyer will want to meet with you to prepare for your testimony in court. Such preparation may include the following:

- The lawyer will review with you all previous testimony, examinations and written or oral statements. The lawyer will attempt to determine if your present recollection differs in any way from your previous statements.
- The lawyer will review with you all exhibits that you will identify or authenticate.

---

[32] *Ibid.*

- The probable testimony of other witnesses will be reviewed to see if any inconsistencies exist.
- With respect to preparation for your direct examination, the lawyer will attempt to ensure that you can establish the foundation for all necessary exhibits. The lawyer should explain that he or she cannot use leading questions in direct examination. Preparation should continue until you are thoroughly familiar with the lawyer's questions and you can answer them in the clearest, most accurate way. However, preparation should not continue to the point where the testimony sounds memorized or rehearsed.
- The nature of cross-examination should be reviewed. The lawyer should prepare you for the areas that he or she anticipates the cross-examination will cover. The lawyer should explain the different rules that apply to cross-examination and the purposes of the examination. The lawyer should also emphasize that you should maintain the same demeanour and attitude on cross-examination as you had on direct and should answer only the question asked.
- The lawyer should explain to you how the courtroom is arranged, where the judge, counsel, court reporter, clerk and spectators sit, where and how you will take the oath or affirmation and where you will sit while giving your testimony.[33]

Attendance in Court

Whether you have been subpoenaed by a third party to attend at court or you are a party to the proceedings, there are general principles which apply regarding your attendance in court. Observing the following guidelines may favourably affect the way the court will evaluate and weigh your testimony:

- Dress neatly and conservatively, with clothes appropriate to your position.
- Listen carefully to every question. Answer only that question. Do not ramble on or volunteer information. Speak clearly and loudly so that the judge can hear you.
- If you do not understand a question, say so and counsel will rephrase it. If you cannot remember the answer to a question, say "I can't recall". If you do not know an answer, say "I don't know". If you can only recall approximate dates, times and distances, give only your best approximation. Provide positive, clear and direct answers to every question, whenever possible. Answer the questions with the words you normally use and feel comfortable with.
- Be serious and polite at all times. Do not exaggerate or understate the facts. Do not give cute or clever answers. Never argue with counsel or the judge. Never lose your temper. Counsel on cross-examination may attempt to draw you into an arguement or make you lose your temper. Resist these provocations.

---

[33] T.A. Mauet, D.G. Casswell and G.P. Macdonald, *Fundamentals of Trial Techniques*, Canadian ed. (Toronto: Little, Brown and Company, 1984), at p. 10.

- You will be allowed to testify only as to what you personally saw, heard and did. You generally cannot testify as to what others know, or to conclusions, opinions and speculations.
- Above all, always tell the complete truth according to your best recollection of the facts and events involved.[34]

Overall, in a legal proceeding, a witness's conduct and evidence are constantly being evaluated and compared to that of other witnesses. Throughout the proceeding, the judge is attempting to assess the credibility and veracity of each witness. From the moment that a witness enters the courtroom, he or she should show respect for the court and maintain a proper degree of courtesy and formality.

MUNICIPAL FREEDOM OF INFORMATION AND PROTECTION OF PRIVACY ACT

In addition to the privacy provisions of the *Education Act,* principals as leaders of public institutions must also comply with privacy legislation of more general application such as the *Municipal Freedom of Information and Protection of Privacy Act*[35] (the "*MFIPPA*"). Educators can collect and keep any type of record, provided that this collection and retention is permitted by the provisions of the *MFIPPA*. A principal and his or her staff often collect and retain information about a student which does not form part of that student's OSR. Such information will not be subject to the restrictions of the *Education Act,* but must be managed in accordance with the *MFIPPA*. However, though the *Education Act* does not affect records outside of a student's OSR, the *MFIPPA* does place restrictions on the use of information which is collected and retained pursuant to the *Education Act*. As a result, the management of the OSR is subject to the *MFIPPA* to the extent that the *MFIPPA* does not conflict with the *Education Act*.[36] Thus, as we review the restrictions that the *MFIPPA* places on the use of any information by an institution such as a school, we will also note where the provisions of the *MFIPPA* affect the creation and retention of a student's OSR. In those cases, educators must comply with both the *Education Act* and the *MFIPPA*.

The *MFIPPA* is divided into two main parts, each serving a distinct purpose. In the context of a school, these purposes are:

- to provide the public with a right of access to information in the possession and control of a school board; and

---

[34] *Ibid.*, at p. 11.
[35] R.S.O. 1990, c. M.56.
[36] A.F. Brown and M.A. Zuker, *Education Law*, 2nd ed. (Toronto: Carswell, 1997), at pp. 205-206.

- to protect the privacy of individuals, such as students, teachers or principals, with regard to personal information about themselves which is held by a school or school board.[37]

Freedom of Information

The *MFIPPA* establishes a right of access to existing "records" in the custody or under the control of an institution. The term "record" is defined in the *MFIPPA* to include any record of information however recorded. It includes correspondence, minutes, reports, photographs and computer tapes and any other recorded information regardless of medium or format.[38]

An access request under this legislation would *only* apply to records or recorded information in the custody or under the control of a school board. Therefore, it is important to recognize that an access request would *not* apply to any oral comments, discussions or deliberations.

A principal's written notes made at a meeting or interview or in the context of an investigation will, in most cases, be considered a record within the meaning of the *MFIPPA*. As with records in the OSR, students and parents will have a right to review these notes where they contain personal information pertaining to the student and they are specific and identifiable.

Under the *MFIPPA*, any person may make a request for information held by a school board. The *MFIPPA* sets out a procedure for handling such requests. Requests for information are made to "heads" of institutions. The head is responsible for administering the *MFIPPA* and complying with the access and privacy provisions of the legislation. The duties of a head include responding to access requests, adhering to time limits and notice requirements, and making decisions about the disclosure of records.

Most school boards in Ontario have designated the chairperson of the board as the head and he or she in turn has delegated certain powers and duties to the director of education and other board officials. The decisions of the head are subject to independent review by the Information and Privacy Commissioner.

A request must be made in writing and an individual making such a request must provide sufficient detail to enable an experienced employee to locate the record. The access scheme in the *MFIPPA* sets out specific time limits – usually 30 days – within which institutions must respond to requests for access to information. In addition, a school board must have information available which describes how the board is organized and its general responsibilities. Furthermore, the school board must provide a list of the general classes or types of records in its custody or control.

Under the *MFIPPA*, an individual has a *prima facie* right of access to *any* "personal information" about himself or herself in the custody or under the control

---

[37] E.M. Roher, "Freedom of Information and Protection of Privacy in a School Setting", *Education Law News* (Fall, 1995) (Toronto: Borden & Elliot).
[38] *MFIPPA*, s. 2(1).

of an institution with respect to which the individual is able to provide sufficient specific information to make it reasonably retrievable by the institution. All records containing personal information must be retained for the shorter of one year after use or the period set out in a resolution made by the school board.

"Personal information" is defined in the *MFIPPA* as recorded information about an identifiable individual. Such personal information can include recorded views or opinions of other individuals about a student. However, as previously indicated, the *MFIPPA* does not apply to oral comments, discussions or deliberations.

Notwithstanding an individual's general right of access to personal information, there is a broad range of exemptions where information need not be disclosed. For example, the *MFIPPA* provides that an institution shall not disclose personal information in its custody or under its control except:

- if the person to whom the information relates has identified that information in particular and consented to its disclosure;
- for the purpose for which it was obtained or compiled or for a consistent purpose;
- if the disclosure is made to an officer or employee of the institution who needs the record in the performance of his or her duties and if the disclosure is necessary and proper in the discharge of the institution's functions;
- if disclosure is to an institution or a law enforcement agency in Canada to aid an investigation undertaken with a view to a law enforcement agency proceeding or from which a law enforcement proceeding is likely to result; or
- in compelling circumstances affecting the health or safety of an individual if upon disclosure notification is mailed to the last known address of the individual to whom the information relates.

For these reasons, where a school maintains records containing personal information in its custody and under its control on students who are interviewed as part of an investigation, such students and/or their parents would likely have access to such records under the *MFIPPA*. Parents and guardians are entitled to exercise the rights and power conferred by the *MFIPPA* on behalf of children who are under 16 years of age.

Interviewing Prospective Employees

Principals interview prospective employees on a regular basis. The principal generally makes a recommendation to the school board as to whether a candidate should be hired for a particular position. A principal may wish to obtain information from previous employers and references with respect to a prospective employee's job performance. However, under the *MFIPPA*, a problem may arise in obtaining such information.

Under the *MFIPPA*, an institution must collect personal information directly from the individual to whom the information relates *unless* the individual authorizes another manner of collection. To avoid a problem in obtaining references, it is suggested that board officials ensure that the employment application includes an appropriate authorization to be signed by the prospective employee. Such authorization would permit the school board to obtain personal information from previous employers to assist in determining a prospective employee's suitability, eligibility or qualifications for employment with the board. It is further suggested that, when principals write to previous employers and any other references given, they clearly indicate that the information requested will be held in confidence by the school board.

During the interview process, it is not uncommon for the principal to make personal notes with respect to each applicant. These personal notes, which constitute personal information about the applicant, could be the subject of an access request under the *MFIPPA*. To avoid such access request, it is advised that the principal or vice-principal be extremely careful in making such notes during the interview process. It is suggested that a principal not include third-hand information, rumours or irrelevant comments about a teacher or prospective teacher in his or her personal notes. A principal's own file which contains personal information about an individual could be the subject of an access request.

The *MFIPPA* is not intended to replace informal procedures or other methods of access to information which are currently available. For example, the procedures set out in teacher collective agreements and the *Education Act* regarding access to certain information remain intact. The *MFIPPA* is intended to be used by board employees and the public in cases where information cannot be obtained through the usual channels.

In summary, principals and other board officials should recognize:

- The *MFIPPA* only applies to recorded information; it does not apply to any oral comments, discussions or deliberations.
- All records of meetings and interviews should be factual and avoid rumours, gossip or speculation.
- A principal's personal notes should not include irrelevant or third-hand information.
- Personal notes should be objective, direct and forthright and avoid subjective comments or innuendo or any other indirect meaning.
- To the extent possible, information contained in a record should be based on the first-hand knowledge of the record maker.
- As a rule, information in a record should not be disclosed to a third party unless the individual in charge of the record is certain that an exception under the *MFIPPA* permits disclosure.

CONFIDENTIALITY

Confidentiality relates to whether and under what conditions persons holding information communicated to them in confidence, or obtained with an expectation of confidence, may voluntarily disclose such information to a third party.[39] Confidential information may exist in many forms. For instance, it may be oral, in writing or by way of diagram. In addition, the information may be partly public and partly private. Whether or not a communication will be recognized as confidential depends on such factors as the nature of the information, the context in which the information was provided and the relationship between the parties exchanging the information.[40] Communications of a personal and private nature or communications between professionals and their clients will more readily be recognized as confidential, but the information does not necessarily have to be private or personal to the person making the communication.[41] A student, for example, may provide information about a fellow student or complain about the conduct of a teacher with an expectation that the communication will be kept confidential.

A duty of confidentiality may be imposed by common law, statute or professional codes of ethics. An action for breach of confidentiality may arise at common law if confidential communications are disclosed to the detriment of the person from whom the communication originated. Legislation relating to education, child welfare and health care commonly contains confidentiality provisions which, if breached, will also give rise to a cause of action.

Confidentiality in a School Setting

Confidentiality issues commonly arise in a school setting when a student confides in a guidance counsellor, social worker, psychologist or other such professional. The goal of having these services available to students is to develop a rapport and maintain trust with students. Indeed, teachers and principals may also receive confidential information while serving as an advisor or confidant for students. However, anyone serving in the capacity of a counsellor should be made aware that private discussions with students cannot always remain confidential. Many people do not appreciate that parents, principals, teachers, ministers, physicians or psychologists, who are given information in the strictest confidence and who would never divulge this information voluntarily, may be compelled to do so in a court of law or other legal proceedings. In most jurisdictions, if a guidance counsellor or other staff member refuses to divulge information on the basis that it is confidential, he or she could be required to do so by court order, and failure to do so could result in contempt of court charges.

---

[39] Roher, *op. cit.*, footnote 3.
[40] *Coco v. A.N. Clark (Engineers) Ltd.*, [1969] R.P.C. 41 at p. 48 (Ch.).
[41] Roher, *op. cit.*, footnote 3.

Confidentiality, Privilege and Student Records

The issue of an educator or other school professional being compelled to disclose confidential information pursuant to a court order raises the issue of privilege in communications. Privilege relates to whether and under what circumstances confidential information can be compelled by the state. This may occur even where student information is communicated with an expectation of confidentiality. The scope of privilege which will attach to student communications will usually be decided on a case-by-case basis according to the principles developed at common law.

A four-factor test has been developed to determine whether there is a privilege against disclosure of certain communications. A court will consider these factors in various contexts involving confidential communications, and it is likely they will also be considered to determine whether statements by students will be kept confidential:

- Did the communication originate in the confidence that it would not be disclosed?
- Was the confidentiality essential to the full and satisfactory maintenance of the relationship between students and teachers, principals, counsellors and therapists?
- Was the relationship between them one which the community feels should be diligently fostered?
- Would the injury to the relationship caused by the disclosure of the information be greater than the benefit to be gained by a correct determination of the issues in litigation?[42]

Whether a particular communication between a student and his or her confidant will ultimately be privileged depends on the answer to the fourth question: Would the benefit in disclosing the information outweigh the harm done to the relationship? For example, if a school counsellor receives information from a student about a violent crime or learns that a student has been the perpetrator or victim of violence, the disclosure of that information may bring an end to the problem and outweigh the loss of confidence in the relationship.

As a practical matter, the qualified privilege of confidentiality is very infrequently invoked in civil proceedings.[43] In addition, the standard four-part test of privilege may not apply in some types of civil and criminal cases. In the civil context, for example, the Supreme Court of Canada has held that, in addition to the express waiver of confidentiality which is found in most standard form of insurance policies, there may be an implied waiver of confidentiality where a person's physical, emotional or mental condition is at issue in lawsuits such as

---

[42] *Slavutych v. Baker* (1975), 55 D.L.R. (3d) 224 at p. 228, [1976] 1 S.C.R. 254.
[43] "Compelling Student Records Before Trial", *Edulaw for Canadian Schools* (Calgary: Edulaw, June, 1994).

those relating to personal injury, medical malpractice and insurance.[44] If a student or former student is the plaintiff in such an action, relatively broad access to relevant information in that student's school record is likely to be ordered, particularly when the court is attempting to determine damages for loss of future income. A student's pre-injury academic performance and emotional and psychological stability, for example, will impact on that student's lost earning potential for which the student may have to be compensated.[45]

Criminal Proceedings and Confidentiality

Other factors may also be relevant in certain proceedings under the *Criminal Code*. For instance, in *R. v. O'Connor*,[46] the Supreme Court of Canada considered what level of disclosure of records held by persons other than a Crown Attorney is appropriate for the purpose of a criminal defence. Psychological assessments and counselling records held by schools, for example, may be quite relevant to a student's competence to testify or to a student's credibility when testifying against another student. These documents, which rest in the hands of third parties such as schools and school boards, can be compelled if they are found "likely to be relevant" to an issue at trial or to the competence of a witness. This would protect the right of an accused to make full answer and defence to the charges against him or her. Once found "likely to be relevant", the judge will examine and weigh the salutary and deleterious effects of an order to compel the disclosure of a record, balancing the right to privacy against the right of an accused to mount a full defence. The Supreme Court of Canada has held that the following factors must be considered when balancing these rights and determining whether the record should be produced:

- the nature of the reasonable expectation of privacy vested in the record;
- whether the request for production of the record is based on any discriminatory assumptions, stereotypes, beliefs or biases;
- the potential prejudice to the dignity, privacy or security of the person to whom the record relates, balanced against the potential detriment to the accused if the records are not produced;
- whether the person seeking disclosure can obtain the information by any other reasonable means; and
- the amount of information which would be necessary for the accused to make full answer and defence.[47]

In response to the *O'Connor* decision, the federal government made certain amendments to the *Criminal Code* relating to the disclosure of records containing

---

[44] *Frenette v. Metropolitan Life Insurance Co.* (1992), 89 D.L.R. (4th) 653, [1992] 1 S.C.R. 647.
[45] "Privacy and Confidentiality of Student Records", *Edulaw for Canadian Schools* (Calgary: Edulaw, March, 1996).
[46] (1995), 130 D.L.R. (4th) 235, 103 C.C.C. (3d) 1 (S.C.C.).
[47] *Supra*, at pp. 256-8.

personal information pertaining to a complainant or witness in sexual offence proceedings.[48] In these amendments, the restrictions on disclosure relate to any record which contains personal information for which there is a reasonable expectation of privacy, including medical, counselling, education and employment records, as well as records containing personal information, the disclosure of which is protected by any other Act of Parliament or a provincial legislature.[49] Such records of witnesses or complainants in the specified sexual offence proceedings can only be disclosed in accordance with the specified sections of the *Criminal Code*.[50] The accused must make an application for the production of the given records to the judge before whom the accused is being tried. In a closed hearing, the judge will then determine whether to order the production of all or part of the records, considering the salutary and deleterious effects of the determination on the accused's right to make full answer and defence and on the right to privacy and equality of the complainant or witness, and any other person to whom the records relate. In making this determination, the trial judge must also take into account the following factors set out in section 278.5(2) of the *Criminal Code*:

- (a) the extent to which the record is necessary for the accused to make a full answer and defence;
- (b) the probative value of the record;
- (c) the nature and extent of the reasonable expectation of privacy with respect to the record;
- (d) whether production of the record is based on a discriminatory belief or bias;
- (e) the potential prejudice to the personal dignity and right to privacy of any person to whom the record relates;
- (f) society's interest in encouraging the reporting of sexual offences;
- (g) society's interest in encouraging the obtaining of treatment by complainants of sexual offences; and
- (h) the effect of the determination on the integrity of the trial process.

Unlike in the case of *R. v. O'Connor*, the criteria listed in the *Criminal Code* are to apply whether or not the records are in the possession of the Crown Attorney or a third party for the specific sexual offences. Thus, in the case of sexual offences, the ability of a court to order disclosure of certain records in the possession of a school or school board has been diminished by these amendments. Recently, it was decided by the Supreme Court of Canada that these amendments to the *Criminal Code* do not infringe the *Canadian Charter of Rights and Freedoms* by denying the accused in a sexual offence the right to a fair trial or the right to make full answer and defence to criminal charges.[51]

---

[48] *An Act to Amend the Criminal Code (Production of Records in Sexual Offence Proceedings)*, S.C. 1997, c. 30.
[49] *Criminal Code*, s. 278.1.
[50] *Criminal Code*, s. 278.2.
[51] *R. v. Mills* (1999), 180 D.L.R. (4th) 1, 139 C.C.C. (3d) 321 (S.C.C.).

Professional Ethics and Confidentiality

Professional codes of ethics also establish duties of confidence for professionals providing services in schools. These professionals range from the teachers themselves to social workers and psychologists. The handling and release of confidential information communicated by students is of prime importance to all of the professionals who render services in a school setting. As such, various codes of ethics and standards of professional conduct provide a further method whereby confidentiality is maintained regarding the data contained in school records[52] and other information provided by students.

In Alberta, for example, the *Teaching Profession Act*[53] provides that the Alberta Teachers' Association may pass by-laws concerning standards of professional conduct and the establishment of a discipline committee to discipline members for breaches of those standards. Accordingly, the Alberta Teachers' Association has published guidelines for ethical behaviour which are intended to direct teachers in providing guidance and counselling services. Furthermore, the Code of Professional Conduct of the Alberta Teachers' Association contains a provision pertaining to confidentiality. Other provinces across Canada have similar statutory enactments and codes of professional conduct which govern the conduct of teachers in relation to confidentiality.

In Ontario, the duty of confidentiality is imposed on teachers by the *Teaching Profession Act*[54] which provides that the board of governors may make regulations prescribing a code of ethics for teachers.[55] Accordingly, section 14 of the regulation[56] provides that a member of the Ontario Teachers' Federation shall "refuse to divulge beyond his [or her] proper duty confidential information about a pupil".

Additionally, non-teaching professionals such as social workers and psychologists must adhere to their professional ethical standards while working in schools. Their respective codes of ethics also provide obligations regarding confidentiality which will apply in their dealings with students. For social workers, these standards are provided by the Canadian Association of Social Workers. In the case of psychologists, the Canadian Psychological Association Code of Ethics is applicable.

---

[52] E. Carruthers, "Student Records: Confidentiality and Privacy Rights" (paper presented to the Canadian Association for the Practical Study of Law in Education, Edmonton, May 5 to 7, 1991), in W.F. Foster and F. Peters, eds., *Education & Law: Strengthening the Partnership* (Welland: Editions Soleil Publishing, 1993).
[53] R.S.A. 1990, c. T-3.
[54] R.S.O. 1990, c. T.2.
[55] The definition of "teacher" in s. 1 of the *Teaching Profession Act* expressly excludes a principal or vice-principal.
[56] Section 1 of the *Regulations Act*, R.S.O. 1990, c. R.21, expressly excludes regulations made pursuant to the *Teaching Profession Act* from the application of the *Regulations Act* and, as such, they are not required to be published in *The Ontario Gazette*. Accordingly, the Regulation made under the *Teaching Profession Act* does not have a conventional numerical citation.

Other Confidentiality Problems

These issues of confidentiality take on a greater significance where a student confides in a principal, teacher or other education professional regarding the student's involvement in criminal activity. For example, a counsellor who has been informed of a student's involvement in dangerous or criminal activities may be obligated to contact police. In addition, in the event of criminal proceedings, that counsellor could be called upon to testify in court. Where a student confides about relatively minor alleged criminal conduct, it is appropriate to encourage the student to tell his or her parents and advise the student that if he or she does not do so within 24 hours the student's parents will be contacted. It could also be suggested that the student go to a Legal Aid Clinic for advice or, in appropriate circumstances, personally retain a lawyer. A school's staff should be advised that, depending on the circumstances of the individual case, they should consider contacting the school principal, superintendent or school board lawyer for guidance.

The obligation of confidentiality can also create tension with other duties and responsibilities of school principals. A common example of the potential breach of confidentiality in the school context occurs where a student provides information to a teacher, principal or guidance counsellor that the student does not want disclosed to a parent. For instance, a student may run away from home but remain in attendance at school. In view of a teacher's duties under the code of ethics and an education professional's common law duty of confidentiality, it is likely that information provided in confidence by a student who has run away, such as the student's current residence or health status, would likely give rise to an obligation of confidence. Thus disclosure of such information to the student's parent could contravene a duty of confidentiality to the student.

However, a competing obligation might arise which could make the issue of confidentiality extremely difficult to resolve. As was seen in Chapter 2, "Negligence and Liability", school authorities have a responsibility to provide for the supervision of students in their care. The standard of care of a reasonably careful or prudent parent in the circumstances imposes a responsibility on school authorities to protect the pupil from all foreseeable risks of harm. In the context of a runaway, where there may be reasonable grounds to believe that the student will be harmed or injured, a competing obligation arises to inform the student's parents and/or relevant authorities. Thus, where a principal or teacher is informed by a student in confidence of an event or action which could cause foreseeable damage or harm to the student or a third party, the principal or teacher has a duty to use reasonable care to prevent such damage or harm.[57] School principals should exercise common sense to resolve this dilemma appropriately in the particular circumstances of each case. Principals may wish to seek the advice of their superintendent and/or their school board's legal counsel for assistance.

---

[57] Roher, *op. cit.*, footnote 3.

4

Documenting Teacher Performance

INTRODUCTION[1]

The evaluation of teacher performance can be a difficult undertaking for a school principal. There are a number of reasons why this may be the case. For instance, it necessarily involves communicating deficiencies in performance as they occur, which is never a comfortable task for any manager. Also, at a time when principals in the Province of Ontario are freshly removed from the teachers' bargaining units, teacher evaluation may be one instance in which the principal's role as a school board representative creates tension in relationships with teachers. The evaluation process will test a principal's mettle as a collaborative leader.

An additional difficulty for the principal lies in the dual purposes of teacher performance evaluations, purposes which are seemingly at odds with each other. On the one hand, evaluations are designed to help teachers identify any weaknesses in their performance so that assistance can be offered to allow teachers to improve to an acceptable level. Thus, the first purpose of the evaluation process is to assist principals in meeting their mandate to improve the instruction provided to students. On the other hand, the evaluation process also serves the purpose of providing the necessary documentation for the principal to recommend termination to the school board or providing an incentive for voluntary resignation for those teachers whose performance is inadequate despite their best efforts at improvement.[2] These two aspects of performance evaluations require a school principal to perform a delicate balancing act.

In this chapter, we will examine the law's influence on the process of teacher performance evaluations. The law intersects with this part of a principal's job by creating a legal duty to evaluate teacher performance and setting out the procedural requirements for a system of evaluation.

---

[1] The authors are indebted to C. Hoglund, whose paper, "On the Improvement Track: Documenting Teacher Performance" (paper presented to the annual conference of the Canadian Association for the Practical Study of Law in Education, April, 1999) [unpublished], was instrumental in the creation of this chapter.

[2] E.M. Roher, "Reading, Writing and Recording: Documenting Teacher Performance", *Education Law News* (Spring, 1996) (Toronto: Borden & Elliot), p. 1.

From a legal perspective, the key for any principal in effectively completing teacher evaluations is adequate *documentation*. Meeting the law's requirements for documentation of teacher performance will be very helpful to the principal. It will help the principal create clear and concise materials with which to warn a teacher in writing, giving him or her assistance and allowing the teacher a reasonable time to improve.

Judge Marvin Zuker has said that proper documentation is founded on the concept of communication. He has stated that its goal is to "humanize the evaluation and documentation process with the ultimate objective of improving a teacher's performance to an acceptable level".[3]

Should adequate improvement not be forthcoming, clear documentation will also help justify any recommendations to school board officials and, perhaps, an arbitration board. Further, developing a healthy habit of consistently documenting performance will make a principal a more effective evaluator and remove some of the stress from the task.

One shortcoming of the provisions set out in the *Education Act*[4] pertaining to teacher evaluation is that they are focused on the relationship between teachers and the school board as opposed to the relationship between teachers and their students. While performance evaluations are based on teacher conduct in the school, the law is focused on the process of evaluation and not the effect of various teaching methods and conduct on students. However, the well-being of students is not lost on the legal process. A judge presiding over a Board of Reference decision in Ontario observed:

> I cannot complete these reasons without making one further observation. I was completely dismayed throughout the course of this hearing that no mention whatsoever was made about the responsibility of the teacher and/or the Board to the pupils who are attending classes. It was only in the latter part of the evidence that anyone made reference to the welfare of the students. Surely the welfare of the students should be utmost in our minds and in the minds of the teacher and the Board. Many documents that have been written and produced would show the protection afforded to the teacher and it is rightfully so that teachers should be protected from boards that would not act in all instances in good faith. Also there are limitations and protections provided to school boards which again is justified in our system of education. However, it is the utmost obligation of the Board to see to the well-being and proper education of the students under its control. To fail to do this would, in my view, be a serious breach of the Board's obligation to the citizens of its community.[5]

Obviously, in meeting the law's requirements for performance evaluations, all parties should keep their focus on the benefit to students of an effective evaluation system.

---

[3] M. Zuker, *The Legal Context of Education* (Toronto: Ontario Institute for Studies in Education, 1988), at p. 127.

[4] R.S.O. 1990, c. E.2.

[5] *Chevalier and Ottawa Roman Catholic School Board (Re)* (unreported, September 30, 1986, Bd. Ref., Flanigan J.), at p. 5.

A DUTY TO EVALUATE AND DOCUMENT

In order to meet the needs of students effectively, improve the quality of instruction and assist the teacher in self-evaluation, the law requires that principals and other school administrators undertake and document teacher performance. In this regard, the law attempts to ensure some uniformity of approach. Education statutes, collective agreements between school boards and their teachers and arbitral jurisprudence stemming from teacher discipline or dismissal all demand that fair evaluation of teachers take place and that proper documentation occur. These legal sources also contain the basic procedural requirements for teacher performance evaluations. The remaining procedural details are generally provided by each school board's individual evaluation policies and guidelines, which should also adhere to the law's requirements.

Education Act

In Ontario, the *Education Act* and its regulations set out the duty of supervisory officials and principals to carry out and document teacher performance. Section 286 of the Act sets out the general duties of supervisory officers. Under section 286(1) of the *Education Act*, it is the duty of the supervisory officer:

> (a) to bring about improvement in the quality of education by assisting teachers in their practice;
>
> . . . . .
>
> (c) to visit schools and classrooms . . . as the board may direct;
> (d) to prepare a report of a visit to a school or classroom . . . when required by the board and to give to a teacher referred to in any such report a copy of the portion of the report that refers to the teacher;

Section 265 of the *Education Act* sets out the duties of principals. It provides, in part:

> 265. It is the duty of a principal of a school, in addition to the principal's duties as a teacher,
> (a) to maintain proper order and discipline in the school;
> (b) to develop co-operation and co-ordination of effort among the members of the staff of the school;
>
> . . . . .
>
> (i) to furnish to the Ministry and to the appropriate supervisory officer any information that it may be in the principal's power to give respecting the condition of the school premises, the discipline of the school, the progress of the pupils and any other matter affecting the interests of the school, and to prepare such reports for the board as are required by the board;

Regulation 298[6] under the *Education Act* also details a principal's duties with respect to teacher evaluations. The duties of a principal are set out in section 11 which provides, in part:

---

[6] *Operation of Schools – General*, R.R.O. 1990, Reg. 298.

11(3) In addition to the duties under the Act and those assigned by the board, the principal of a school shall, except where the principal has arranged otherwise under subsection 26(3),
- (a) supervise the instruction in the school and advise and assist any teacher in co-operation with the teacher in charge of an organizational unit or program;

. . . . .

- (g) where performance appraisals of members of the teaching staff are required under a collective agreement or a policy of the board, despite anything to the contrary in such collective agreement or board policy, conduct performance appraisals of members of the teaching staff;
- (h) subject to the provisions of the policy of the board or the provisions of a collective agreement, as the case may be, in respect of reporting requirements for performance appraisals, report thereon in writing to the board or to the supervisory officer on request and give to each teacher so appraised a copy of the performance appraisal of the teacher;
- (i) where the performance appraisals of members of the teaching staff are not required by board policy or under a collective agreement, report to the board or to the supervisory officer in writing on request on the effectiveness of members of the teaching staff and give to a teacher referred to in any such report a copy of the portion of the report that refers to the teacher;
- (j) make recommendations to the board with respect to,
   - (i) the appointment and promotion of teachers, and
   - (ii) the demotion or dismissal of teachers whose work or attitude is unsatisfactory;

. . . . .

(4) *A principal shall only make a recommendation to the board under subclause 3(j)(ii) after warning the teacher in writing, giving the teacher assistance and allowing the teacher a reasonable time to improve.*

(Emphasis added.)

Section 11(4) deals with the duties of the principal regarding how an evaluation is to be carried out. It sets out at least four duties a principal is required to perform, as follows:

- Identify the work or attitude which is unsatisfactory.
- Warn the teacher that such work or attitude is unacceptable.
- Spell out in the report any suggestions for improvement and how the teacher can obtain assistance (it might be from another teacher, the department head or a consultant, but the principal should ensure that the persons named are available to assist).
- Give the teacher a reasonable time to try the suggestions, obtain the assistance and improve.

While section 11(4) speaks only to the duties of principals, in the authors' view, the direction outlined in the provision would apply to anyone who is documenting the performance of a teacher. As a matter of policy, the legislation seeks to ensure that principals assist teachers in meeting their own statutory duties to "teach diligently" and "encourage the pupils in the pursuit of learning".[7]

Collective Agreement

The requirement to evaluate a teacher's performance will also likely arise as a result of a provision set out in a collective agreement negotiated by the school board and teacher representatives. Such collective agreements often contain procedural protections regarding the evaluation process. For example, provisions in a relevant collective agreement may require a minimum number of evaluations for probationary teachers. A collective agreement may require a specified number of evaluations over a defined period for permanent teachers. In addition, provisions in a collective agreement may set out guidelines for the evaluation procedure.

It is strongly advised that principals and other school administrators review the requirements set out in the relevant collective agreement before embarking on the documentation process. The requirements set out in collective agreements regarding documentation of teacher performance vary from no requirement to very elaborate provisions. Some requirements which are often contained in collective agreements include:

- a provision requiring the principal or other school administrator to notify the teacher in advance when he or she intends to make a classroom visit;
- a provision requiring that the teacher be evaluated in his or her "area of specialty"; and
- a provision requiring that the evaluation not be shown to anyone else before it is discussed with the teacher.[8]

It is arguable as to whether failure to comply with one of those requirements will result in a principal or supervisory officer being unable to tender his or her report in evidence at a board of arbitration hearing. For example, the collective agreement may contain a provision stating that the evaluation is not to be shown to anyone else before it is discussed with the teacher. If a principal does not comply with this requirement and shows a particular evaluation to a supervisory officer before discussing it with the teacher, in the authors' view, it is unlikely that a board of arbitration would rule that such evaluation is inadmissible. Overall, it should be emphasized that where requirements regarding the process of documentation are specifically set out in a collective agreement, every effort should be made to understand, review and follow the proper procedures.

Arbitral Jurisprudence

Many collective agreements contain a just cause provision. In this circumstance, an employee cannot be terminated from his or her employment unless the

---

[7] *Education Act*, s. 264(1)(a) and (b).
[8] Roher, *op. cit.*, footnote 2, at p. 2.

employer can demonstrate just cause. Thus, where the cause a school board is alleging is the incompetence or unsatisfactory performance of a teacher, the board will not succeed in front of an arbitrator unless it has documented the shortcomings in the teacher's performance appraisal. In this regard, a "paper trail" is important in order to demonstrate that the teacher has been informed of the unsatisfactory work, has been given an appropriate warning and has been given a reasonable time to obtain assistance and improve. Where circumstances permit, the file should show a progressive escalation over time of responses to the concern.

It should be noted that, in certain circumstances, documentation may play no role whatsoever in the termination of a teacher. For example, there may be a situation where a teacher is convicted for the sexual assault of a child. Where the act is proved and the teacher is convicted, there is nothing to be gained from documentation – the offence is either serious enough to justify termination or it is not.

Arbitral jurisprudence has not set out black and white rules regarding how an evaluation should be carried out. However, a review of recent arbitration decisions provides some suggestions regarding the evaluation process:

- Evaluations must not only be done justly, but they must be seen to be done justly. Teachers should be evaluated on the basis of their observed performance over a reasonable period of time. Where a teacher is assigned to a new position, the school administrator should build additional time into the evaluation process to allow for this change in assignment.
- The teacher should be given adequate advance notice of the intention to evaluate. The teacher should be evaluated in the areas of teaching in which the teacher spends the most time. The results of the evaluation should be discussed with the teacher as promptly as possible. A written report should be given to the teacher within a reasonably short period of time. The teacher should be given the opportunity to respond to the evaluation in writing. Only relevant factors should be included in the evaluation process.
- The school administrator should ensure that the form being used to evaluate or document teacher performance uses appropriate language or definitions. One should consider the commonly understood meaning of the terms used. It is extremely difficult to explain to an arbitrator that a "good" rating does not mean good.
- Once an appropriate form of documentation is developed, the school administrator should be honest and frank in the evaluation. In other words, call a spade a spade. In general, it is our experience that people do not like to be critical of others. However, a principal cannot expect to give a glowing review of a teacher today, and six months from now convince an arbitrator that the principal really did not mean it and that he or she was just trying to be nice.
- If the evaluation is unfavourable, the principal has a duty to give the teacher assistance and allow the teacher a reasonable time to improve. Such assistance should be meaningful and effective in attempting to remedy perceived difficulties.

- Communication with all parties is essential. Where a disciplinary letter from a principal to a teacher is prepared, copies should be forwarded to the appropriate supervisory officer, the teacher's personnel file and, where appropriate, the teacher's representative.

In circumstances where the performance evaluation of a teacher becomes the subject of a grievance arbitration, it is the role of the arbitrator to ensure *fairness* in the process. Where a termination is involved, the arbitrator is interested in whether the school board has established "just cause" for that termination. The arbitrator will review documented evidence which demonstrates that the evaluation was open and fair to the teacher at all stages, rather than examining the quality of the conclusions in the evaluation from an educational perspective. Questions that an arbitration board may review include the following:

- Was the teacher fairly evaluated?
- Was the teacher given suggestions for improvement, assistance to improve, and time for the improvement to occur?
- Was the teacher made aware of the consequences of a failure to improve?
- Has the evaluation policy been followed?
- Is the evaluation procedure professionally sound?
- Was the evaluator biased?[9]

Clear and concise communication and documentation of the entire process are the key to demonstrating that each of these issues has been properly addressed.

IMPLEMENTING AN EVALUATION POLICY

Each school board should have in place a policy or guideline for completing teacher performance evaluations. While no two guidelines will be entirely alike, they should all have certain qualities. Generally speaking, these evaluation policies will be designed to assist the vast majority of teachers whose performance meets or exceeds expectations. The evaluation process should be applied consistently and fairly. The purpose of an evaluation system is, among other things, to foster excellence in teaching, improve the quality of instruction, acknowledge effective teaching strategies and assist the teacher in self-evaluation.[10]

The product that every school board evaluation policy will generate is a written evaluation report. This document can then be used to affirm a teacher's skills, assist the teacher in improvement, track his or her performance over time, indicate progress or justify any discipline which may be required. In reaching this end

---

[9] T. Ulrich, "Teacher Dismissal for Unsatisfactory Performance: Meeting the Legal Requirements", in W.F. Foster, ed., *Rights, Responsibilities & Reasonableness: Striking the Balance in Education* (Chateauguay: Lisbro, 1995), p. 237, at p. 241.

[10] Roher, *op. cit.*, footnote 2, at p. 1.

product, an effective policy should clearly identify everyone's role in the process, including that of the teacher being evaluated. The policy should state the frequency with which evaluations will occur, keeping the requirements of any collective agreement in mind, and set out the time lines for each stage in the process. An open and effective policy, which is clearly communicated to teachers at the outset, will help to ensure that the process is fair and efficient for all involved.

Once a policy is in place, it should be carefully followed by principals and those responsible for its implementation. This is so for obvious reasons, such as a consistent and non-arbitrary application of the process to all teachers.

Each evaluation policy or guideline will describe its stages differently and may have its own unique characteristics. However, most share the following steps in common in order to meet both academic and legal obligations:

- the initiation of evaluation procedures;
- teacher self-evaluation;
- a pre-conference with the teacher;
- classroom evaluation(s);
- a post-conference with the teacher;
- the offer of assistance in a plan for improvement; and
- the preparation of a written evaluation report.

Generally, it is the responsibility of the principal to implement this process at the school level. While the established guidelines must be adhered to, factors within each school may require flexibility from the principal and his or her staff to properly complete teacher evaluations. These factors may include the size of the school, the grade levels taught, academic streams, class subjects, the experience and skill of the staff, parental input, labour relations and staff morale, board policies, collective agreements and past performance of the school's teachers.

The Initiation of Evaluation Procedures

Every board policy regarding teacher performance will require the completion of evaluation reports in a specified and timely manner. However, part of a principal's leadership role in monitoring teacher performance is to determine when it is appropriate to launch a formal evaluation procedure other than as required by the board's time lines. This will require the consideration of information received regarding a teacher's conduct in light of its seriousness and impact on the quality of instruction. Sources of concern with regard to deficiencies in a teacher's performance include the principal or vice-principal's own observations, parents, students, and a teacher's self-evaluation or request for assistance.

An interesting question principals may face is whether the complaints of a parent may be used in documenting the performance of a teacher. This may be appropriate, provided that the complaint is relevant to the teacher's performance, the complaint is not anonymous and the consent of the complaining parent is sought so that the teacher may view and respond to the complaint. While a parent's complaint should not form the sole evidence in an evaluation report, it may be useful for a teacher to understand the source of any concerns.

The decision as to whether to commence a formal evaluation procedure should not be made before completing some preliminary inquiries. An initial discussion of any complaints regarding teacher performance or conduct should be held with the teacher in question. The concerns should be clearly expressed and the teacher should have an opportunity to respond. The teacher's explanation may reveal extenuating or personal circumstances. That possibility should be canvassed and the teacher should be provided with an opportunity to provide an explanation.[11]

A classroom visit may be appropriate, perhaps to offer assistance or to assess the veracity of the complaint. Accurate and detailed notes regarding any discussion with the teacher and any classroom visits should be made. Where a formal process is initiated, the record of these events should form part of the report.

Teacher Self-evaluation

Many effective evaluation policies include a form of self-evaluation at the outset of the process. A questionnaire will prompt a teacher to consider and list the strengths and weaknesses of his or her performance. This approach allows the teacher to participate in focusing the evaluation and makes the teacher a greater stakeholder in the process. It also provides an opportunity for reflection, time for which is often not included in a teacher's busy schedule. The results of this self-evaluation should be communicated to the evaluator and also form part of the final report. Even where there is no formal opportunity for self-evaluation in the relevant school board policy, a principal may wish to provide teachers with an opportunity to offer their input.

A Pre-conference with the Teacher

A pre-conference to be held in advance of a classroom visit by the evaluator is a vital step in the process. In allows the teacher to participate in his or her own evaluation. It is also a forum for continued communication which is the hallmark of a formal evaluation process. The overall goal of the pre-conference is to review the evaluation process with the teacher and to agree upon any matters which require input from the teacher in question. Both the evaluator and the teacher must be on the same page as the evaluation commences and this should be evidenced in the documentation.

There are a number of considerations which should be discussed with the teacher in the pre-conference. These include:
- the objectives of the evaluation process;
- adequate notice of the evaluation;

---

[11] K.C. Miles and J.P. Reynolds, "Dealing With Unsatisfactory Teacher Performance" (Scarborough Board of Education, May, 1992).

- the logistics of "when" and "where" the evaluation will take place to avoid scheduling conflicts (where evaluations of all the teacher's subject areas will not be undertaken, the subject-matter where most of the teacher's time is spent should be evaluated);
- the number of classroom visits which will be made (the board's policy may establish a required number of visits);
- the criteria for judging the teacher's performance, including the indicators for each criteria, the method of measurement and the acceptable level of performance (the criteria for evaluation should be expressed in specific language to the teacher, *e.g.*, vague phrases such as "student-teacher relations" or "classroom climate" should be avoided and replaced with details regarding what a teacher may do well or poorly to create such an environment); and
- the procedure for follow-up and feedback once the evaluation has been completed.[12]

In addition, documentation of the matters considered and the conclusions reached at the pre-conference should be prepared. A copy of this summary should be provided to the teacher for confirmation to avoid misunderstandings at the beginning of the process. The results of this conference should also be copied into the teacher's personnel file and be included in the final evaluation report.

On a practical note, the evaluation guideline of the Toronto Catholic District School Board provides some useful suggestions for principals to lead effective principal-teacher conferences:

- Be prepared, and make sure that the teacher is prepared.
- Allow plenty of time for an uninterrupted conference.
- Create a comfortable atmosphere in an appropriate setting.
- Let the teacher know the purpose of the conference (in advance).
- Invite the teacher to fully participate.
- Clarify specific expectations.
- Build trust by being open and honest.
- Be a good listener.
- Accentuate the positive.
- Be specific about concerns or praise.
- Judge performance, not the person.
- Discuss staff goals.
- Recognize your impact.

---

[12] *Ibid.*, at p. 9; E.S. Hickox, "Tiger by the Tail: Administrative Vulnerability in Teacher Evaluation", *Field Development Newsletter*, Vol. 12, No. 2, p. 4; H. Goldblatt, "The Role of Principals in Teacher Evaluations", *Ontario Public School Teachers' Federation*, Vol. 7 (Toronto: October, 1991), p. 3; "Appraisal, Growth and Improvement in Teaching Practices" (Toronto Catholic District School Board, 1998); E.M. Roher, "The Documentation Process as a Formal Legal Procedure" (address to the Ontario Council for Leadership and Educational Administration, "Documenting Teacher Performance: Legal and Management Issues", February 19 to 20, 1990), at p. 8.

- Establish a plan of action.
- Summarize and conclude on a positive and constructive note.[13]

Classroom Evaluation

The first task in any classroom evaluation of teacher performance is to select the appropriate evaluator. At the outset, a consideration of whether only principals and vice-principals should undertake teacher evaluations should be made. Other possible evaluators include qualified administrators or teachers, such as department heads.[14] Any delegation of teacher evaluations should be done selectively. The evaluator should be properly trained to carry out the job effectively. An evaluator who is seen to be unqualified may lead to the reversal of a school board's dismissal or disciplinary decision upon review by an arbitration board.[15]

Anthony Brown and Judge Marvin Zuker have indicated some of the skills required by administrators who carry out teacher performance evaluations.[16] These include:

- the ability to describe and analyze what is happening in the classroom;
- the ability to provide an unbiased rating of a teacher's performance;
- the ability to diagnose the cause(s) of a teacher's poor performance;
- the ability to prescribe remediation which is appropriate to the teacher's classroom deficiencies;
- the ability to conduct conferences with teachers regarding their instructional performance;
- the ability to document the above matters; and
- knowledge of the legal bases for evaluating and dismissing incompetent teachers.

In addition, the evaluator should be familiar with the relevant subject areas and the board's evaluation policy or guideline.

There are a number of issues to consider with regard to the fairness of the classroom evaluation itself. A teacher should be evaluated on the basis of his or her observed performance over a reasonable period of time.[17] This means that each visit to the classroom must be of a reasonable length, sufficient to make and record useful observations. It also means that the total time spent in all visits to a teacher's class must be sufficient to permit reasonable conclusions regarding the teacher's performance. More time should be built into an evaluation in certain circumstances. These include circumstances where a teacher is working with a

---

[13] "Appraisal, Growth and Improvement in Teaching Practices", *ibid.*, at p. 3-19.
[14] Hickox, *op. cit.*, footnote 12, at p. 4.
[15] S. Tracy, "Performance Supervision and Evaluation – A Resource Guide for School Administrators" (Metropolitan Toronto Separate School Board, 1987).
[16] A.F. Brown and M.A. Zuker, *Education Law*, 2nd ed. (Toronto: Carswell, 1997), at p. 285.
[17] Roher, *op. cit.*, footnote 2, at p. 3.

new class or subject area, where the teacher is new to the school or where interruptions, such as fire alarms or illness, prevent proper conditions for an evaluation.

There may also be matters which require investigation by an evaluator. For the most part, these are matters which can be discovered with a few simple inquiries. For instance, where poor classroom management is evident in an evaluation, the evaluator may wish to inquire as to whether the children in question present problems in other classes as well. This investigation can serve to explain the teacher's problems or refute the excuse of a "bad day". The classroom visit has obvious limits as an evaluation tool since it only reveals the lesson as a final product. It cannot reveal the elements of planning and the reasoning behind the instruction decisions made by the teacher. An evaluator should combine his or her observations in the classroom with information gained at the pre-conference and be prepared to ask follow-up questions of the teacher to tie up any loose ends which become evident in the classroom.

In addition, where the classroom visit or other observations lead to a reasonable belief that there may be a personal, medical or psychological cause for a teacher's poor performance, inquiries should be made of the teacher. Serious employment decisions should not be made improperly on the basis of a teacher's health. It should be noted that section 5(1) of the Ontario *Human Rights Code*[18] provides:

> 5(1) Every person has a right to equal treatment with respect to employment without discrimination because of race, ancestry, place of origin, colour, ethnic origin, citizenship, creed, sex, sexual orientation, age, record of offences, marital status, same-sex partnership status, family status or handicap.

The definition of "because of handicap" under the *Human Rights Code* includes any degree of physical disability or infirmity caused by a bodily injury or illness, a condition of mental impairment or a mental disorder.[19] Allowance should be made for the existence of any such conditions. In the event that a teacher is injured or suffering from an illness, the principal should consider postponing the evaluation in favour of offering the teacher assistance or counselling from available resources.

The Toronto Catholic District School Board's evaluation policy offers some practical advice for principals and others entering classrooms to perform evaluations. These pointers include:

- Prepare carefully for each classroom visit.
- Enter the classroom as unobtrusively as possible.
- Participate in the activity in progress, where deemed appropriate.
- Concentrate on the whole learning situation.
- Attempt to discover the strong points in the learning situation.
- Suggestions for improving the lesson should not be made in the classroom unless the teacher asks for them at the time.

---

[18] R.S.O. 1990, c. H.19.
[19] *Human Rights Code*, s. 10(1).

- Make your presence in the classroom as comfortable as possible for the pupils and the teacher.
- Details of room management are important to observe.
- During the visit, show approval of positive events happening in the classroom.
- Make notes on each classroom observation, with the teacher's knowledge. These notes should be used to formulate a written report to the teacher.[20]

A Post-conference with the Teacher

The post-conference should be scheduled before the classroom visits occur and take place shortly thereafter. This will allow the participants to recall the classroom visit or visits while the details are fresh in their minds. Also, making the teacher aware of the post-conference in advance of the classroom visit will allow the teacher to prepare his or her thoughts for the meeting and reflect on his or her performance in advance. This will make other goals of the post-conference easier to accomplish. The post-conference should occur in advance of the preparation of the final report. This allows the teacher to contribute to the content of the report, building fairness into the process. Also, the teacher will be more likely to feel as though he or she has been dealt with fairly upon receiving the report.[21]

A conference with the teacher following one or more classroom visits can serve a number of purposes. It permits the evaluator to communicate his or her thoughts and concerns to the teacher for the first time. Observations made in the classroom should be discussed in light of the previous conference and self-evaluation. The contents of a draft report can be discussed so that the teacher will understand the conclusions to appear in the final report. The evaluator and teacher can also discuss weak areas of performance and develop attainable goals for improvement. To this end, the principal can begin to meet his or her statutory duty by offering various forms of assistance and agreeing upon a reasonable amount of time for improvement. What constitutes a reasonable period of time will vary in each circumstance, but a period of some weeks or a few months offers a reasonable guideline. The post-conference will also permit the teacher and evaluator to ask any questions which arose during the classroom visit, and the teacher should be invited to ask questions.

As always, the results of the post-conference should be accurately documented. The teacher should be sent a copy of the results and should acknowledge receipt of the copy. The conclusions reached in the post-conference should also appear in the final report and a copy should be placed in the teacher's personnel file.

A Plan for Improvement

A plan for improving a teacher's performance should be offered in good faith and the elements of the plan should be well documented. The plan should be developed in conjunction with the teacher and should specify areas of weakness in

---

[20] "Appraisal, Growth and Improvement in Teaching Practices", *op. cit.*, footnote 12.
[21] Goldblatt, *op. cit.*, footnote 12, at p. 3.

the teacher's performance. One arbitrator has affirmed the assistance plan offered to a poorly performing teacher, indicating that the assistance offered was congruent with the problem areas the evaluator identified.[22] The assistance included help from other staff with respect to classroom management and lesson plans, observing other teachers in class and helpful materials. The assistance plan should identify the problem areas and make specific suggestions for improvement. Attainable goals should be set, permitting the teacher a reasonable time frame in which to achieve them.

Anthony Brown and Judge Marvin Zuker provide a useful model for assisting teachers with their performance.[23] Creating a plan to assist the teacher could include the following steps:

- Tell the teacher honestly of the areas which require improvement.
- Express concerns completely to the teacher with verifiable data or information if necessary. The evaluator and teacher should use this information to determine how improvement will be recognized and measured.
- Gather data on how to assist the teacher with his or her particular difficulties. Potential sources for information include other principals and vice-principals, administrators, teachers, professional literature and consultants. This information should then be provided to the teacher.
- Specify the assistance to be provided in the plan, identifying the individuals who will participate.
- Specify the expected outcomes of the plan and state the time frame for that improvement.

The plan should also indicate how the improvement process will be monitored and how feedback on improvement will be provided. This may occur through additional classroom or supervisory visits and conferences with the teacher in question. The frequency of such monitoring and follow-up should be made clear to the teacher.[24]

The Evaluation Report

The most important element in documenting teacher performance is the written evaluation report. This report should be representative of the entire evaluation process. In other words, the report should be open, honest, constructive, clearly worded, focused on its objectives and fair. The document should form a summary of the process from the beginning, listing the conclusions reached by the evaluator and teacher at each step. The written report is the main document from which a teacher will attempt to improve his or her performance. Therefore, the report must provide a reference point for the teacher's weaknesses and goals for improvement.

---

[22] *Board of Education for the City of York and O.S.S.T.F., District 14 (Re)* (March 18, 1993, Marcotte), E.R.C. # 480.
[23] The "TIGHT" Method of Evaluation, as noted in Brown and Zuker, *op. cit.*, footnote 16, at p. 286.
[24] "Appraisal, Growth and Improvement in Teaching Practices", *op. cit.*, footnote 12.

Where a case is reviewed by an arbitrator, a clear and objective evaluation report will indicate that the teacher was dealt with fairly and was given every opportunity to improve. The report will demonstrate that the evaluator was aware of his or her legal obligations and took every reasonable step to meet them. The importance of properly documenting the process should not be underestimated.

There are a number of factors to consider in preparing an evaluation report:

- The report should be written in plain language so that persons without backgrounds in education can also understand its contents.
- The report should list the dates of each meeting, conference or other step in the evaluation process, and describe the general conclusions of each stage.
- The report should list any objections the teacher had at a particular stage.
- The evaluation should make factual and measurable observations with respect to each of the criteria established before the classroom visit, judging the teacher's performance as satisfactory or unsatisfactory based on those observations.
- The evaluation report must identify the particular work or attitude which is problematic and warn the teacher that the work or attitude is unacceptable. The teacher should also be made aware of the potential consequences, in plain language, should the work or attitude not improve.
- The report should make specific suggestions for improving performance in each criteria where required and make note of the resources or assistance offered to the teacher.
- The report should note the reasonable time period agreed upon for improvement.
- The report should make note of the specific context in which the teacher is being evaluated.
- The report should avoid extraneous or inflammatory language and stick to observations which are relevant and verifiable.
- The report should recognize positive aspects of a teacher's performance where applicable.
- The teacher should receive a copy of the report and a copy should be placed in the teacher's personnel file.[25]

The principal should ensure that the teacher has been permitted to sign a copy of the report, indicating his or her acknowledgement of its contents and that it has been discussed with the evaluator. The signature need not indicate the teacher's agreement with the report's conclusions.

Teacher performance evaluations are a time-consuming but vital part of a principal's job. A lot is at stake, including the professional development of teachers and their ability to effectively meet the needs of their students. Key objectives in undertaking the evaluation process are to foster and recognize excellence in teaching and to assist teachers in improving professional

---

[25] Miles and Reynolds, *op. cit.*, footnote 11, at p. 9; Goldblatt, *op. cit.*, footnote 12, at p. 5; Roher, *op. cit.*, footnote 2; Ulrich, *op. cit.*, footnote 9.

competencies. Where severe deficiencies in a teacher's performance persist, the evaluation process will provide the necessary documentation for the principal to recommend termination to the school board. It may also provide an incentive for voluntary resignation for teachers whose performance continues to be unsatisfactory despite their best efforts at improvement. Overall, in meeting the law's requirements for performance evaluations, all parties should continue to focus on the well-being and proper education of students under the school board's care.

5

Dealing with the Problem Parent

INTRODUCTION

School councils, advisory committees and community partnerships are examples of the trend towards increased parental involvement in the education system. Funding cutbacks have resulted in more and more parents participating as volunteers in the day-to-day operation of schools. Parental involvement in the education of children is of paramount importance. Proper values are instilled early in life and need to be supported and nurtured by schools and parents working as a team. Generally, parents are encouraged to attend meetings, co-operate with school personnel and do their part to assist their children.

Parental co-operation has become a vital issue in our schools. Many of today's parents are demanding, involved and vocal, all of which can be positive qualities. However, from time to time, there are some parents who consistently refuse to follow the rules. The question then arises as to what the response of a teacher or principal should be when a parent makes excessive demands. What steps should a school official take when a parent stirs up discontent or behaves in an inappropriate manner? What actions can an educator take when a parent attempts to threaten or intimidate?

In a recent incident, a Toronto parent, who was upset that his son did not make a certain position on the school football team, commandeered the principal's office, called the police and alleged that the school was involved in child abuse. This parent also made a death threat against the physical education teacher involved in selecting the team. The parent was charged by the police with three counts of threatening to cause bodily harm.

While this type of threat is a rare occurrence, it has become increasingly common for a parent or a group of parents to intimidate or harass a particular teacher. A parent or group of parents may, from time to time, hold meetings, lobby trustees and circulate petitions to demonstrate their discontent with a teacher, in an aggressive and confrontational manner.

Increasingly, schools have taken the initiative in bringing problem parents into line. Some schools have instituted disciplinary action, providing a warning to the parent and effectively placing him or her "on probation". In circumstances where a principal believes that a parent's presence in the school would be detrimental to the physical or mental well-being of the pupils, the principal could invoke the *Trespass to Property Act*[1] to prevent the parent from entering onto school property.

PARENTAL HARASSMENT

In a recent paper, Alberta lawyer, Daniel Carroll, points out that "parental harassment" is not a technical term recognized in law.[2] Carroll defines parental harassment in a school context as "the use by parents of confrontational tactics which attack a teacher or which have the consequence of reducing a teacher's ability to conduct himself effectively within the school and which harm the teacher's well-being or professional reputation".[3]

An appropriate definition of parental harassment could also include the following:

- unwanted comments, interferences or suggestions;
- various forms of intimidation and aggressive behaviour;
- verbal threats;
- verbal and emotional abuse;
- the application of force or physical assault;
- "bullying" which is an attempt to undermine an individual through cruel or humiliating behaviour; and/or
- "mobbing" which involves a collective effort to psychologically harass a person.

It should be recognized that there are parents with legitimate concerns who feel that they have no choice but to become confrontational when their concerns are not addressed. Assessing whether certain conduct is inappropriate is often a difficult balancing act. A school official does not want to discourage healthy dissent, such as valuable feedback from parents who are helping to keep the school on track. The teacher or principal also does not want to penalize a good student for the poor judgment of his or her parents.

As an educator, it is clear that dealing with difficult people from time to time is an integral part of the job. However, a principal must recognize that under section 265(a) of the *Education Act*,[4] he or she has a duty to maintain proper order and discipline in the school.

The aim of this chapter is to outline the various steps that the educator may take in order to deal with a problem parent. The increased role that parents now play in

---

[1] R.S.O. 1990, c. T.21.
[2] D. Carroll, "Parental Harassment: When Reasonableness Fails", in W.F. Foster and W.J. Smith, eds., *Reaching for Reasonableness: The Educator as Lawful Decision-Maker* (Chateauguay: Lisbro, 1999), p. 257.
[3] *Ibid.*, at p. 257.
[4] R.S.O. 1990, c. E.2.

the educational process will be discussed, followed by the various strategies that may be used by school administrators when a parent crosses the line and becomes a negative influence in the school setting.

Increased Parental Involvement Through School Councils

In 1995, the Ministry of Education and Training released "Policy/Program Memorandum No. 122"[5] (the "Policy") which mandated the creation of school councils. The Policy sets out the background and rationale for the program and outlines requirements for the composition and operation of school councils. The purpose of school councils is to advise principals and school boards on educational issues and matters relating to individual schools. In terms of membership, the school council must include parents and guardians of children enrolled in the school, the principal, a teacher, a student representative in the case of secondary schools, a non-teaching school staff member, and representatives from the community. Parents and guardians must make up the majority of the school council.

Consequently, parents and guardians can exert a great deal of influence through the school council, which, as part of its advisory function, may advise the principal or school board on a wide variety of matters including: school year calendars; codes of student behaviour; curriculum priorities; programs and strategies to improve school performance on provincial and school board tests; preparation of the school profile; school budget priorities; communications to parents and the community; extra-curricular activities; community use of the school, and community programs and services provided at the school through school-community partnerships; school board policies which will affect the school; and the selection of principals.

While the increased parental involvement which arises from the participation of parent-driven school councils is to be encouraged as a welcome source of advice and constructive criticism, on occasion, it may also be co-opted by disgruntled parents as a means of airing grievances in public and channelling discord in their campaign against targeted educators. Whether a parent acts alone or as part of a school council to harass or otherwise disrupt the proper functioning of the school environment, school administrators must be prepared to respond quickly and appropriately to the problem parent.

DEVELOPING AN APPROPRIATE RESPONSE

Since teachers have the most direct contact with students, it is often teachers who first bear the brunt of a problem parent's attack. Teachers should learn to recognize potential problems when warning signs appear. For example, a problem parent will often go to the principal, superintendent, other parents or a local

---

[5] Ontario Ministry of Education and Training, "Policy/Program Memorandum No. 122: School Board Policies on School Councils" (issued April 12, 1995).

newspaper before a real attempt is made to raise and deal with a concern directly with the teacher. Or a problem parent might overreact to a situation, creating an atmosphere of animosity and confrontation instead of one geared towards an amicable resolution.

In developing an appropriate response, it is important to determine the source and nature of the problem and the social, political and personal dynamics of the situation. Daniel Carroll suggests that educators make an early assessment of who is complaining and their history:

> Is this just one parent or is there a group? If it is a group, who is the ringleader? What is motivating this harassment? In particular, what are the complaints and what evidence is there to support and meet those complaints? What is the previous history of the relationship of the school and this parent and in particular of the teacher or staff member and this parent? To the extent complaints have been voiced, are they legitimate and what can be done to address them in a non-confrontational fashion?[6]

In preparing an appropriate response to a possible incident of harassment, the school should consider the following:

- *Communicate early in the process* – Whether or not the complaint comes to the teacher or the principal, they should speak to each other early in the process. A teacher who anticipates a problem should consult with his or her principal and, where appropriate, the relevant superintendent of education. The teacher should not wait until the situation gets out of control before contacting school officials.
- *Provide backup and support to the teacher and principal* – A complaint heard from time to time is that the school board considers these issues to be the responsibility of the principal *alone* and does not provide sufficient backup. Senior administration should remember that principals are acting on behalf of the board. A strategy for responding to the concerns raised should be developed consensually between the principal and appropriate superintendent. Senior administration should attempt to ensure consistency in responding to situations across the board's jurisdiction. The principal should inform the relevant superintendent of education of the nature of the allegations and keep the superintendent informed as events unfold. Parents will often solicit the support of individual trustees as part of their campaign. It is important for school board administration to be aware of events in order to respond effectively to trustee concerns.
- *Document* – Both principals and administrators should carefully document all telephone calls and meetings. In preparing notes, educators should be objective, factual and accurate in setting out a description of events. School personnel should avoid language which appears to make judgments or inferences. Educators should also record the dates and times of events and make note of the names of individuals who attended relevant meetings.
- *Contact professional association* – The teacher may contact his or her professional association for assistance. The association can be of assistance in providing counselling and advice.

---

[6] Carroll, *op. cit.*, footnote 2, at p. 259.

- *Investigate allegations* – Where appropriate, the principal should undertake an investigation into the parent's allegations. Principals should interview the complainant and meet with relevant witnesses. If there is more than one complainant, the principal should meet with each one individually. The principal may ask the parents if they have raised these issues directly with the teacher. In appropriate circumstances, the principal should suggest that the parents speak to the teacher directly to review a particular concern. The principal should also meet with the teacher and obtain his or her response to the allegations. The principal should take notes of these meetings and, where appropriate, consult with the relevant superintendent of education.
- *Meet parents at early stage* – The school administration should attempt to intervene at an early stage. Where appropriate, the principal or relevant superintendent could attempt to meet with the parents or the ringleader of the parent group in order to mediate a resolution of the dispute. In organizing this meeting, school officials would provide a forum for the legitimate expression of the parents' concerns. Before this meeting is organized, the parties should understand and agree to predetermined ground rules. Such ground rules would include the location and time of the meeting, the purpose of the meeting and the parties which will attend (such as whether a translator, legal counsel or family friend will accompany the parents and whether the superintendent or relevant teacher will attend with the principal).
- *Three "V"s* – In the meeting with parents, the educator should consider practising the three "V"s: ventilate, validate and verify. The educator should permit the parents to ventilate their concerns and fully outline their position. The administrator should validate that the school board recognizes that the parents have certain concerns, listen carefully and acknowledge that he or she understands the parents' position. The educator should also verify the importance of the parent-teacher relationship, that both parties are working in the best interests of the student and outline possible steps which can be taken to resolve the issue.
- *A timely letter* – In some cases, a letter to the parent or parents from the principal, superintendent of education, director or trustee explaining the circumstances can resolve certain issues. In circumstances where the parent requests an apology, but the principal and/or teacher have done nothing wrong and do not believe an apology is warranted, in the spirit of reconciliation, the principal may consider preparing a "letter of regret". In this letter, the principal would indicate her or his regret regarding the circumstances which gave rise to the complaint.
- *Maintain confidentiality* – A letter of complaint directed at a particular teacher should be kept in confidence, subject to the ability to conduct a full investigation. It is important not to widely disclose the letter's contents. In general, the contents of the letter should be shared on a need-to-know basis. The fewer people who know, the better. The principal or superintendent should determine early on who will be included when sharing information. Where there has been wide distribution of an anonymous letter with derogatory or

personal comments, it may be prudent to advise the school staff as to what is being done. Any such communication should be very general without revealing the school's strategy.
- *Summarize outcome of meetings and course of action* – The school administration should confirm the outcome of the meetings or its course of action in a letter to the relevant parents. This letter should provide a summary of the events, confirm the school's position and set out the results of what the parties have agreed to. Such letter must be carefully drafted with respect to tone and content to ensure that it does not create additional hostility and further provoke the parents. In addition, school administration should inform the teacher, who was the target of the complaint, of the outcome or terms of resolution of the incident.

In addition to the remedies of negotiation and mediation, depending on the individual circumstances, there are a range of other, more severe remedies a school board may consider in dealing with a problem parent. These remedies include exercising one's rights under the Ontario *Trespass to Property Act*, the commencement of a civil action and/or proceedings under the *Criminal Code*.[7]

Trespass to Property Act

In extreme situations, where a parent has been involved in harassing conduct, he or she may persist in attempting to enter onto school property with the intent to threaten or harm students or staff. Schools should be aware of their rights and responsibilities to these unwelcome individuals and should make every effort to ensure that the safety of students and staff within the school is protected.

The provisions of both the *Education Act* and the *Trespass to Property Act* are of assistance to principals who wish to have a problem parent removed from school premises. The *Education Act* provides in section 265(m) that a principal has a duty to "refuse to admit to the school or classroom a person whose presence in the school or classroom would in the principal's judgment be detrimental to the physical or mental well-being of the pupils".

The provisions of the *Education Act* enacted by the *Safe Schools Act, 2000*[8] (Bill 81) specifically deal with access to school premises. Section 305(2) provides that no person shall enter or remain on school premises unless he or she is authorized by regulation to be there on that day or at that time. Under section 305(4), a principal may direct a person to leave school premises if the principal believes that the person is prohibited by regulation or under a board policy from being there.

On September 1, 2000, the regulation governing access to schools came into force.[9] Section 2(1) of the regulation sets out who is permitted to be on school premises, including a person enrolled as a pupil in the school, a parent or guardian of such a pupil or a person employed or retained by the school board. The

---

[7] R.S.C. 1985, c. C-46.
[8] S.O. 2000, c. 12.
[9] *Access to School Premises*, O. Reg. 474/00.

regulation also gives principals and boards the right to restrict access to their schools. Section 3(1) provides that a person is not permitted to remain on school premises if, in the judgment of the principal or vice-principal or another person authorized by the board, his or her presence is detrimental to the safety or well-being of a person on the premises.

The regulation does not limit the ability of a principal to restrict access to the school, even for individuals who are permitted by the regulation to be on school premises. In this regard, a principal may restrict a parent's access to school premises in extreme cases of harassment, threats or other offensive conduct. Unauthorized persons on school property will face fines of up to $5,000, on conviction.[10]

The *Trespass to Property Act* also provides a framework for translating the principal's duty into action when necessary. School boards in Ontario can be characterized as "occupiers" in respect of school sites and thus have all the rights and duties which come with being classified as such. Most notably, the Act makes trespassing an offence punishable by a fine of up to $2,000, on conviction.

One situation in which this becomes an issue is where an individual insists on unauthorized access to school property.[11] For instance, a parent may attempt to gain access to his or her child's classroom without the consent or authorization of school administration. A parent involved in harassing or threatening a particular teacher could attempt to use these visits as a springboard to reinforce allegations about the teacher's performance.

In general, a parent should not have a right of access to a child's classroom without the express permission of school administration. There is no problem with parents having access to a classroom for a special event, open house or class production. However, on a day-to-day basis, parents should not be permitted to attend a child's classroom without the consent of the teacher or principal. Where a parent wilfully interrupts or disquiets the proceedings of a school or class, he or she may be subject to prosecution under the provisions of the *Education Act* and the *Trespass to Property Act*.

In order to meet the requirements of the *Trespass to Property Act*, a school should give notice to the problem parent that, in the principal's judgment, the parent's presence in the school would be detrimental to the physical or mental well-being of the pupils and that, as a result, the parent is prohibited from entering onto school property. The notice should indicate that, if the individual trespasses on school property in the future, he or she may be prosecuted for any such action to the full extent of the law.

The school, a police officer or a person authorized by the school may arrest without warrant any person he or she believes on reasonable and probable grounds to be trespassing on the premises. While principals clearly have the power to

---
[10] *Provincial Offences Act*, R.S.O. 1990, c. P.33, s. 61.
[11] See *R. v. Burko* (1968), 3 D.L.R. (3d) 330, [1969] 3 C.C.C. 72 (Ont. Co. Ct.); *Serup v. School District No. 57* (1989), 57 D.L.R. (4th) 261, 54 B.C.L.R. (2d) 258 (C.A.); *Nagel v. Hunter*, [1995] 6 W.W.R. 246, 83 W.A.C. 233 (Alta. C.A.), leave to appeal to S.C.C. refused 102 W.A.C. 398*n*, 174 A.R. 398*n*.

arrest, it is recommended that the police be called in to do so in order to ensure that the arrest is done properly and that relevant provisions of the *Canadian Charter of Rights and Freedoms* are complied with.

A trespasser who resists an attempt by the principal to prevent his or her entry or to remove him or her from the property is deemed to have committed an assault without justification or provocation. The prudent course of action when there is no imminent danger is to begin by asking the trespasser to leave peacefully. It is important to note that, unless the trespasser is committing a violent act, or is otherwise an immediate threat, the principal may not use force against the trespasser which may cause serious harm.

CIVIL PROCEEDING

Restraining Order

In extreme situations, where physical harm has been threatened, an alternative course of action is to commence a civil action by way of a statement of claim and, upon affidavit evidence, apply *ex parte* before a judge for a restraining order to halt intimidating and harassing behaviour. In two cases, restraining orders were issued against defendants who were persistently calling the complainant[12] or distributing defamatory pamphlets[13] as part of their campaign against school administrators. In these circumstances, the school board must demonstrate to the judge that the matter is an emergency and that mischief would arise if notice of the application was given to the parent. In general, if such orders are granted, they are of limited duration.

In taking a proactive approach, it may be sufficient to put the problem parent on notice that his or her conduct may attract a civil lawsuit. A demand letter, often prepared by school board counsel, would put the parent on notice that his or her conduct in threatening or intimidating a particular teacher must cease. The letter would provide a summary of meetings which have taken place and would assure the parent that both the teacher and the school encourage parents to discuss their concerns. It would confirm that the parent's efforts to gather the support of other parents to prevent the teacher from continuing to teach at the school exceed the bounds of productive dialogue. The letter would indicate the parent's campaign is not only disrupting the operation of the school, but also injuring the teacher's professional reputation and undermining his or her ability to maintain the confidence of parents and students.

This demand letter should be orchestrated in concert with an effort by school administration to work with the parents to remedy the situation. In this regard, the school would take a "dual track" approach. On one hand, the school board's

---

[12] *Peel District School Board v. Taurozzi* (unreported, October 15, 1998, order of Campbell J.).
[13] *Peel Board of Education v. Gradek* (unreported, November 23, 1994, order of Carnwath J.).

lawyer would send a letter which demands that the parent cease and desist in his or her conduct and which outlines the school's legal remedies. Simultaneous with this letter, the principal or relevant superintendent would work with the parents to try to reach an amicable resolution.

Where these approaches do not work and the disruptive behaviour continues, the teacher or the school administration may consider filing a statement of claim for either defamation, where the problem parent is affecting the educator's professional reputation or personal integrity, or nuisance, where the problem parent is a threat to the educator's right to privacy, as an appropriate response.

Defamation

The law of defamation is an attempt to balance the competing values of individual freedom of expression and the right to privacy and protection of one's reputation. Its purpose is to "prevent or discourage wrongful attacks on honour and reputation, and [correct], [redress], and [check] the abuses of a powerful communications media".[14] Carroll sets out the three phases of a typical defamation lawsuit as: (i) the plaintiff's case; (ii) the defendant's case; and (iii) the plaintiff's response.[15]

- *The plaintiff's case* – There are essentially three factors which the plaintiff must prove in order to establish a case for defamation.[16] First, the plaintiff must establish that the offending statement was communicated or published to a third party. Secondly, the plaintiff must show that the offending statement refers to the plaintiff. Thirdly, the plaintiff must show that the offending statement is defamatory, in that it is false and discredits the plaintiff[17] by either lowering him or her in the estimation of community members or by exposing him or her to ridicule, contempt or hatred.[18]
- *The defendant's case* – The defendant has three main defences available to a defamation claim, namely, truth, fair comment and qualified privilege. The truth or justification defence is a complete defence wherein the defendant bears the burden of establishing to the court's satisfaction that the content of the offending statement is true and therefore not defamatory.[19] It is worth noting here that this defence will only be successful where the defendant can establish that the offending statement is, in fact, true. It will not assist a defendant where the offending statement is not true, even if the defendant honestly believes it to

---

[14] R. Brown, *The Law of Defamation in Canada*, 2nd ed. (Scarborough: Carswell, 1994), at p. 1-4.
[15] Carroll, *op. cit.*, footnote 2, at pp. 264-5.
[16] M.P. Fitzgibbon, "Defamation in a School Context", *Education Law News* (Winter, 1999) (Toronto: Borden & Elliot).
[17] A. Gahtan, M. Kratz and J.F. Mann, *Internet Law: A Practical Guide for Legal and Business Professionals* (Scarborough: Carswell, 1998), at p. 278.
[18] *Botiuk v. Toronto Free Press Publications Ltd.* (1995), 126 D.L.R. (4th) 609, [1995] 3 S.C.R. 3.
[19] *Hiltz and Seamone Co. v. Nova Scotia (Attorney General)* (1999), 172 D.L.R. (4th) 488, 173 N.S.R. (2d) 341 (C.A.).

be so. The defendant may also use the fair comment defence. This defence is characterized as a statement which is "an expression of an honestly held opinion founded on true facts on a matter of public interest".[20] The elements of this defence are that the statement is: (i) a comment or opinion; (ii) based on facts which are true; (iii) made honestly and fairly; (iv) made without malice; and (v) a matter of public interest.[21] Alternatively, a defendant may rely on the defence of qualified privilege which, under certain circumstances, allows a person to make offending statements which would otherwise be defamatory. The defendant must prove that he or she has a duty, whether it be legal, moral or social, to make the offending statement, and that the person to whom it was made has a corresponding duty to receive it. Because of the notion of duty inherent to this defence, problem parents may attempt to establish that their duty to their school-age children requires the making of statements which are negative and derogatory, and that they are thus entitled to communicate these statements to the community. Accordingly, this defence plays an important role in the educational context.

- *The plaintiff's response* – As mentioned earlier, truth or justification is a complete defence and, once the defence is made out, the defendant will suffer no liability for offending statements. However, the defence of fair comment or qualified privilege may be defeated in two ways. The plaintiff must prove:
  - express or implied malice, either by evidence of improper motive[22] in making the statement, that the defendant spoke dishonestly or with reckless disregard to the truth of the statements, or by inference from the language of the statement itself, or from the circumstances surrounding the making and publication of the statements;[23] or
  - that the offending statement exceeded the limits of the duty to make the statement.[24]

An examination of the cases involving defamation in a school context will demonstrate the operation of these principles. In *Kohuch v. Wilson*,[25] the defendant, Ms. Wilson had conducted a concerted campaign to discredit the professional reputations of the principal and school superintendent. Among other things, her efforts included over 70 letters, a petition, a public meeting against the principal, an open-line radio show, letters to the editor of the local newspaper, and a phone-in complaint line which was advertised in the paper. The court found that statements about the principal and superintendent were defamatory.

In response, Ms. Wilson claimed that the statements were true or, alternatively, that she was entitled to the defence of qualified privilege. The court found

---

[20] Carroll, *op. cit.*, footnote 2, at p. 264.
[21] N. Martin, "Liability for Statements About Employees and Students", in Foster and Smith, *op. cit.*, footnote 2, p. 143.
[22] *Hill v. Church of Scientology of Toronto* (1995), 126 D.L.R. (4th) 129, [1995] 2 S.C.R. 1130.
[23] Brown, *op. cit.*, footnote 14, at p. 1-19.
[24] *Hill v. Church of Scientology of Toronto*, *supra,* footnote 22, at p. 171.
[25] (1988), 71 Sask. R. 33 (Q.B.).

otherwise. Ms. Wilson's allegations were unfounded, given the evidence before the court, and therefore she could not take advantage of the defence of truth. Furthermore, the court ruled that the use of the defence of qualified privilege was defeated by the express malice exhibited by Ms. Wilson's outlandish defamatory statements. In addition to damages awarded to the plaintiffs, the court also ordered an injunction prohibiting Ms. Wilson from publication of further offending statements.

Similarly, in *Wagner v. Lim*,[26] Mr. and Mrs. Lim had engaged in a letter-writing campaign alleging racial discrimination and mistreatment by Mr. Wagner, the principal of the school where their son was a student and where Mrs. Lim worked as a part-time librarian. The Lims sent letters to parents, teachers, students, the newspapers and other members of the school administration and community. The court found that their statements were defamatory.

In their defence, the Lims claimed that the statements were true, protected by qualified privilege or protected under provisions of the Alberta *Individual's Rights Protection Act*. The court considered each of these defences in turn and rejected them all. Upon a review of the evidence of racial discrimination, the court could find no justification for such an allegation. As for the defence of qualified privilege, and the statutory defence, while the letters to the school administration and the Alberta Human Rights Commission might have been protected, their publication to third parties completely unrelated to the dispute (for instance, students, school staff and other members of the community) was not protected since there was no duty to communicate the statements and no corresponding duty to receive them by the third parties. Even if the Lims had been entitled to claim the defence of qualified privilege, the court's finding of malice would have disentitled them to the defence. Accordingly, the court awarded damages and an injunction to the plaintiffs.

In the recent case of *McKerron v. Marshall*,[27] the court held that the problem parent was liable for defamation and intentional infliction of mental suffering for his campaign against the plaintiff teacher. In the 1994-1995 school year, Mr. Marshall removed his son from Ms. McKerron's grade 4 class on the basis of a conversation he had had with another parent. Mr. Marshall alleged that the parent had informed him that Ms. McKerron was "emotionally abusing" children and that two children had already been removed from her class as a result. At trial, that parent's recollection of the conversation was significantly different. She testified that she had told the Marshalls that a child had been removed because the parent felt that her child was getting "lost in the shuffle" of the large class and so she had decided on home schooling. The witness testified that she had not said anything about emotional abuse and was surprised when she found out that the Marshalls had removed their son from Ms. McKerron's class.

Nevertheless, on the basis of that conversation, Mr. Marshall launched a campaign to have Ms. McKerron removed from the school. He met at various

---

[26] (1994), 22 Alta. L.R. (3d) 169, 158 A.R. 241 (Q.B.).
[27] (1999), 92 A.C.W.S. (3d) 166, [1999] O.J. No. 4048 (Q.L.) (S.C.J.).

times with the school principal, a school board trustee and the school superintendent. He consistently alleged wrongdoing by Ms. McKerron and issued ultimatums that she be removed from the classroom or he would be forced to take action. He distributed a letter in which he claimed that Ms. McKerron was:

> "... no longer capable of performing her duties, and in fact children are at risk with her continuing presence . . . These children are at risk of not only falling further behind academically but are also are at risk of further emotional abuse."[28]

The next day, Mr. Marshall draped a four-metre banner with the words, "MRS. McKERRON IS UNSTABLE, REMOVE HER NOW" on his car and parked in front of the school. The banner was up for approximately an hour and a half and Mr. Marshall himself contacted local media who published reports of the disturbance caused.

Mr. Marshall continued his attack on Ms. McKerron's character, widening his scope to include all those who appeared supportive of her. He wrote letters and distributed documents to the principal, the school trustee, the school superintendent, counsel for Ms. McKerron and the board, the Waterloo County Board of Education, the Ontario College of Teachers, the Law Society of Upper Canada, the Ministry of Education and the local media. He communicated with the parents of children in Ms. McKerron's class in an effort to collect information which would discredit Ms. McKerron, going so far as to tape-record his conversations with them. He defied trespass notices and attended at the school regularly, eventually being convicted and fined on two counts of trespassing. Even Ms. McKerron's transfer to a different school in another district did not deter Mr. Marshall in his campaign – he continued to insist on Ms. McKerron's removal from the new school, claiming that she was "unstable" and "emotionally abusive".

At trial, Mr. Justice Reilly commented on the aggressive and insulting behaviour exhibited by Mr. Marshall both before and during the trial, and found that he had indeed defamed Ms. McKerron in the letter quoted here and by the public presentation of the banner denouncing her. The court ruled that the statements in the letter were protected by the defence of qualified privilege since, as a concerned parent, Mr. Marshall had an interest or duty to make the communication, and school officials had a corresponding duty to receive his comments. However, the court concluded that the defence of qualified privilege was defeated in three separate ways. First, the court found that there was overwhelming evidence of malice exhibited by Mr. Marshall toward Ms. McKerron. Secondly, there was an absence of truth or justification for the statements and, indeed, the court found that Mr. Marshall was aware that at least one of his frequently repeated statements was "demonstrably false . . . very early in his campaign". Thirdly, the court found that Mr. Marshall had conducted the campaign for an improper motive unrelated to the legitimate purpose for which the qualified privilege defence is granted. Mr. Marshall's campaign was motivated by the desire for public attention and self-aggrandisement as a defender of young

---

[28] *Supra*, at pp. 17-18 of the judgment.

children. Accordingly, the court awarded Ms. McKerron damages in the amount of $405,000 and a permanent injunction enjoining Mr. Marshall from further defamation or harassment.

Occasionally, it is the teacher who becomes a problem, as in the case of *Campbell v. Cartmell*.[29] In this case, the plaintiffs were five school board officials and the Toronto District School Board and the defendants were a teacher, her husband and their daughter. Over a five-year period beginning in 1994, the defendants engaged in a letter-writing campaign which included postings on a local network. The letters originally dealt with contractual matters between Ms. Cartmell and the board, but later included allegations that the board and its senior members had committed criminal acts. The Cartmells also began referring, in their letters and postings, to the allergy-related death of a student who was the daughter of two of the plaintiffs. The correspondence continued even after an injunction was obtained.

The court found that the defendants had made defamatory statements in that they communicated the statements to third parties, referred to the plaintiffs by name and the statements were false allegations designed to discredit the plaintiffs. Further, the court held that the defendants had acted with malice given the nature of the defamatory statements made, and in consideration of all of the circumstances of the case. The defences of truth and qualified privilege were both rejected since the statements were unfounded and the defendants had failed to act honestly, in good faith and without malice. Accordingly, the court awarded general, aggravated and punitive damages, as well as a permanent injunction restraining the defendants from further defamatory statements involving the plaintiffs.

Defendants have, however, been able to defend themselves successfully in defamation suits. In *Crandall v. Atlantic School of Theology*,[30] Mr. Crandall was a postulant who was refused ordination by the bishop following certain remarks made by a female student, the faculty and the faculty director regarding Mr. Crandall's inappropriate and discomforting behaviour around women and his lack of interpersonal skills which would impact negatively upon his placement in a parish. Mr. Crandall sued for slander but the court found that the statements of the female student were not defamatory because they were merely expressions of how Mr. Crandall made her feel. On the other hand, while some of the statements made by the faculty were indeed defamatory, they were protected by the defence of qualified privilege. The court found that the faculty director had a duty to make the statements to the faculty and the faculty had a corresponding duty to receive the statements. Furthermore, the court concluded that there was "not the merest scintilla of evidence of malice shown" by the defendants which would defeat the defence.

In *Gibbs v. Jalbert*,[31] a teacher sued a student's guardian for a letter that the guardian sent to the principal, the area superintendent, the school board and the teachers' association. The letter contained the following paragraph:

---

[29] (1999), 91 A.C.W.S. (3d) 507, [1999] O.J. No. 3553 (Q.L.) (S.C.J.).
[30] (1993), 38 A.C.W.S. (3d) 1286, [1993] N.S.J. No. 79 (Q.L.) (S.C.).
[31] (1994), 51 A.C.W.S. (3d) 377 (B.C.S.C.), revd 115 W.A.C. 302, 18 B.C.L.R. (3d) 351 (C.A.).

"My house over the past five years has been a safe meeting place for my daughter and friends from [school]. During this period of time Mr Gibbs' name has been brought up on many occasions in a negative and loathsome manner . . . I find it really difficult [not] to speak out when one offensive, foul and abhorrent teacher is allowed to call himself a professional among what I know to be real professionals. Please do something."[32]

At trial, the letter was found to be defamatory. Ms. Jalbert's defence of qualified privilege was defeated by evidence of express malice towards Mr. Gibbs in this paragraph of her letter. However, the Court of Appeal overturned the trial decision with respect to the finding of malice, concluding instead that, as a member of the community, Ms. Jalbert had an interest in "the integrity of the education system and the fitness to teach of those working within the system". The court ruled:

> It is in accordance with that interest that parents and other community members are permitted to raise with the proper authorities their honestly held concerns about alleged mistreatment of students by teachers. Communications made within that context are properly regarded as communications made on an occasion of qualified privilege which are entitled to the protection of the privilege, unless defeated by express malice.[33]

It is important to note that, to be successful, the educator must prove each element of defamation on a balance of probabilities. However, there are circumstances where an educator will not have the required elements for a defamation suit, for instance, publication of offending statements to third parties. In situations where the problem parent continues to harass the teacher, a civil suit may be brought on the basis of nuisance.

Nuisance

Sometimes, a problem parent will conduct his or her harassment campaign in a more private manner, harassing the teacher only, rather than involving third parties. Because of the requirement for publication of defamatory statements before liability will be assessed in a defamation suit, a teacher thus besieged may choose to sue on the basis of nuisance. In *Motherwell v. Motherwell*,[34] the Alberta Court of Appeal extended the common law of nuisance to protect against unwanted invasions of privacy, in this case, by telephone. The court found that the long-term and persistent harassment of the plaintiffs by the defendant at their homes, and in the case of one plaintiff, at his office, was conduct which fell within the principle of private nuisance. The test set out was whether the telephone calls "amounted to undue interference with the comfortable and convenient enjoyment by the plaintiffs of their respective premises".[35] It seems clear that persistent harassment by means of either telephone calls or unwanted visits by a problem

---

[32] *Supra*, at p. 305.
[33] *Supra*, at p. 308.
[34] (1976), 73 D.L.R. (3d) 62, [1976] 6 W.W.R. 550 (Alta. C.A.).
[35] *Supra*, at p. 74.

parent at the teacher's home or place of work would fall within this definition, leading to a range of possible remedies, including damages, an injunction or possible incarceration.

CRIMINAL CODE

Under section 265(1) of the *Criminal Code*, a person commits an assault when "he attempts or threatens, by an act or gesture, to apply force to another person, if he has, or causes that other person to believe upon reasonable grounds that he has, present ability to effect his purpose". An assault is also committed where a person, without the consent of another person, applies force intentionally to that other person, directly or indirectly.

Where a person fears on reasonable grounds that another person will cause personal injury to him or her or will damage his or her property, an application may be made before a provincial court judge or a justice of the peace.[36] After a hearing is held, where the judge or justice of the peace is satisfied by the evidence adduced that the informant has reasonable grounds for his of her fears, the judge or justice of the peace may order that the defendant enter into a recognizance to keep the peace and be of good behaviour for a period of time not exceeding 12 months, or commit the defendant to prison for a term also not exceeding 12 months if the defendant refuses to enter into the recognizance. Other conditions may be attached to the recognizance, including a prohibition against possessing a firearm or a requirement that the defendant stay a specified distance away from the school and cease communications with the informant. Under the provisions of the *Criminal Code*, a person who commits a breach of the recognizance is guilty of either an indictable offence and liable to imprisonment for a term not exceeding two years or an offence punishable on summary conviction.

Alternatively, a charge can be made under the "stalking" or "criminal harassment" provisions of the *Criminal Code*. Under section 264, no person may repeatedly follow a person from place to place, repeatedly communicate with that person, beset or watch that person's home or place of business, or engage in threatening conduct, without lawful authority and knowing that or being reckless as to whether the other person is harassed, which causes the other person to fear for his or her safety. Under the provisions of the *Criminal Code*, a person who contravenes section 264 is guilty of either an indictable offence and is liable to imprisonment for a term not exceeding five years or an offence punishable on summary conviction.

In the leading case of *R. v. Hertz*,[37] the court enumerated seven points relevant to the charge of criminal harassment. The court stated:

(1) The Crown must prove beyond a reasonable doubt that
(a) "that the accused engaged in one or more of the types of conduct found in subs. (2) of the section."

---
[36] *Criminal Code*, s. 810.
[37] (1995), 170 A.R. 139, [1995] A.J. No. 496 (Q.L.) (Prov. Ct.).

(b) "that in doing so it was the intention of the accused to harass the complainant, or the accused was in fact reckless as to whether the conduct did harass the complainant."
(c) "that in all of the circumstances known to the complainant, the complainant had 'reasonable fears' for his or her safety or 'the safety of anyone known' to him or her."

. . . . .

(2) "[T]here is nothing in the section in question that there be actual injury of any kind, either physical or mental, caused to the complainant as a result of the conduct of the accused before the section becomes operative . . . the Crown need not establish that a threat was actually made by the accused to the complainant in order for a finding to be made that the offence has been committed." . . .

(3) "Repeatedly" means "many times over". It means more than once or twice. The circumstances of each case (ie.: the context in which the acts complained of were committed) will determine whether an act has been "repeatedly" performed . . .

(4) "Safety" means "more than freedom from physical harm. It includes a freedom from fear of mental or emotional or psychological trauma" . . .

(5) "Harassment" means the conduct must be unwelcome to the complainant . . . I am also of the view that the term "harassment" includes an element of tormenting the complainant . . .

(6) The test as to whether the complainant fears for his or her safety is objective but only to this extent: would a reasonable person, in the particular circumstances of the complainant, fear for his or her safety or the safety of anyone known to him or her. In my view, if there are circumstances special to the complainant which makes it reasonable for that person to suffer the fear described in the section, then it is necessary for the accused to be aware of those circumstances before a conviction can be entered. It is not enough for the complainant simply to say that he or she was fearful. It must have been reasonable for the complainant to be fearful in his or her particular circumstances.

(7) Further, in considering whether the complainant's fears were reasonably held, one must take into [account] all the evidence (subject to my comments in (6)) including "the gender of the victim and the history and circumstances surrounding the relationship which existed or which had existed, if any, between the accused and the victim" . . .[38]

The circumstances in *R. v. Theysen*[39] demonstrate the application of the law in a school context. In that case, the victim, Ms. Smith, was a secretary at the school where the accused's children attended and where the accused also volunteered. The accused, Ms. Theysen, spoke frequently about her problems with the victim who was initially sympathetic to her struggles as a single unemployed parent. The accused would deliver chocolates and flowers to the victim, despite the victim's request that she discontinue the gifts.

While at first the contact was not unwelcome, following a separate unrelated incident at the school, Ms. Theysen's contact with the victim increased in both its intensity and its frequency. Ms. Theysen began calling the victim at the school and

---
[38] *Supra*, at pp. 149-50 (case references omitted).
[39] (1996), 44 Alta. L.R. (3d) 364, 190 A.R. 133 (Prov. Ct.).

at home at all hours of the day; she delivered written notes, both to the school and to Ms. Smith's home; she exhibited "stalking" behaviour at the victim's residence and in the city in which they both lived; and she attended several times at the school to harass Ms. Smith. She was charged under the criminal harassment section and the court had this to say about the requirements set out by *R. v. Hertz* and the behaviour exhibited by Ms. Theysen:

> (1) the accused knew that her conduct in respect of Ms. Smith caused Ms. Smith to feel harassed. Ms. Theysen knew that her conduct was unwelcome and tormenting and that Ms. Smith wanted it stopped. Ms. Theysen admitted this in writing, she admitted this to the investigating police, she admitted this to Mr. Green, and to Ms. Smith's husband, Mr. Rod Smith;
> (2) the accused engaged in repeated communications with Ms. Smith in person, by telephone, by letter, and by the giving of unwanted gifts;
> (3) the repeated communication with Ms. Smith by the accused caused her to reasonably fear for her safety in the context of fear of psychological trauma. I have concluded that it was reasonable for Ms. Smith to fear for her safety as the consequence of what can only be described as bizarre behaviour by the accused. On occasion the accused was contrite, apologetic and seemly sorry for her conduct. On other occasions she was angry. On yet other occasions she was endeavouring to make the complainant feel guilty with threats of a suicide attempt. Her refusal to listen to the police, the principal of the school, and Ms. Smith's entreaties that she be left alone combined with the erratic nature of her contact with Ms. Smith, at school, by late night telephone calls, by personal attendances at Ms. Smith's home, by enquiries as to Ms. Smith's whereabouts directed to Ms. Smith's neighbours, all caused Ms. Smith to reasonably fear for her safety;
> (4) the contact between the parties was clearly unwelcome both according to the testimony of Ms. Smith and as acknowledged by the accused herself in her letters entered as exhibits at trial;
> (5) a reasonable person in the position of Ms. Smith would, given all the circumstances of the case, fear for her safety as that term is defined in *R. v. Hertz, supra*.[40]

Accordingly, the court found Ms. Theysen guilty of criminal harassment. She was subsequently sentenced to four months' incarceration, followed by a two-year period of probation.

It should be kept in mind that a successful prosecution under either the assault or the criminal harassment section of the *Criminal Code* will require detailed documentation by the complainant of the harassment by the problem parent, and the co-operation and assistance of the local police and Crown counsel.

A PARENT PROTOCOL

Educators must often perform a difficult balancing act in responding to parents' concerns. On the one hand, school administrators do not want to discourage healthy dissent and constructive criticism from the parents and community that they serve. On the other hand, it is clear that a concerted effort by a parent to

---

[40] *Supra*, at pp. 376-7.

threaten or intimidate a teacher is not acceptable. Teachers should attempt to recognize potential problems when warning signs appear. They should bring these issues to the attention of the principal and relevant superintendent at an early stage. It is often critical for educators to understand the social, political and personal dynamics of the situation. Both teachers and school administrators should document telephone discussions and meetings with parents. School officials should develop a strategy and plan of action to respond to the parent's concerns.

In an attempt to minimize hostile or confrontational situations with a problem parent, a school should also consider setting out its expectations of parent conduct as part of its parent handbook. Among other benefits, such a policy would confirm that the school believes that a positive and constructive working relationship between the school and a student's parents is essential to the fulfilment of the school's mission.

An effective parent protocol could also include:

- a policy statement declaring that the school board is committed to providing a workplace free of harassment;
- a statement of the applicability of the policy to all employees in the school workplace;
- a statement of the purpose of the school board in setting out a harassment policy, such as fostering mutual respect between parents and educators and establishing a complaint procedure;
- a comprehensive definition of "harassment" with examples;
- the appointment of advisors to work with school administrators with respect to harassment issues; and
- a procedure for handling and investigating complaints of parental harassment.

Appropriate remedies should be assessed at an early stage depending on the source and nature of the problem. Clearly, it is preferable to resolve these issues through a co-operative, problem-solving approach with the parents. It is important to be proactive and attempt to meet with the parents early in the process, before the issues fester and the situation gets out of control.

In the alternative, in extreme situations, such as where a teacher has been threatened with physical harm, school officials should consider a range of legal remedies. Such remedies include appropriate notice under the *Education Act* and the *Trespass to Property Act*, commencement of a civil action for defamation or nuisance, or, where warranted, proceedings under the *Criminal Code* for criminal harassment.

6

The Rights of Non-Custodial Parents

INTRODUCTION

Family breakdown is a reality faced in every Canadian community. Incidents of divorce or separation can be extremely difficult and divisive, not only for the individuals involved and their children but, in many cases, for school personnel as well. Since teachers and principals have contact with children in their classrooms on a day-to-day basis, they are invariably caught up in the incidents of family breakdown which affect their students.

Teachers and principals are often called upon to give emotional support and attention to students who are attempting to deal with the difficulties and anxieties of a family breakdown. In addition, marriage breakdown can complicate the relationship between the school and parents by adding a variety of legal duties to the already onerous responsibilities of teachers and principals. Furthermore, the separation or divorce of parents may draw teachers or principals into the role of attempting to mediate disputes and confrontations, a role which is not within the normal scope of their duties or expertise.

In the event of a separation or divorce, the custody of a child is determined either by agreement of the parents or by a court of law. Although the "custodial parent" may be responsible for the daily care of the child, the decision-making power with respect to issues such as the child's religion, health and education may be shared by the parents in different ways. As a result, one cannot assume that a non-custodial parent has given up control over certain aspects of a child's life.

Since custody of and access to a child are legal concepts which are settled through separation agreements or an order of a court, a school principal must be aware of certain duties and obligations with respect to the student and the custodial and non-custodial parent. Obviously, no two families, or their custody and access arrangements, are the same. As a result, the challenge for the principal will be to understand the relevant legal principles and to apply them in a common sense manner, taking the particular family circumstances into account. In this way, a principal should be able to discharge his or her legal duties while permitting a child's parents to resolve their own disputes, where they arise. For both school officials and parents, the priority should always be the best interests of the child.

RELEVANT LEGISLATION

In Canada, the relevant legislation regarding a parent's right of access to his or her child is the *Divorce Act*.[1] Section 16(5) of the *Divorce Act* provides:

> 16(5) Unless the court orders otherwise, a spouse who is granted access to a child of the marriage has the right to make inquiries, and to be given information, as to the health, education and welfare of the child.

Provincial family legislation grants similar rights to non-custodial parents with access. For example, section 20(5) of the Ontario *Children's Law Reform Act*[2] provides:

> 20(5) The entitlement to access to a child includes the right to visit with and be visited by the child and the same right as a parent to make inquiries and to be given information as to the health, education and welfare of the child.

In 1983, the Ontario Ministry of Education issued "Policy/Program Memorandum No. 76" which addressed the rights of non-custodial parents.[3] In summarizing its position, the Ministry of Education stated:

> In general, this means that a non-custodial parent of a child is entitled to examine the child pupil's record, under the provisions of subsection [266(3)] of the Education Act, unless a court order or separation agreement states that such parent is not entitled to access to the child; but that only a parent or other person having custody can claim for the child the right to attend school without payment of a fee.[4]

The policy provides that, in accordance with section 20(5) of the *Children's Law Reform Act*, a non-custodial parent is entitled to visit with the child or make inquiries and be given information as to the health, education and welfare of the child, unless a court order or separation agreement states that such parent is not entitled to access to the child.

In the authors' view, the right to information about a child's education includes the right to make reasonable inquiries of the teacher or principal concerning the child's behaviour and performance in the school.

ROLE OF THE SCHOOL

In the event of a separation or divorce, custody of a child and arrangements for non-custodial access will be set out in an agreement of the parents or an order of a court. For school administrators to properly discharge their legal obligations, they need to understand any restrictions that such agreement or court order may place on the rights of a particular parent. General restrictions to a non-custodial parent's

---

[1] R.S.C. 1985, c. 3 (2nd Supp.).
[2] R.S.O. 1990, c. C.12.
[3] Ontario Ministry of Education, "Policy/Program Memorandum No. 76: Custody and Guardianship of Minors" (1983).
[4] *Ibid.*, at p. 2.

access will apply everywhere, including the child's school. However, in many instances, the lack of information provided by a parent regarding custody and access arrangements can prevent a school principal or the school's staff from making informed responses.

Ultimately, the onus is on the parents to inform the school about any family matters or custody and access arrangements which would affect their children and govern the relationship between the parents, their children and the school.[5] The registration forms provided by the school board should inquire as to whether there are any custody, guardianship or access arrangements of which the school should be aware. Where there are such formal arrangements, the school should request a certified copy of any order or agreement to be kept on file and referred to as required. While parents can be encouraged to co-operate in providing these documents to best protect their rights, they are not obligated to provide copies of such documents.[6]

Where a custodial parent objects to access being given to a non-custodial parent regarding information as to the health, education and welfare of the child, the school should require that the custodial parent support his or her claims with appropriate documentation. If such documentation is not provided, schools should attempt to act in the best interests of the child. In the absence of information to the contrary, schools are entitled to treat both parents as if they are married and have joint custody.

Subject to any limitation in a court order or separation agreement between the parents, the custodial parent has the right to control his or her child's education, medical treatment or residence. Accordingly, on a day-to-day basis, the school must deal with the custodial parent as the primary contact person when making decisions about the child's education and health care.

When there is joint custody, those rights and responsibilities are shared and both parents are entitled to take part in important decisions affecting their child. Where there is a dispute which cannot be resolved by parents with joint custody, such as a disagreement as to whether a child should be enrolled in a French immersion program or participate in a particular school excursion, the school should avoid involvement. The principal or teacher should attempt to maintain the status quo until agreement is reached by the parents and conveyed to the principal or teacher or they are provided with a court order which alters the status quo.[7]

---

[5] E.M. Roher, "The Rights of Divorced or Separated Parents to Information Relating to Their Child's Education", in W.F. Foster, ed., *Education & Law: Education in the Era of Individual Rights* (Chateauguay: Lisbro, 1994), p. 114.

[6] "The Non-Custodial Parent: Rights and Privileges", *Edulaw for Canadian Schools*, Vol. 4, No. 6 (Calgary: Edulaw, February, 1993).

[7] E.M. Roher, "Rights of Divorced or Separated Parents", *Education Law News* (Summer, 1993) (Toronto: Borden & Elliot), p. 2.

RIGHTS OF NON-CUSTODIAL PARENTS

Under section 16(10) of the *Divorce Act*, the children of a marriage are entitled to "as much contact with each spouse as is consistent with the best interests of the child" and, for that purpose, the courts must take into consideration the willingness of the person seeking custody to facilitate such contact. Accordingly, parents who do not have custody of their children are usually granted "reasonable" access to them unless it is in the best interests of the children to restrict or deny access.[8]

At common law, unrestricted access simply allows the non-custodial parent the right to visit with the children, including the right to visit with the children away from the custodial home. The right of access does not allow the non-custodial parent the right to control or interfere with the upbringing of the children and it does not confer on the non-custodial parent the right to be consulted about or participate in decisions about the education of the children. Notwithstanding the fact that a non-custodial parent may have unrestricted access to his or her child, it is recommended that all contact with the child on school premises be supervised by school board personnel.

Where the access of a non-custodial parent has been limited, the parent's rights will depend on the exact terms of the court order or separation agreement. For example, where a court order requires that a non-custodial parent must have supervised access, this does not mean that the parent has no rights to information about the health, education and welfare of the child. In attempting to interpret a court order or separation agreement, principals and other school board officials cannot be expected to know the fine points of family law. If there is any doubt about the terms of a court order or separation agreement, clarification should be obtained from the board solicitor.[9]

The situation may also arise where a non-custodial parent, who is only entitled to visit the child on weekends, enters on the school premises on a weekday asking to see the child. In this situation, the parent is in breach of the court order or separation agreement. However, it is not the duty of the principal or other board official to monitor or enforce a parent's respective rights and obligations. It is advised that the custodial parent be contacted as soon as possible and be informed of the situation. It is the responsibility of the custodial parent to enforce the terms of the court order or separation agreement. If the principal or teacher has reasonable grounds to believe that the child may be in danger, he or she should contact the police.

It is clear that not every visit by a non-custodial parent on school premises means that a child is in danger. The response of the principal or teacher in each individual situation will hinge on his or her knowledge of the family background. Is there a history of child abuse in the family? Does the child want to see the

---

[8] *Ibid.*, at p. 2.
[9] A.F. Brown, "Rights of Custodial and Non-Custodial Parents in the School Setting", *Viewpoint*, Vol. 3 (Ontario Public School Teachers' Federation, March, 1990).

parent? Has the custodial parent warned school personnel that this visit might occur?

Where a non-custodial parent arrives at the school to visit his or her child and school officials have been provided with a court order denying access to that parent, school personnel should prevent contact with the student, pointing out that the visit appears to be in breach of the express terms of the court order. The principal or his or her designate should contact the custodial parent and outline the circumstances surrounding the non-custodial parent's arrival at the school. Counsel for the custodial parent should attempt to resolve this matter with counsel for the non-custodial parent. Ultimately, in the event that the non-custodial parent would like access to the student either at lunch or after school, it is the non-custodial parent's responsibility to provide the school with a revised court order which permits such access. In this regard, school officials should request an amended court order which reflects the requested change. It is not the responsibility of the principal or other school personnel to act as a mediator or conciliator in this situation.

In the event that a parent arrives on school property and proceeds to use offensive language, profanity or threats towards school personnel, the principal has the authority under the *Education Act*[10] to refuse to admit such parent to the school or classroom. Section 265(m) of the *Education Act* provides that it is the duty of a principal of a school, subject to an appeal to the board, to "refuse to admit to the school or classroom a person whose presence in the school or classroom would in the principal's judgment be detrimental to the physical or mental well-being of the pupils". The principal may be called upon to exercise this duty in circumstances where a non-custodial parent becomes disruptive in the school. It should also be kept in mind that, under section 212(1) of the *Education Act*, it is an offence to *wilfully* interrupt or disquiet the proceedings of a school or class. A conviction can lead to a modest fine of up to $200.

If a non-custodial parent must be denied access to the school, especially where the parent becomes disruptive, the principal must ensure that adequate notes are taken regarding the incident. This information may be important should any charges be laid under the *Trespass to Property Act*[11] or the *Criminal Code*.[12] It may also help to refute any accusation which may be made by the parent in question.

Clearly, difficult situations such as these should be resolved with common sense and good judgment and the use of the police or confrontational denials of access to a parent are not ideal solutions. However, where a parent refuses to act reasonably in the circumstances or presents a threat to the safety of students or staff, the use of school security personnel or the police is advisable. Where the school is aware of a court order denying access to a parent outright, or at certain times, then the school should attempt to prevent the release of the child to the non-custodial parent while doing everything reasonably possible to ensure the

---

[10] R.S.O. 1990, c. E.2.
[11] R.S.O. 1990, c. T.21.
[12] R.S.C. 1985, c. C-46.

safety of the children. Principals can try to prevent confrontations by obtaining as much information regarding the particular family situation and access arrangements as they reasonably can.[13]

Request of Non-custodial Parent to be Consulted

Related to the right of a custodial parent to determine matters of his or her child's education are the occasional demands of the non-custodial parent to be consulted on such matters. In some instances, the demand to be consulted is made through a school principal or teacher. Generally speaking, the right of access to the child does not include the right to be consulted regarding day-to-day educational decisions, such as participation in extra-curricular activities, school excursions or athletic events, and any such consultation is at the discretion of the custodial parent. However, there has been some limited judicial support for the ability of a non-custodial parent to be consulted regarding important decisions involving the child.

For instance, in the case of *Abbott v. Taylor*,[14] an appeal regarding a custody and access order before the Manitoba Court of Appeal, the court stated that provincial legislation granted a non-custodial parent the same right as a custodial parent to reports, including school reports, regarding their child and anticipated the consultation of the non-custodial parent for important decisions regarding the child's life. However, the court also indicated that the ultimate responsibility for making decisions regarding the child was that of the custodial parent.[15]

The Ontario case of *Lebel v. Walter*[16] involved an application by a child's mother to vary a joint custody arrangement due to ongoing disagreements regarding the religious upbringing and education of the child. The court granted the application, awarded custody to the mother and affirmed the custodial parent's sole right to determine the religious upbringing and education of a child. However, the father had concerns about the possibility that the child had a learning disability. In granting the mother's application, the court gave some direction to the mother to address the father's concerns about the child's possible special needs.[17]

For school principals, however, the key principle to remember is that the custodial parent is ultimately responsible for decisions regarding the child's education, regardless of what level of consultation the custodial parent engages in with the non-custodial parent. Where the school principal is aware of a custody and access arrangement for divorced or separated parents, the principal and the school staff must comply with those arrangements insofar as they affect the school. Should the non-custodial parent make a request of the school which

---

[13] "The Non-Custodial Parent: Rights and Privileges", *op. cit.*, footnote 6.
[14] (1986), 28 D.L.R. (4th) 125, 2 R.F.L. (3d) 163 (Man. C.A.).
[15] See discussion in A.F. Brown and M.A. Zuker, *Education Law*, 2nd ed. (Toronto: Carswell, 1997), at pp. 149-50.
[16] (1996), 62 A.C.W.S. (3d) 324, [1996] O.J. No. 1099 (Q.L.) (Prov. Div.).
[17] See "Limited Rights of Non-Custodial Parents", *Education Law Reporter*, Vol. 7, No. 10 (Calgary: Edulaw, June, 1996), p. 76.

conflicts with the established arrangements, school officials should request documentation which reflects the requested change and, if necessary, confirm that change with the custodial parent.

Rights and Privileges of the Non-custodial Parent

A natural desire of non-custodial parents is to be more involved in their children's education. This may include receiving information about extra-curricular activities, attending concerts or athletic events on school property or becoming active as a volunteer in the school. A non-custodial parent may make a request to a teacher or principal for a greater level of involvement. The question of the appropriate rights and privileges of a non-custodial parent with respect to such activities has been considered by the courts.

In the Alberta case of *Moss v. Boisvert*,[18] the father of two children had been granted access in a divorce, while the mother had custody. In the access order, the father was given the rights to "liberal and generous" access, to make inquiries, to be given information as to the health, education and welfare of the children and to be told by the mother in writing of the medical concerns and problems of the children.

The father made allegations in a statement of claim that the mother, school district and school employees had interfered in the relationship with his children and with the normal parental rights of access to the school. He also alleged that he had been defamed by the individual defendants, who, he stated, had spread a false story that he had entered the school office with his son without permission and rummaged through school files. Further, the father alleged that he had been prevented from attending school functions, such as the Christmas concert, and helping in the school as a volunteer.

The father sued for a declaration that he was entitled to access to his son's school, to be involved in school activities and functions, to volunteer supervision in school activities on terms no less restrictive than those of any other parent and to be consulted before either of his children were involved in school activities, such as field trips, which would conflict with his normal access time. He also sued for damages of $100,000.

In striking out the father's claim, the court held that the father's rights as a non-custodial parent were limited to access, to make inquiries and to be given information as to the health, education and welfare of his children, and to be told in writing by the mother of the children's medical concerns and problems. The court indicated that the father did not have a right of access to the school and to be involved in activities at the school. No person has the right to enter on to school property or to be involved in activities in the school, except as permitted by the school board, as provided in the legislation. In effect, the court was stating that the father could not circumvent the limits of his access rights in the divorce order by demanding certain other rights in the context of his children's school. Further,

---

[18] (1990), 74 Alta. L.R. (2d) 344, 107 A.R. 385 (Q.B.).

since the school board had the power to control access to the school, arguing that the divorce order itself did not prevent access to the school or participation in school activities did not carry the day for the father.

With respect to the father's request to be consulted about field trips, the court held that the non-custodial parent had no right to be consulted about these activities or to object to or prevent the children's participation in them. It was observed that the father's rights to inquire into and receive information about the children's education and welfare could reasonably include the right to receive notice or information about the children's school activities.

The court also ruled that the non-custodial parent did not have the right to prevent participation in school activities during his access time. It was determined that the best interests of the child were paramount and that children must be permitted to participate in school activities, including field trips, which "occasionally" cut into the non-custodial parent's access time. In addition, it was emphasized that a divorce order is between the parents and does not involve the school. Accordingly, whether these activities should be permitted to interfere with the non-custodial parent's access time is really a matter for the parents and the courts to decide.

Furthermore, the court ruled that a non-custodial parent does not have the same right as a custodial parent to be involved in school activities and functions and to volunteer for supervision of school activities. The court stated:

> Where one parent only has custody of the children by order of the court the school of necessity must deal only with the custodial parent. If non-custodial parents had the right that the plaintiff [father] here advocates (as against schools), schools would be in impossible situations.[19]

The court concluded that there was nothing disclosed which would, in law, give the father the right to access and participation in school activities that he claimed.[20]

STUDENT NAMES

A corollary but emotional issue for separating parents is what surname the child will use after the parents' relationship has come to an end. The father, in the case of *Moss v. Boisvert*, also sought a court injunction which would compel the mother and the school to require the children to use the father's surname, Moss, exclusively. This contentious issue can also arise in the context of remarriage of the custodial parent. Obviously, school administrators can be caught in the middle of a dispute between parents regarding a student's name.

At common law, a person may use any name he or she wishes provided that it is not chosen for a wrongful purpose, such as fraud. In certain circumstances,

---

[19] *Supra*, at p. 351.
[20] See Roher, *op. cit.*, footnote 5, at pp. 117-19; "The Non-Custodial Parent: Rights and Privileges", *op. cit.*, footnote 6.

specific requirements regarding the surname to be used by the children may be set out in a separation agreement or court order. Subject to provincial legislation, a school may take at face value the name provided for use by a custodial parent. Any disputes regarding the surname of a student should be settled between the parents.[21]

In Ontario, the *Change of Name Act*[22] governs the change of surnames. Section 3(2) of that Act provides that, within 90 days after a marriage is dissolved by divorce, annulment or death, the former spouse may elect to resume the surname that the spouse had immediately before the marriage. The Act also contains special provisions regarding the change of a child's name. The person with lawful custody of the child is the person who may apply to change the child's name, subject to any court order or separation agreement which prohibits such a change.[23] In addition, such an application requires the consent of any person whose consent is necessary in accordance with a court order or separation agreement, and the consent of the child if the child is 12 years of age or older.[24] The Act also provides that any applicant seeking to change the name of a child must provide notice of the application to any person who is lawfully entitled to access to the child.[25]

As a result of this legislation, a non-custodial parent should not be caught by surprise by a change of the child's name. Therefore, should a parent make demands of a school regarding the child's name, it is reasonable and appropriate for school administration to require disclosure of relevant documentation, such as a change of name certificate or new birth certificate. Section 9 of the *Change of Name Act* provides that a person whose name has been changed under the Act is entitled to have the change noted on any public or private record or document which mentions that person's name. Specifically, the section provides:

> 9. A person whose name has been changed under this Act is entitled to have the change of name noted on any public or private record or document that mentions the person's name, on payment of any applicable fee prescribed by law and on producing satisfactory proof of identity and the change of name certificate or new birth certificate.

Principals in Ontario have specific obligations regarding the change of a student's surname. The *Ontario Student Record (OSR) Guideline, 2000*[26] (the "Guideline"), issued by the Ontario Ministry of Education, sets out certain requirements which must be met when a student's surname changes as a result of marriage or law (such as a divorce order). With respect to a change of surname by marriage, section 10.2 of the Guideline provides:

---

[21] "The Non-Custodial Parent: Rights and Privileges", *op. cit.*, footnote 6.
[22] R.S.O. 1990, c. C.7.
[23] *Change of Name Act*, s. 5(1).
[24] *Change of Name Act*, s. 5(2).
[25] *Change of Name Act*, s. 5(6).
[26] Ontario Ministry of Education, *Ontario Student Record (OSR) Guideline, 2000* (March, 2000).

> When a principal receives a document that establishes that a student for whom the principal maintains an OSR has had his or her surname changed by marriage, the principal will file the document, a copy of the document, or a verification of his or her knowledge of the document in the documentation file, and will change the surname of the student on all current and future components of the OSR.[27]

With respect to a change of surname by law, section 10.3 of the Guideline provides:

> When a principal receives a document that establishes that a student for whom the principal maintains an OSR has had his or her surname changed in accordance with the law of the province, state, or country in which the document was made, the principal will file the document, a copy of the document, or a verification of his or her knowledge of the document in the documentation file, and, on request, will change the surname of the student on all components of the OSR so that the record will appear as if originally established in the new surname.[28]

Therefore, where possible, a principal should obtain a copy of any legal document which evidences the change of name of one of his or her students as a result of a separation or remarriage of that student's parents. A copy of that document will be filed in the student's OSR. In appropriate circumstances, the principal will change the surname of the student on all current and future components of the OSR.

MANAGING SCHOOL RELATIONSHIPS

From a practical point of view, the onus is on the parents to inform the school about any family matters which may affect their children and govern the relationship between parents, their children and the school. As indicated earlier in this chapter, it is advised that school registration forms specifically request information as to whether there are any family matters, custody, guardianship or access orders or court agreements of which the school should be aware. The onus rests with the custodial parent to provide the school with a certified copy of any order, judgment or separation agreement.

Overall, school personnel have an obligation to make decisions in the best interests of the child. If a teacher or principal has reason to believe that a child may be in danger, a parent's request for access to the child should be denied. In certain cases, it may be necessary to call the police. Obviously, not every visit by a non-custodial parent poses a danger to the child. The responses of an individual teacher or principal will depend on a range of factors, such as his or her knowledge of the family situation, the age of the child, any history of abuse and any warnings from the custodial parent.

Managing the relationships between separated parents, their children and the school, while protecting the best interest of students, is a challenging undertaking for any principal. Like any issue which involves potential conflict, these family

---

[27] *Ibid.*, section 10.2, at p. 23.
[28] *Ibid.*, section 10.3, at p. 23.

issues call on the principal's ability to communicate effectively and use common sense and good judgment.

Since many issues involving the custodial and non-custodial parent of a student must be resolved between the parents directly, or through alternate means such as a mediator or court, it is even more important for a principal to properly understand his or her role. By permitting disputes to be resolved by the parties, respecting the rights of the parents and intervening where the law or the safety of students or staff demands, a principal should be able to minimize the divisive impact of any custody and access dispute on the school.

7
School Attendance

INTRODUCTION

In 1846, educator Egerton Ryerson recognized the importance of compulsory school attendance. He stated:

> The branches of knowledge which it is essential that all should understand should be provided for all, and taught to all; should be brought within the reach of the most needy and forced upon the attention of the most careless.[1]

In suggesting that education should be "forced upon the attention of the most careless", Ryerson, in his *Report on a System of Public Elementary Instruction for Upper Canada*, laid the foundation for the obligation to attend school. Since 1871, education legislation in Ontario has contained a provision making school attendance compulsory for pupils of certain ages.[2]

From time to time, educators are faced with the dilemma of parents who, for whatever reason, refuse to send their children to school or students who themselves may unilaterally decide not to attend school. A number of questions arise. Is there an obligation on parents and guardians to ensure that their children attend school? What are the responsibilities of school administrators to enforce school attendance? What is the role of the school attendance counsellor in monitoring and enforcing compulsory attendance? What remedies are available at law to prosecute individuals who contravene the compulsory attendance provisions under the education legislation? What policies and procedures are suggested to respond to the issue of deficient school attendance?

---

[1] E. Ryerson, *Report on a System of Public Elementary Instruction for Upper Canada* (Montreal: Lovell & Gibson, 1846).
[2] P. Lauwers, "Attendance and Discipline" (paper presented to the Canadian Bar Association-Ontario), in *The A,B,C's of Education Law in Ontario* (1986), p. 13.

OBLIGATION TO ATTEND SCHOOL

Section 21(1) of the *Education Act*[3] sets out the basic obligation of a child to attend school. The *Education Act* establishes that there will be compulsory school attendance for children between the ages of six and sixteen. The statute provides that:

- A child who attains the age of six years on or before the first school day in September must attend school on every school day from the first school day in September in that year until he or she reaches the age of 16 years.
- If the child attains the age of six years after the first school day in September, he or she must attend school as of the first school day in September in the following school year until the last school day in June of the year in which he or she attains the age of 16 years. The child may finish the school year, but has no obligation to start the next September even if his or her 16th birthday lies somewhere between September and December.[4]

Section 21(2) of the *Education Act* contains a number of exemptions from attending school. These exemptions include:

- The child is receiving satisfactory instruction at home or elsewhere. The *Education Act* does not define "satisfactory instruction". It is the duty of a school board, through its local school attendance counsellor, to ensure that all children of compulsory school age in the board's jurisdiction attend school unless legally excused. In this regard, a board has an obligation to find out if absent children are being educated. The Supreme Court of Canada has confirmed that it is the parents' legal responsibility to ensure that their child attends school as required.[5] Given the parents' obligation to send their children to school, in the authors' view, they have the onus to demonstrate to school board officials that their child is legally excused.[6]
- The child is unable to attend school by reason of sickness or other unavoidable cause. It should be noted that if medical reasons require that a child be educated at home, the principal can arrange for "home instruction", to be provided by a board teacher. Home instruction, which is provided by the board, is separate and distinct from home schooling.
- Transportation is not provided by a board and there is no school that the child has a right to attend within a certain distance.
- The child has obtained a secondary school graduation diploma or has completed a course which gives equivalent standing.
- The child is absent for the purpose of receiving music instruction, and the period of absence does not exceed one-half day per week.

---

[3] R.S.O. 1990, c. E.2.
[4] A.F. Brown, *Legal Handbook for Educators*, 4th ed. (Toronto: Carswell, 1998), at p. 32.
[5] *R. v. Jones* (1986), 31 D.L.R. (4th) 569, [1986] 2 S.C.R. 284.
[6] Brown, *op. cit.*, footnote 4.

- The child is suspended, expelled or excluded from attendance under any Act or regulation.
- The child is absent on a day regarded as a holy day by the church or religious denomination to which the child belongs.
- The child is absent or excused as authorized by the *Education Act* and its regulations. For example, under section 23(3) of Regulation 298,[7] parents may temporarily withdraw a child from school with the permission of the principal.

RESPONSIBILITY FOR ENFORCING SCHOOL ATTENDANCE

The *Education Act* provides a detailed system for enforcing school attendance. It should be noted that students themselves have a duty to ensure regular school attendance. Section 23(1)(d) of Regulation 298 provides that a pupil shall attend classes punctually and regularly. The *Education Act* also sets out the duties and responsibilities of a parent or guardian, the principal and the school attendance counsellor.

Duty of the Parent or Guardian

Section 21(5) of the *Education Act* provides that the parent or guardian of a child who is required to attend school must ensure that the child attends school. In addition, section 23(2) of Regulation 298 requires that, when a pupil returns to school after an absence, a parent of the pupil, or the pupil, where the pupil is an adult, must give the reason for the absence orally or in writing as the principal requires.

Principal's Responsibility

Section 28 of the *Education Act* sets out the principal's duties:

> 28(1) The principal of every elementary and secondary school shall,
> (a) report to the appropriate school attendance counsellor and supervisory officer the names, ages and residences of all pupils of compulsory school age who have not attended school as required;
> (b) furnish the school attendance counsellor with such other information as the counsellor requires for the enforcement of compulsory school attendance; and
> (c) report in writing to the school attendance counsellor every case of expulsion and readmission of a pupil.

Section 265(c) of the *Education Act* requires that the principal register pupils and ensure that the attendance of pupils for every school day is recorded either in the register supplied by the Minister of Education or in such other manner as is approved by the Minister. Furthermore, section 11(3)(n) of Regulation 298

---

[7] *Operation of Schools – General*, R.R.O. 1990, Reg. 298.

provides that the principal must report promptly any neglect of duty or infraction of the school rules by a student to the parent of guardian of the student.

Responsibility of a School Attendance Counsellor

In order to enforce and monitor compulsory attendance, section 25 of the *Education Act* requires each school board to appoint one or more school attendance counsellors. The school attendance counsellor appointed by a board has jurisdiction and is responsible for the enforcement of compulsory school attendance in respect of every child who is required to attend school, "except a child who is under the jurisdiction of a person appointed under section 119 of the *Indian Act* (Canada)".[8]

DEALING WITH THE PROBLEM OF NON-ATTENDANCE

Suggested steps in dealing with a problem of non-attendance are as follows:

- The principal should monitor and identify possible attendance problems.
- Before a problem becomes acute enough to be referred to the school attendance counsellor, the principal or his or her delegate may attempt, on an informal basis, to discover the reason for the attendance problem and to resolve it. If the reason for lack of attendance is the illness of a student, a program of home study may be arranged. Successful intervention is often dependent upon referrals being made *before* the student's absence becomes chronic or habitual. The proactive use of counselling and the involvement of board resource personnel, such as guidance counsellors, social workers and/or psychologists, will often produce better results than reactive intervention.
- If the truancy problem persists, the matter should be referred to the school attendance counsellor. The school attendance counsellor should ensure that the parent or guardian is aware of the student's absence by conducting a home visit, leaving a notice at the student's place of residence or by making telephone contact in the evening.
- The primary objective of the attendance counsellor is to arrange for the student's quick and receptive return to school. The act of forcibly returning an absentee student to class is not the most productive approach when dealing with attendance issues nor is it conducive to producing a long-term solution. As the title implies, the function of the attendance counsellor is to provide counselling services.[9]
- It should be noted that parental consent is not required prior to a home visit by the attendance counsellor. When responding to a referral, the counsellor will offer recommendations and assistance. Investigation by the attendance

---

[8] *Education Act*, s. 25(5).
[9] Board of Education for the City of Scarborough, "Attendance Regulations" (January 20, 1997).

counsellor will often reveal that there exists a variety of chronic or severe social, emotional and/or educational issues which, if left unresolved, may preclude any long-term solution to the problem. Case management may dictate that the counsellor arrange for the involvement of other school board resource personnel, community agencies or clinics.
- Under section 26(4) of the *Education Act*, a school attendance counsellor is required to inquire into every case of failure to attend school within his or her knowledge or when requested to do so by the appropriate supervisory officer, the principal of a school or a ratepayer. The counsellor must also:
  - give written warning of the consequences of such failure to attend school to the parent or guardian of the child who is not attending school;
  - give written notice to the parent or guardian to cause the child to attend school immediately; and
  - advise the parent or guardian in writing of the provisions in the *Education Act* regarding the process by which an inquiry is undertaken by the Provincial School Attendance Counsellor.
- Where a school attendance counsellor has reasonable and probable grounds for believing that a child is illegally absent from school, he or she may, at the written request of the parent or guardian of the child or of the principal:
  - take the child to the child's parent or guardian; or
  - take the child to the school from which the child is absent provided that, if exception is taken to the school attendance counsellor entering the home, he or she must not enter.
- Where the parent or guardian of a child considers that the child is excused from attendance at school under section 21(2), and the appropriate school attendance counsellor or the Provincial School Attendance Counsellor is of the opinion that the child should not be excused from attendance, the Provincial School Attendance Counsellor must appoint one or more persons, who are not employees of the school board operating the school that the child is attending, to inquire into the validity of the reason or excuse for non-attendance and other relevant circumstances.
- The Provincial School Attendance Counsellor may, by order in writing signed by him or her, direct that the child attend school or be excused from attendance at school, and a copy of the order must be delivered to the board and to the parent or guardian of the child.
- A principal may suspend a pupil because of persistent truancy.

Court Prosecution

The school attendance counsellor may, when circumstances warrant, initiate court proceedings with respect to children who are habitually absent or who refuse to attend school. Parents may be prosecuted for the failure to cause their child to attend school. If a child is under the age of 12 years, he or she cannot be charged under the *Provincial Offences Act*;[10] only the parent or guardian can be charged with failing to cause a child to attend school. If the child is 12 or more years of age, then the child can be prosecuted as well.

The school attendance counsellor first appears before a justice of the peace who swears the information and then issues a summons to the defendant (the parent or guardian or child) setting out the offence in respect of which the defendant is charged and requiring the defendant to attend at court at the time and place stated in the summons. The summons is served by a provincial offences officer, pursuant to section 26(2) of the *Provincial Offences Act*.

The prosecution is conducted in the Ontario Court of Justice. Court procedure is governed by the *Provincial Offences Act*. Where the charge is brought against the parents, the general provisions of the Act apply; where a child is charged, Part VI of the *Provincial Offences Act* applies.

Section 31 of the *Education Act* creates a number of evidentiary short cuts which can be used by the school attendance counsellor in conducting the prosecution. These short cuts include:

- A certificate as to the attendance or non-attendance at school of any child, signed or purporting to be signed by the principal of the school, is proof in the absence of evidence to the contrary of the facts stated therein without any proof of the signature or appointment of the principal.
- If the child appears to the court to be of compulsory school age, the child will, for the purposes of such prosecution, be considered to be of compulsory school age unless the contrary is proved.
- An order made under section 24(2) of the *Education Act* shall be admitted in evidence in a prosecution only where the prosecution is in respect of the school year for which the order was made.

The onus is on the school attendance counsellor to prove the offence. In recent years, the courts have held that the offences regarding compulsory attendance are public welfare offences. Public welfare offences involve the protection of public and social interests (such as the education of children). Public welfare offences fall under the category of strict liability offences. In a strict liability offence, the fact that the act prohibited in the offence was done (such as not attending school) is enough to prove that the prohibited act under the offence occurred. As a result, it is only open to the defendant to prove that he or she took all reasonable care (referred to as the due diligence defence). This involves consideration of what a reasonable person would have done in the circumstances. The defence will be available if:

- the accused reasonably believed in a mistaken set of facts, which, if true, would render the act or omission innocent; or
- the accused took all reasonable steps to avoid the particular event.

---

[10] R.S.O. 1990, c. P.33.

After hearing the case, the justice may:

- dismiss the charge;
- refer the matter to the Provincial School Attendance Counsellor if it appears to the court that the child may have been excused from attendance at school under section 21(2) of the *Education Act*; or
- make a finding of guilt.

In prosecutions of parents or guardians, section 30(1) and (2) of the *Education Act* authorizes the court to impose a fine of not more than $200 and, in addition to or instead of imposing the fine, requires the parent or guardian to submit a personal bond in the sum of $200 with one or more sureties on the condition that the person shall cause the child to attend school. A child who is required by law to attend school and who refuses to attend, or who is habitually absent from school, is guilty of an offence and on conviction is liable to the penalties under Part VI of the *Provincial Offences Act*.

Relevant Case Law

In a 1995 case before the Ontario Court (Provincial Division), a mother was charged under the *Education Act* for failing to cause her nine-year-old son to attend school.[11] The school notified the mother that the permission for her son to attend the school's supervised, alternative program had been revoked and directed her to apply to another one of the local board's schools which operated the program or to send her son to his home school. A month later, the mother attended two meetings at which time the school outlined its position with respect to her son. A few weeks later, the school issued a warning letter to the mother.

The mother's defence was that she was still seeking further information and evidence as to why the school removed her son from the special program, blaming the local board for its indifference to her son's education. The court held that a parent's failure to make his or her child attend school was a strict liability offence, to which the normally available defence is that of due diligence. The court held that, in this case, there was no evidence of due diligence.

The court convicted the mother and ordered the production of a pre-sentencing report. The court ruled that, although parents have a natural interest in avoiding disruption in their child's education, it does not follow that a school's refusal to allow a pupil to continue in an alternate training program constitutes a hindrance to the child's education.

Judge Marvin Zuker recognized the interests of parents in the education of their children and expressed his view of the relationship between parents and school officials as follows:

> The court is mindful of the fact that judicial deference has, in more recent years, moved towards providing more of an expansive discretion in educational decisions to be made by educational officials. Courts have recognized that public schools have

---

[11] *R. v. Thompson* (1995), 29 W.C.B. (2d) 33, [1995] O.J. No. 3140 (Q.L.) (Prov. Div.).

an inculcative function in their own right. Absent any clear legislative mandate, the normal parent-and-school relationship is permissive. That is, schools may respond to parents' requests or demands regarding their children's education, but cannot be required to accommodate the request.[12]

Following this decision, the mother failed to co-operate in preparing a pre-sentencing report and, thus, the probation officer could not carry out the court's order. Since she was unemployed, ordering a fine as provided for under the *Education Act* would have been futile. Accordingly, the court suspended sentence and placed the mother on probation for two years.

PREVENTING ATTENDANCE PROBLEMS

In the 1986 Supreme Court of Canada case of *R. v. Jones*,[13] the court recognized the importance of compulsory education. It held:

> Whether one views it from an economic, social, cultural or civic point of view, the education of the young is critically important in our society. From an early period, the provinces have responded to this interest by developing schemes for compulsory education.[14]

Essential to the process of preventing school attendance problems is early intervention by school personnel. When irregular attendance is identified by school officials, intervention by the principal, teachers, guidance counsellors and/or attendance counsellor at an early stage will be beneficial to both the school and the child. Poor attendance patterns are often developed early in a child's educational career. Successful intervention is dependent upon referrals being made *before* the student's absence becomes chronic or habitual. Proactive use of counselling and guidance services is generally advisable prior to a formal process under the *Education Act*.

An investigation by a principal or school attendance counsellor will often reveal that there exists a variety of chronic or severe social, emotional and/or educational issues, which, if left unresolved, may preclude any long-term solution to the problem. Case management may dictate that the school official or counsellor arrange for the involvement of other school board resource personnel, community agencies and/or clinics.

In this regard, the following guidelines are suggested:

- To prevent attendance problems, educators should be aware of warning signs such as persistent lateness, student fatigue, poor work performance and erratic absenteeism.

---

[12] *Supra*, at p. 3 of the judgment.
[13] *Supra*, footnote 5.
[14] *Supra*, at p. 592.

- The principal and/or relevant teacher should consult with the parents and/or guardians at an early stage to inquire about any social, emotional or educational problems.
- Where appropriate, educators should consult and work with school resource personnel, such as guidance counsellors and social workers who may provide assistance.
- If attendance problems persist, the principal should contact the school attendance counsellor and report the names, ages and residences of all pupils of compulsory school age who have not attended school as required.
- Educators should recognize and understand their respective duties and responsibilities under relevant legislation with respect to compulsory school attendance.
- The school board should develop policies and procedures with respect to early intervention and prevention of attendance problems, as well as a policy regarding the enforcement of compulsory school attendance legislation.

8

Managing Medication in Schools

INTRODUCTION

With the passing of each school year, the management and administration of medication in schools have become a greater concern for school principals. In Canadian schools, it seems that an increasing number of parents are requesting that medication be administered to their children during the average school day. There are a number of possible reasons for this trend. Medical advances have allowed children suffering from various health problems to remain in or return to regular classes provided they receive proper medication. Shifts in societal attitudes have moved towards accepting the integration of special needs students into regular class streams. This has required schools to consider the necessity of administering medication to students who could not otherwise attend regular classes.[1] More students also take medication now to adjust their behaviour patterns or to assist them in retaining an adequate attention span to make attending classes a productive experience.[2] For example, drugs such as Ritalin or Dexedrine are now commonly prescribed for attempts at controlling hyperactivity or hyperkinesis and dosages are often required during a school day.[3] Additionally, the simple reality of a busy, modern family frequently leads parents to request that school administrators assist in ensuring that their child receives proper medication during the school day.

Another growing problem is the number of students who may require ongoing or emergency medication because of an allergic reaction to food, insect bites or other foreseeable items in a school setting. For example, many students in Canadian schools are highly allergic to peanut products. In certain situations, even inadvertent touching of a smudge of peanut butter can lead to a life-threatening

---

[1] W.F. Foster, "Medication of Pupils and Related Issues", in W.F. Foster, ed., *Education in Transition: Legal Issues in a Changing School Setting* (Chateauguay: Lisbro, 1996), p. 176.
[2] A.F. Brown and M.A. Zuker, *Education Law*, 2nd ed. (Toronto: Carswell, 1997), at pp. 141-2.
[3] E.M. Roher and J.J. Morris, "Managing Medication in Schools", *Education Law News* (Spring, 1995) (Toronto: Borden & Elliot), p. 1.

reaction. Overall, 1% to 2% of the Canadian population is at risk for serious allergic reactions to insect stings and foods[4] while the Allergy Asthma Information Association reports that the rate of severe allergies has grown by 40% in the last decade. Such allergy rates make the presence of susceptible students a practical certainty in the majority of Canadian schools. In this regard, parents of such students often provide the relevant teacher and school office with an adrenaline auto-injector ("epi-pen") to be administered only in emergency circumstances.[5]

Taken together, these realities can cause a certain level of discomfort for school administrators as the school year approaches. This is especially the case where schools are no longer provided with the expertise of a nurse whose primary responsibility is to administer care, as needed, to students. A number of questions surely occur to principals as their minds turn to addressing these issues. Such questions may include:

- Under what circumstances should the school agree to manage and/or administer medication to a student?
- What form of consent to administer medication is necessary from the student and/or the parents involved?
- Can the principal require school staff to participate in the management and/or administration of medication to students?
- When is training for staff regarding the use of medication necessary?
- What are the legal risks involved in a program of medication management? How can these risks be minimized for the students, staff, school, board and principal?
- What is the extent of a school's responsibility in the case of an emergency?
- Does the principal have complete and satisfactory information regarding the allergies or medical needs of the student population? If not, to what extent should inquiries regarding these facts be made?
- What are the components of an appropriate policy regarding medication in schools?

This chapter will address these concerns and attempt to make some practical suggestions for managing medication in a school setting.

DUTY AND STANDARD OF CARE IN ORDINARY CIRCUMSTANCES

The starting point for determining the duties of teachers and other school board employees is the applicable legislation. In all jurisdictions in Canada there is legislation governing education which sets out the duties of teachers and other school board employees. In general, the legislation does not prescribe positive

---

[4] Canadian Society of Allergy and Clinical Immunology, *Anaphylaxis in Schools and Other Child Care Settings* (August, 1995).
[5] See Roher and Morris, *op. cit.*, footnote 3.

duties to administer medical treatment. However, each statute does require that school board employees adequately supervise the students under their care.[6]

Some statutes explicitly require teachers or principals to monitor the health or safety of students. For example, section 265(j) of the Ontario *Education Act*[7] provides that a principal has a duty "to give assiduous attention to the health and comfort of the pupils". Section 26(1)(n) of the Nova Scotia *Education Act*[8] requires teachers to "attend to the health, comfort and safety of the students". The Prince Edward Island *School Act*[9] requires both teachers and principals to attend to the health, comfort and safety of students. In Alberta, the *School Act*[10] requires principals to "direct the management of the school" and "maintain order and discipline in the school".

In the authors' view, these and related provisions in each statute impose an obligation on school administrators to assist in or manage medical treatment where doing so is in the best interests of the student, is reasonable and can be carried out without special skills or training. There does not appear to be any prohibition on the delegation of this task to teachers, or even to non-teaching personnel, such as a school secretary.

In special circumstances, where the administration of medical treatment is not commonly assumed by ordinary laypersons, training in this area should be afforded to the individuals who will be responsible for supervising the student.

School Policy and Procedure

In September, at the beginning of the school year, the school registration forms sent home should request, where applicable, that parents inform the school as to relevant medical problems their children may have, any treatment which is required and any limitations on the children's activities. With respect to administration of prescribed medication, it is suggested that a written authorization be provided to the school by the student's parents with clear instructions from the student's physician.[11] In this regard, a specific administration of medication form should be prepared by the school board to be completed when the principal concurs with a parent's request for the school to administer or manage the administration of medication.

A new form should be completed at the beginning of each school year and/or when a student's medication changes. In the form, the physician should specify particulars as to the name of the medication, the reason for its use and the method of administration. The parent should provide the medication to the school in a

---

[6] E.M. Roher, J.J. Morris and M.A. Warner, "Managing Students with Diabetes in Schools", *Education Law News* (Summer, 1999) (Toronto: Borden & Elliot).
[7] R.S.O. 1990, c. E.2.
[8] S.N.S. 1995-96, c. 1.
[9] S.P.E.I. 1993, c. 35 (c. S-2.1), ss. 98(f) and 99(m).
[10] S.A. 1988, c. S-3.1, s. 15.
[11] Roher and Morris, *op. cit.*, footnote 3, at p. 1.

156   An Educator's Guide to the Role of the Principal

container clearly labelled by a pharmacist with instructions regarding its storage (*e.g.*, refrigeration).

There are a number of other elements which should be considered for inclusion in a school or board policy for medication management in order to reduce the risks associated with managing medication. These include:

- There should be language in the administration of medication form which sets out limitations and warnings in relation to the school's activity.
- In addition to the standard disclaimer, the form could specify that it is neither the objective nor purpose of the school to administer medication to students and the school is prepared to undertake this activity as a last resort to assist the student to continue to attend school.
- Where possible, medication should be delivered to the school in its original bottle and with its original label.
- Responsibility for its safe storage, under lock and key where necessary (there should be access to emergency or allergy medication), should be delegated to specific persons. A detailed inventory of the stored medication should be kept at all times.
- As a matter of policy, it may be preferable that only school nurses dispense medication to students. However, most schools are without nurses. In the absence of a nurse, the principal may choose to designate a person or persons to supervise the administration of medication and where it will be stored in the school.
- The person administering or supervising the administration of medication to the student should complete an entry on a daily record form each time medication is administered. The record of the administration of medication should include the pupil's name, the date and time of the provision of medication, the dosage given and the name of the person administering the medication.
- The telephone number of the student's parents and physician should be readily available to the person administering the medication or supervising the student.
- For persons who have been delegated the responsibility of administering medication or supervising a student's self-administration of medication, principals may wish to consider providing necessary training. This may be necessary in special circumstances where the method of administration is not commonly used by a layperson.
- A safe and private area should be provided for the administering of medication if requested. Every effort should be made to make the taking of medication a seamless part of a student's day. If the student or parent expresses any discomfort with the administering of the particular medication in the presence of others, a more private setting should be found.[12]

---

[12] In Ontario, the Ministry of Education, "Policy/Program Memorandum No. 81: Provision of Health Support Services in School Settings" (Toronto: Ministry of Education, July 19, 1984), at p. 2, states that medication should be administered "in a manner which allows for sensitivity and privacy and which encourages the pupil to take an appropriate level of responsibility for his or her medication".

- Procedures for dealing with emergencies arising out of the administering of medication should be developed in advance of the school year. These can then be communicated to parents and students at the beginning of the school year. Principals way wish to consider including these procedures in medication authorization forms in order to obtain consent to them in advance of any emergency.
- Any policy must include effective methods for communicating its requirements to students, parents and staff. This includes a mechanism for informing substitute or rotating teachers (such as music teachers or librarians) of the medical needs of the students for whom they are responsible and the regular procedures for meeting those needs.
- There should be a protocol for contacting parents when the administering of medication is refused by the student or is no longer possible for any reason. This is especially the case where the parents have come to rely on the school to administer their child's medication.[13]

Wherever possible, physicians should be requested to prescribe medication which can be administered outside of school hours. There may be circumstances, however, where certain medication is essential for a student to continue to attend school and such medication must be taken during school hours. There are different risks and degrees of expertise required in administering different types of medication. For example, the risk and expertise required in giving a student a pill prescribed by a physician is different from the risk and expertise required in administering a hypodermic needle.

Depending on the type of medication required by a student, it may be prudent to ensure that the individuals assigned to the task of administering certain medication have appropriate training. Where it is a simple matter of reminding a student to take medication in the form of a pill or giving cough syrup with a spoon from a bottle, the administration is relatively straightforward and would seem to require no special training or qualifications. On the other hand, where there is a significant risk that a teacher may be called upon to administer an injection of glucagon to a student who has gone into insulin shock, the teacher may require some training or qualifications.[14]

Criteria to Consider

As previously indicated, school administrators are under an obligation to assist in or manage medical treatment where doing so is in the best interests of the student, is reasonable and can be carried out with no special training or skills. When is it reasonable for school administrators to provide this assistance? A number of factors should be considered in each case. It is ultimately the principal's

---

[13] *Ibid.*, at p. 2; Roher, Morris and Warner, *op. cit.*, footnote 6; Roher and Morris, *op. cit.*, footnote 3; Foster, *op. cit.*, footnote 1, at p. 204; Brown and Zuker, *op. cit.*, footnote 2, at p. 144.

[14] Roher and Morris, *op. cit.*, footnote 3.

responsibility to determine whether medication management is appropriate in the circumstances.

Even if a parent or student consents in writing to the management and administering of medication, there is some risk in agreeing to manage the medication. In fact, the principal or school board might consider whether there is a need to take on the responsibility in every case. When possible, for example, the student's medication schedule may be adjusted so as not to involve school personnel. As well, the type of medication involved may make a difference in a principal's decision to administer it.

Overall, there are a number of criteria that a principal should examine when considering whether to undertake the management of a student's medication. These include:

- the type of medication (this can include a consideration of whether the medication can be taken outside of school hours, the probability of serious side effects, the frequency of required dosages, the difficulty of storage and whether it is appropriate for the student to administer his or her own medication);
- the availability of qualified personnel at the school to administer the particular medication;
- the number of students in the school who require support services for medication or other treatments;
- the degree to which the administering or management of medication interferes with the normal duties of the principal and school staff (this criteria can be considered in the context of both the needs of individual students and the needs of all students in the school taken together);
- the timing and location of administration (*e.g.*, can the medication or treatment be administered at the appropriate time and/or in an appropriate location);
- the method of administration (*i.e.*, whether the method of administration is within the expertise of the average layperson, requires special training or expertise or is simply too risky an exercise for the staff to undertake);
- other risks associated with the services (the potential risks associated with providing health services are many, including the potential consequences of failing to give a dosage or giving an incorrect dosage, the side effects of medication, injuries or infections occurring while administering medication, contamination of medication and escalating costs of providing the services); and
- the seriousness of the condition (*i.e.*, whether the medication is essential for a student to continue to attend school – should the health condition requiring medication be extremely serious, the associated risks with taking responsibility for its medication may be too great).[15]

---

[15] J.J. Morris, "Managing Medication in Schools" (address to the Canadian Association for the Practical Study of Law in Education Conference, April 26, 1999) [unpublished];

Obviously, the principal of the school will be in the best position to decide whether school resources should be used to assist a student in receiving certain medical treatment. Provided the principal receives adequate information, a balancing of these and other criteria in the circumstances must be undertaken in order to reach a reasonable course of action.

The Risks in Managing Medication

Clearly, there are risks associated with undertaking the management of medication or medical treatment in the school setting. The practical difficulties of such an undertaking were crystallized in a 1997 British Columbia case involving injuries sustained at school by an eight-year-old child.[16] The student had slight mental disabilities, attention deficit disorder and was hyperactive. The student had been integrated into a grade 2 class. To make this integration possible, a full-time care worker was to be in close proximity to the child to respond to his sudden and unpredictable behaviours. The child also received a regular dosage of Ritalin, including a dosage at school. When the child acted up, he was permitted to leave the room and exert some energy in the school's gym. This occurred on the day in question and the child's care worker followed him closely down the school's hallway. The child opened the heavy door to the gym. During the moment when the care worker hesitated to avoid the door swinging back, the child climbed a railing. The care worker lunged to stop him but the child fell over the railing and suffered significant facial injuries.

The student, through his litigation guardian, sued the school board in negligence. The statement of claim alleged that the care worker failed to stay in close proximity to the child, leading to the accident, and that the failure of the school to administer Ritalin to the child on the day in question caused his subsequent injuries. The court found that the care worker was not negligent in her care of the child that day. With respect to the medication, it was provided under prescription and, as was the procedure in previous school years, the school required parental authorization to administer Ritalin to the child once at each lunch hour. On the day of the injuries, no Ritalin was given to the child as the authorization for the current school year had not been completed.

The court found that the school authorities were negligent in failing to inform the child's parents that no consent to the administering of medication had been completed and that the medication could not be administered. This was especially the case since school personnel were well aware of the importance of medication to this child. Though the school board was found to be negligent, no liability ensued since the court determined that the accident may have happened even if the child had received his medication.

E.M. Roher, *Medication in Schools: Workbook* (Aurora: Canada Law Book Inc., 1998); North York Board of Education, "Health Issues", in *Safe Schools Resource Book* (North York: September, 1995), p. 1.

[16] *Crosby (Guardian ad Litem of) v. Prince Rupert School District No. 52* (1997), 73 A.C.W.S. (3d) 551, [1997] B.C.J. No. 1937 (Q.L.) (S.C.).

This case clearly demonstrates that, once the decision to undertake the management of medication has been made, it must be completed with reasonable care and due diligence. Also, once parents come to rely on a school to administer medication to their child, it is the school's responsibility to communicate with the parents in the event that the school is unable to continue administering the medication.[17]

Once approval for administering medication has been given, meeting the appropriate standard of care of a prudent parent in these circumstances involves a number of steps. First, a proper authorization form must be completed. A proper form will contain satisfactory consent to the treatment, details of the services provided and adequate disclaimers of the school's liabilities. Next, appropriate personnel must be designated to manage the medication. In situations where a school nurse is not available, the issue of whether staff can be required to administer medication may be raised. Finally, the program of medication management itself must be properly designed and implemented to minimize the risks for all involved. Throughout the process, communication with the students, parents and staff is vital.

DUTY AND STANDARD OF CARE IN AN EMERGENCY

The common law generally provides that a person who attempts in good faith to assist someone in peril exposes himself or herself to potential civil liability if the attempt is bungled, whereas the person who stands idly by without lifting a finger incurs no liability. Thus, there is no general civil duty to render assistance to individuals in danger.[18]

In the authors' view, however, this general principle which encourages passive inaction does not apply to the special relations between a school and its students. Our courts have held that a school has a special responsibility towards its students which, in our view, imports an additional obligation to engage in positive conduct for the students' benefit.

At common law, the standard of care that a teacher is expected to show towards a child under his or her charge is such care as would be exercised by a reasonably careful or prudent parent. This standard of care requires, in the authors' view, no more than would be reasonable in the particular circumstances having regard to the relationship between teacher and student.

Our courts have held that a person who makes a reasonable decision as to a course of action in an emergency will not be treated as having acted negligently if the course of action ultimately turns out to be wrong. All that is necessary is that the decision was not unreasonable, taking the exigencies of the particular situation into account. There is no absolute standard of care, but rather the standard of care

---

[17] E. Doctor, "Negligence for Failure to Administer Medication" (1997), 9 *Education Law Reporter* 9.

[18] Roher and Morris, *op. cit.*, footnote 3, at p. 2.

varies according to the circumstances and the risk involved. In providing emergency medical treatment, a teacher or other school board employee should first make a determination that an emergency in fact exists and that immediate emergency care is necessary.

In emergency situations, the issue of consent to treatment becomes important. An emergency may necessitate immediate medical action either by the supervising teacher or on his or her authorization. Acquiring parental consent in these circumstances may be impractical, if not impossible.

At common law, an individual under the age of 18 can consent to his or her own medical treatment. As a basic rule, unless there is contrary evidence, the law presumes that a person is legally and mentally capable of giving consent. Whether a student can consent depends on the individual in question, his or her mental ability and the treatment or procedure that the individual is asked to understand.

In an emergency, the teacher should talk to the student and find out what type of medication, if any, the student takes or what is required for treatment. If the student is mentally capable of consenting to the administration of medication, the student's consent should be obtained. On the other hand, if the student is not mentally capable of providing consent (*i.e.*, does not understand or is unconscious), it is not necessary to obtain consent from the student.[19]

Excursions

From time to time, as part of a student's education program, an excursion may be offered by the school, such as a canoe trip, horseback riding or an outdoor education program.[20] Such excursion could bring with it an assumption of certain risks. It is normal for most students, including students with severe allergies or asthma, to want to participate in such excursions. Where a life-threatening medical condition has been reported to the school, the directions for treatment have been indicated by a physician and appropriate authorization has been provided by the parent or guardian, it may be appropriate for teachers to carry the medication provided by parents. The school board should ensure that the staff have appropriate training in administering the relevant medication and in responding to possible allergy or asthma reactions before such students are able to participate. In the case of a life-threatening medical condition, it is advised that the principal and/or teacher have an in-depth discussion with the parent or guardian and consider all aspects of risk, including the distance from medical assistance.

If the administration of medication is too complicated, or if school personnel do not have sufficient training, the principal or teacher may suggest to the child's parents that it would be inappropriate for the child to attend. In certain circumstances, it may be prudent to exclude a student from a particular excursion. One alternative which could be considered would be for the parent or guardian to attend the excursion to provide the necessary medical care and monitoring for the child.

---

[19] *Ibid.*
[20] *Ibid.*, at p. 3.

Teachers who are in charge of field trips should be specially trained to deal with emergencies. This is self-evident based on the special risks involved in travelling with large groups and the potential for the group to be far from hospitals or emergency medical services.

ASSIGNMENT TO ADMINISTER MEDICATION

In most schools, there will inevitably be more than one student with a requirement to receive medication during the school day. This fact, combined with the myriad of other duties a principal must attend to, demands that a school principal delegate the responsibility of administering care and medication to other members of his or her staff. For many, including various teachers' associations,[21] the question of whether teachers and other school staff can be *required* to participate in the administration of medication and other care to students remains.

Legislation respecting education in various provinces prescribes duties for teachers which help to form a sort of statutory job description. For instance, Ontario's *Education Act* includes a duty for teachers "to maintain, under the direction of the principal, proper order and discipline in the teacher's classroom and while on duty in the school and on the school ground".[22] Statutory descriptions of teachers' duties are written in general terms such that the reasonable delegation of various non-teaching activities is contemplated by the legislation. Additionally, the legislation of many provinces provides that teachers must also undertake duties assigned to them, in addition to the listed statutory duties.[23] Unless the administering of medication or medical care is specifically listed in the legislation, or as a duty in the contract or collective agreement of a particular staff member, any requirement to undertake such activities must form an implied obligation of the employment relationship. However, it must be noted that there is nothing in the Acts or regulations with respect to education which *prevents* the principal from delegating this task to teachers. In addition, a principal may choose to assign this task to non-teaching personnel, such as a school secretary.[24]

The issue of what activities may form implied duties of a teacher's contract has been considered by Canadian courts. Again, in these decisions, there has not been any finding of law which prevents a principal from delegating to teachers the administering of medication or care to students. In a 1975 decision of the Supreme Court of Canada,[25] then Chief Justice Laskin considered whether noon-hour

---

[21] See Foster, *op. cit.*, footnote 1, at pp. 190-91.
[22] *Education Act*, s. 264(1)(e).
[23] See Foster, *op. cit.*, footnote 1, at pp. 191-2. For an example, see *Operation of Schools – General,* R.R.O. 1990, Reg. 298, s. 20.
[24] Roher and Morris, *op. cit.*, footnote 3, at p. 2.
[25] *Winnipeg Teachers' Assn. No. 1 v. Winnipeg School Division No. 1* (1975), 59 D.L.R. (3d) 228, [1976] 2 S.C.R. 695. See also *School District of Snow Lake No. 2309 v. Snow Lake Local Assn. No. 45-4 of the Manitoba Teachers' Society*, [1987] 2 W.W.R. 348, 46

supervision of students by teachers was a voluntary activity or an implied term of the teachers' contract. The teachers had withdrawn from noon-hour supervision in the midst of a labour dispute. In this case, noon-hour supervision, like the administering of medication, was not an express duty under the teachers' contract. Before finding specifically that the teachers were required to provide noon-hour supervision as assigned, Chief Justice Laskin considered how the determination of implied contractual duties should be made, and stated:

> Contract relations of the kind in existence here must surely be governed by standards of reasonableness in assessing the degree to which an employer or a supervisor may call for the performance of duties which are not expressly spelled out. They must be related to the enterprise and be seen as fair to the employee and in furtherance of the principal duties to which he is expressly committed.[26]

Thus, in determining whether a teacher can, for example, be required to administer medication, it must be decided whether the employment relationship will permit the assignment of duties not expressly set out in the legislation or contract. Such assignment will be possible in the vast majority of situations, with the possible exception of where the contract in question forbids such an assignment. The assignment must be fair and reasonable in the circumstances. It must relate to the enterprise and further to the principal duties to which a teacher is expressly committed.[27] The decision is not as complex as this reasoning may imply. Generally speaking, the administration of medication in schools is in furtherance of the education of the students who require the service. Many of these students could not attend classes if they did not receive medication during school hours. For the most part, the manner of administering medication to students does not make unreasonable demands of the designated staff member. It usually involves administering oral medication which can be done simply and quickly. Only where the manner of administration becomes overly complex, risky or lengthy would this assignment likely be considered unreasonable.

W.F. Foster has suggested some factors to consider when asking whether the assignment of the duty is fair and reasonable to an employee in particular circumstances.[28] These factors include:

- the availability of other school personnel to administer medication;
- the number of pupils requiring medication in class;
- the degree to which administration and record-keeping interfere with the teacher's other duties;
- the timing and location of the administration;
- the method of administration;
- the training, if any, required to administer the medication;

Man. R. (2d) 211 (Q.B.), affd [1987] 4 W.W.R. 763, 46 Man. R. (2d) 207 (C.A.), leave to appeal to S.C.C. refused 57 Man. R. (2d) 159, 86 N.R. 400*n*.

[26] *Supra*, at p. 235.
[27] Brown and Zuker, *op. cit.*, footnote 2, at p. 143.
[28] Foster, *op. cit.*, footnote 1, at pp. 196-7.

- the care the student may require after receiving the medication;
- the risks involved in administering the medication or if an error of dosage occurs; and
- the statutory or contractual protections in place to protect teachers or staff from potential liability, and the insurance available to them and the school.

Generally speaking, there is nothing to absolutely prevent the assignment of medication management or other appropriate medical care to teachers and other school staff. As with other decisions a principal makes, this one must be made in a reasonable manner and in furtherance of the education of students who require the service.

MANAGING STUDENTS WITH DIABETES[29]

Diabetes mellitus is a disease characterized by the body's inability to produce insulin, or the body's inability to properly use the insulin that it does produce. There are two main types of diabetes – type 1 and type 2. Approximately 10% of people with diabetes have type 1, in which the body produces little or no insulin. This form of diabetes is often diagnosed early in life. People with type 1 diabetes must take insulin injections every day, and must also learn to use meal planning, physical activity and self-monitoring to help them control their diabetes. In type 2 diabetes, the body does produce some insulin, but is unable to use it properly. This form of diabetes may develop later in life and can usually be controlled by diet alone or with oral medication.

Approximately 6% of Canadians suffer from diabetes. In 1995, there were approximately 7,500 children with type 1 diabetes in the school system in Ontario. In general, these children can participate fully in all school activities, including field trips, school sports and extra-curricular activities. It is critical, however, that educators be aware of the special needs of children with diabetes. Specifically, educators need to be aware of what duties they have, if any, with respect to insulin injections, blood glucose testing, the monitoring of food intake, and recognizing and treating hypoglycemia and hyperglycemia.[30]

School Policies and Procedures

The school registration forms sent to parents at the beginning of each school year should solicit information regarding a child's diabetes. This includes not only the fact of the child's condition, but also what treatment is required and any limitations on the student's activities. Parents should also be invited to provide specific information about their child to school administrators and key school

---
[29] See Roher, Morris and Warner, *op. cit.*, footnote 6.
[30] Canadian Diabetes Association, *Standards of Care for Children with Type 1 Diabetes in Schools* (1999).

personnel. All school personnel who are in contact with the student with diabetes should then be educated about the student's condition and any emergency and treatment procedures. Finally, a copy of the student's photograph, together with emergency and treatment procedures, should be readily available for all staff to refer to.

Insulin Injections

School personnel should not be responsible for administering insulin injections. There may be circumstances, however, where a student requires insulin during school hours. If this is the case, the student and his or her family should be responsible for performing this aspect of diabetes care. It may be reasonable to require school personnel to ensure that students with diabetes are provided with the time and a clean, private space to self-inject insulin if necessary. It would also seem reasonable that arrangements be made for the safe storage of insulin and syringes, and the safe disposal of lancets and syringes.

Monitoring Food Intake

In order to maintain appropriate levels of glucose in the blood, a child's insulin dose and food intake must be balanced. Therefore students with diabetes must generally eat the same amount of food each day, and eat meals and snacks at the same time each day.

Young children with diabetes may require extra supervision in the lunch room to ensure that they eat all or most of what they have been provided. A child with diabetes may also require regular snacks during the day. Where possible, these can be co-ordinated with recess or class snack times. If it should come to the attention of a teacher that a student has missed a meal or snack or has been eating inadequately, the parents should be notified.

Blood Glucose Monitoring

Students with diabetes need to monitor the level of glucose in their blood through simple blood tests. Unless students are especially young or have special needs, they should be expected to perform such testing themselves. It may be reasonable that, as with insulin injections, students be given the time and a clean, private space for performing the test. It may also be reasonable for arrangements to be made for the safe storage and disposal of lancets and needles, and the disinfecting of blood glucose monitoring areas.

Hypoglycemia (Low Blood Glucose)

Hypoglycemia is an emergency condition caused by low blood glucose. Low blood glucose is usually the result of: insufficient food due to a delayed, missed or incomplete meal; more exercise or activity than usual without a corresponding increase in food; and/or too much insulin.

Parents or guardians must discuss the causes, prevention, symptoms and treatment of hypoglycemia with school personnel. Parents or guardians should also provide their diabetic child with an extra snack and a constant supply of fast-acting sugar sources such as pop, fruit juice, packets of sugar, oral glucose tablets or honey. Students should be permitted to take oral glucose to prevent or treat low blood glucose at any time anywhere on school property or during school-sanctioned activities.

In an emergency, a child who is experiencing severe hypoglycemia may require an injection of glucagon. Generally, a glucagon injection should only be performed by a trained health professional, such as a school nurse. It is possible, however, that a school may not have a school nurse on site, or that emergency medical services may be unable to respond quickly enough. These circumstances raise difficult issues. Is this a circumstance, provided that school personnel and parents agree, where teachers or other personnel should be trained to administer glucagon injections? To the extent that teachers undertake to provide emergency treatment in this situation, does it set a precedent for other forms of emergency treatment to be administered by teachers or school administrators? Is a student better served by a teacher, albeit trained, who attempts to administer life-saving treatment as opposed to emergency treatment by qualified paramedics or ambulance personnel who are called in on an emergency basis? Whatever the answer to these questions – and this may differ depending on the particular emergency – no school personnel should engage in the administration of medication or emergency treatment unless they are trained and competent.

Hyperglycemia (High Blood Glucose)

Hyperglycemia refers to high blood glucose. If a student with diabetes experiences increased thirst and urination – the most obvious symptoms of hyperglycemia – the parents should be notified to assist them in long-term treatment. However, hyperglycemia is not generally an emergency requiring immediate treatment.

MANAGING STUDENTS WITH ALLERGIES

As noted earlier in this chapter, approximately 1% to 2% of the Canadian population is at risk for serious allergic reactions to insect stings and foods. There is a slightly lower reported risk for persons allergic to certain drugs or latex. Based on this rate of risk, every principal can be relatively certain of having students with life-threatening allergies in his or her school.

The life-threatening reaction for those with allergies is called an anaphylactic reaction or anaphylaxis. This refers to a collection of symptoms, the most serious of which are related to breathing difficulties, a drop in blood pressure or shock, each of which can prove to be fatal. Other symptoms include hives, itching, swelling, red watery eyes, vomiting, diarrhea, change of voice, difficulty swallowing, a sense of doom, dizziness, fainting or a change in colour.[31] Though anaphylaxis is a rare event, it is also a foreseeable one in a school setting. For this reason, appropriate policies and procedures should be put in place to minimize the risk of an anaphylactic reaction.

Preventing Severe Allergic Reactions

The first step in preventing severe allergic reactions is to identify the students at risk of anaphylaxis. A principal never feels completely secure in the knowledge that all students at risk have been identified or that all pertinent information about them has been gathered. However, the school should make an effort to solicit information about the relevant medical problems of students. Registration forms must include questions designed to solicit the names of students with allergies. Once identified, parents should be encouraged to send their child to an allergy specialist for an assessment of the seriousness of their child's condition. Not every student's reaction will be life-threatening. Therefore, it is important to identify those students at risk of a serious reaction. Requesting a written "prescribed action plan" from the student's physician will provide the school with the necessary information regarding the student's condition, as well as the appropriate response to a reaction.[32]

Once received, this information should be circulated to the appropriate school personnel. School staff must be able to identify the students in question. Suggesting that these students wear Medic-Alert bracelets will help in this regard. In large schools, identification sheets with the child's name, photograph, specific allergy, warning signs of a reaction and appropriate elements of emergency treatment could be posted in the staff room or distributed to staff. Circulation of this information should be accompanied by instruction with respect to the potentially severe nature of a reaction and its proper treatment. This information can be provided to staff at an in-service program at the beginning of each school year, and periodically before special activities.[33] Once this information has been circulated, staff will be in a better position not only to respond to an allergic reaction, but to participate in prevention.

There are a number of measures which can be taken to reduce the exposure of allergic students to certain foods. Such measures include:

- Try to ensure that food-allergic children only eat the lunches and snacks which have been prepared for them.
- Where appropriate, have students with severe food allergies eat lunches and/or snacks in a separate or supervised eating area.

---

[31] See Canadian Society of Allergy and Clinical Immunology, *op. cit.*, footnote 4.
[32] E. Doctor, "Peanut Allergies: A Medico-Legal Perspective", in W.F. Foster and W.J. Smith, eds., *Navigating Change in Education: The Law as a Beacon* (Chateauguay: Lisbro, 1998), p. 351, at p. 355.
[33] Roher, *op. cit.*, footnote 15.

- Emphasize that food, food utensils and food containers should not be traded or shared.
- Encourage students to wash their hands both before and after eating.
- Surfaces such as, tables, chairs and trays should be washed clean of contaminating foods.
- The use of foods in craft classes or cooking classes should be restricted in appropriate circumstances.
- School, staff and parents should consider restrictions on certain food products at school-related activities such as class parties, snacks or lunches.[34]

Severe allergic reactions to peanuts have been identified as the leading cause of food-induced anaphylaxis.[35] Since the peanut is such a common food product, peanut allergies require very thorough prevention plans. The Canadian Society of Allergy and Clinical Immunology has identified particular strategies for preventing severe peanut reactions in school and child-care settings. These include:

- In the earlier public school grades, a ban on peanuts, peanut butter or foods containing peanuts should be instituted since it is difficult to avoid accidental ingestion. This will reduce but not eliminate the risk of accidental exposure and parents should be aware of that fact.
- In higher grades and high school, a complete ban may be impractical. However, no peanut foods should be allowed in common eating areas when there are peanut allergic students. Allergy-free classrooms may be necessary. Students and staff should be educated regarding the dangers of peanut allergies and requests for restricting peanut use in schools should be made.
- Training for teachers, staff and students regarding nut allergies should be incorporated into first aid courses.
- Foods served by the school for snacks, special programs and other events should not contain peanuts when allergic students are present.[36]

Some schools have instituted a complete ban on peanuts due to the presence of allergic students. For example, Armour Heights Public School in Toronto instituted such a ban while a severely allergic child was in attendance. This was done despite the fact that the child in question did not eat lunch at the school. While the ban did meet with some resistance from parents at the outset, it eventually gained a general level of acceptance. For those students who occasionally forgot about the policy and brought food containing peanuts to school, a supply of peanut-free food was kept on hand.[37] While such a plan may meet with initial

---

[34] *Ibid.*; Canadian Society of Allergy and Clinical Immunology, *op. cit.*, footnote 4; Toronto French School, "Policy on Allergic Reaction", in *Parents' Handbook 1999/2000* (Toronto), p. 11.

[35] Canadian Society of Allergy and Clinical Immunology, *op. cit.*, footnote 4, at p. 2.

[36] *Ibid.*, at p. 2.

[37] V. Galt, "Severe food allergies sticky topic for schools", *The Globe and Mail* (September 23, 1995), p. A1.

resistance, clearly explaining the potential consequences of exposure to peanuts for a student with severe allergies should lead to co-operation from students, staff and parents.

Precautions can also be taken to avoid allergic reactions to insect bites. Eating areas can be restricted to indoors, garbage can be well stored and insect nests can be searched for and removed from school property.[38] Also, where students are taken on nature-based excursions, parents should be informed so that precautions, such as the use of an insect repellent, can be taken.

Preparing for Allergy-based Emergencies

The Canadian Society of Allergy and Clinical Immunology has determined that epinephrine (or adrenaline) is appropriate medication for the emergency treatment of anaphylaxis. Epinephrine is administered through the use of a plastic-encased auto-injector, often referred to as an "epi-pen". Though other modes of injection are available, the epi-pen is recommended as the easiest to use. It can be self-administered or administered by another by simply injecting the epi-pen into the thigh of the patient. Since most fatalities from severe allergic reactions occur while the victim is away from home or due to delay in administering epinephrine, schools should develop procedures to ensure that at-risk students can be properly treated should an adverse reaction occur.[39]

To ensure a student's access to an epi-pen, schools should consider the following:

- Students and their parents should provide a prescribed epi-pen to the school. This should be labelled with the student's name and stored in a readily available, unlocked location. This location should be in relatively close proximity to students at risk. All staff should be made aware of this location.
- Since epinephrine has a shelf life, a protocol for checking the age of the epi-pens in storage should be adopted to be certain that none become stale-dated.
- Students who are old enough and able to self-administer an epi-pen should also be encouraged to carry their own at all times. These students should be informed of where other epi-pens are located within the school.
- Information sheets regarding at-risk students can also be placed at the location(s) where the epinephrine injectors are stored.
- First-aid kits located in common areas, such as gymnasiums and lunch rooms, should also contain epi-pens.[40]

Given the obligation of a principal and a teacher to act as prudent and reasonable parents, it is expected that they will demonstrate reasonable care and

---

[38] Canadian Society of Allergy and Clinical Immunology, *op. cit.*, footnote 4, at p. 2.
[39] *Ibid.*, at p. 1.
[40] *Ibid.*, at p. 3; Doctor, *op. cit.*, footnote 32, at pp. 357-8.

due diligence in responding to an allergy emergency. Acquiring parental consent in these circumstances may be impractical, if not impossible.

As indicated earlier, in an emergency, the principal or teacher should talk to the student and find out what type of medication, if any, the student takes. If the student is mentally capable of consenting to the administration of medication (such as an epi-pen), the student's consent should be obtained. If the student is not mentally capable of providing consent, it is not necessary to obtain consent.

With respect to the school's course of action in the event of a severe allergic reaction, the following should be considered:

- Epinephrine should be administered as early as possible after the onset of symptoms of a severe allergic reaction. Since symptoms occur unpredictably, epinephrine should be administered at the beginning of any reaction, and immediately after an allergic contact for those with a history of severe cardiovascular collapse.
- Where physician-prescribed action plans are available, they should be referred to in an emergency. Such a plan may contain details of the student's risk level and history of reactions, assisting those responding to administer epinephrine appropriately, thus eliminating any "guesswork".
- All persons who have received emergency epinephrine must be immediately taken to hospital since further treatments and observation may be necessary. The student should be taken by ambulance following a 911 call. Should more than one epinephrine injection be required before emergency medical services arrive, such injections can be administered every 15 to 20 minutes.
- School staff must be alerted to any allergic reaction immediately upon its occurrence. If an ambulance is delayed in arriving, a principal or teacher should be prepared to transport the student to hospital by car.
- Principals should be prepared to send students who appear to be having a severe allergic reaction to hospital, with or without parental consent.
- Even for those students who are able to self-administer epinephrine, adult supervision is absolutely necessary. Symptoms of the reaction may overcome the student's ability to inject the epinephrine.[41]

CONCLUSION

Overall, relevant legislation imposes an obligation on school administrators to assist in or manage the administration of medication where doing so is reasonable, is in the best interests of the student and can be carried out with no special training or skills. On the other hand, training should be provided to individuals called upon

---

[41] Canadian Society of Allergy and Clinical Immunology, *op. cit.*, footnote 4, at p. 3; Doctor, *op. cit.*, footnote 32, at pp. 357-8; Toronto French School, *op. cit.*, footnote 34, at pp. 1-2.

to administer medication in situations where the administration is not something in which ordinary laypersons commonly engage.

The common law standard of care that a principal is expected to show towards a child under his or her charge is such care as would be exercised by a reasonably careful or prudent parent. This standard of care requires, in the authors' view, no more than would be reasonable in the circumstances having regard to the relationship between educator and student. The degree of care for the safety of others in an emergency, involving, for example, diabetes or an allergic reaction, varies according to the circumstances. There is no absolute standard of care, but rather the degree of care varies directly with the risk involved. An understanding of the legal issues surrounding the management and administration of medication in schools will provide principals with the foundation to effectively carry out their duties in providing assiduous attention to the health and comfort of students under their care.

9

Suspensions and Expulsions

INTRODUCTION

Canadian schools are committed to providing students with opportunities to grow in self-esteem in an environment conducive to the development of respect for oneself and others. Disciplinary policies and practices reflect a commitment to providing safe and healthy environments for teaching and learning. School officials have a duty, under relevant legislation, to maintain proper order and discipline in the school. They also have a duty to protect students in their charge from foreseeable risks of harm.

A necessary corollary to these duties is the power to discipline students whose conduct endangers other students or represents an infraction which cannot be condoned by the school. Across Canada, legislation pertaining to school boards provides the authority and process for the most serious of these disciplinary powers – the removal of a student from school by suspension or expulsion.

In Ontario, on June 23, 2000, the *Safe Schools Act, 2000*[1] (Bill 81) received Royal Assent. This legislation is intended to increase respect and responsibility, and to set standards for safe learning and safe teaching in schools. Bill 81 also paves the way for the *Ontario Schools Code of Conduct*[2] (the "Code"), which establishes standards of behaviour on a province-wide basis.

The Code may be divided into two general categories: the purposive, in which the government sets out the guiding principles, standards of behaviour and roles and responsibilities of the various stakeholders, including school boards, principals, teachers, school staff, students, parents, police and community members; and the substantive, in which the government proposes changes which require legislative amendment. The substantive changes will be implemented by Bill 81.

---

[1] S.O. 2000, c. 12.
[2] Ontario Ministry of Education, *Ontario Schools Code of Conduct* (Toronto: Queen's Printer, 2000). The Ministry of Education released the Code on April 26, 2000. Effective September 1, 2000, the Code became a policy of the Minister.

In terms of substantive requirements, the Code provides that a student will be immediately suspended and proceed to an expulsion hearing in the following circumstances:

- possession of a weapon, including but not limited to firearms;
- trafficking in drugs or weapons;
- robbery;
- use of a weapon to cause bodily harm, or to threaten serious harm;
- physical assault causing bodily harm requiring professional medical treatment;
- sexual assault; and/or
- providing alcohol to minors.

Immediate suspension is the minimum penalty for:

- uttering a threat to inflict serious bodily harm;
- possession of illegal drugs;
- acts of vandalism causing extensive damage to school property or property located on school premises.
- swearing at a teacher or other person in authority;
- being in possession of alcohol; and/or
- being under the influence of alcohol.

This chapter will review the relevant procedural steps involved in the suspension and expulsion of students under the provisions of Bill 81. It will examine the new statutory scheme which is set out and provide suggestions as to ways to ensure procedural fairness. The chapter will conclude with guidelines for educators regarding preventative steps which may be taken, on a proactive basis, to avoid formal school discipline.

Bill 81

Bill 81 implements the substantive provisions of the Code and also creates a number of other important changes to the suspension and expulsion process. In general, the most sweeping change is that Bill 81 repeals section 23 of the *Education Act*[3] and replaces it with an entirely new regime for suspensions and expulsions. Most significantly, Bill 81 removes the discretion of the principal to determine, in specific enumerated instances, whether misconduct by a student warrants suspension or expulsion. It should be noted that, although Bill 81 has been given Royal Assent as of the date of writing, the sections relating to suspensions and expulsions have not been proclaimed in force.[4]

---

[3] R.S.O. 1990, c. E.2.
[4] The Ministry of Education has indicated that it expects the sections pertaining to expulsions (ss. 309 to 311 of the *Education Act*) will be proclaimed in force in February, 2001. In addition, it expects the sections on suspensions (ss. 306 to 308 of the *Education Act*) will be proclaimed in force in September, 2001.

THE SUSPENSION PROCESS

Mandatory Suspensions

Bill 81 implements the mandatory suspension provisions of the Code. Section 306(1) of the *Education Act* provides that:

> 306(1) It is mandatory that a pupil be suspended from his or her school and from engaging in school-related activities if the pupil commits any of the following infractions while he or she is at school or is engaged in a school-related activity:
> 1. Uttering a threat to inflict serious bodily harm on another person.
> 2. Possessing alcohol or illegal drugs.
> 3. Being under the influence of alcohol.
> 4. Swearing at a teacher or at another person in a position of authority.
> 5. Committing an act of vandalism that causes extensive damage to school property at the pupil's school or to property located on the premises of the pupil's school.
> 6. Engaging in another activity that, under a policy of the board, is one for which a suspension is mandatory.

A principal has a duty to suspend a student in such circumstances for a period of between one and twenty school days. Similarly, a teacher has a duty to suspend a student or report any infraction for which a suspension is mandatory to the principal. A teacher may suspend a student for a maximum of one day. However, if the teacher who suspends a student is of the opinion that a longer suspension is warranted, the teacher has a duty to recommend to the principal that the suspension be extended.

Section 306 also permits teachers and principals to consider certain mitigating factors. Section 306(5) provides that, despite section 306(1), the suspension of a pupil is not mandatory in such circumstances as may be prescribed by regulation. At the date of writing, this regulation has not been released by the Ministry.

Section 306(2) provides that the government may pass regulations varying the duration of a suspension and establishing different standards for different circumstances or different classes of persons. Although it remains to be seen whether regulations will be established, it would be possible for the government to return some local discretion to principals through a regulation. Section 306(11) provides that the Minister may issue policies and guidelines to school boards to assist principals and teachers in interpreting the section.

Bill 81 also sets out a requirement to provide prompt notice. The teacher or principal who suspends a student must ensure that written notice of the mandatory suspension is given promptly to the student and, if the student is a minor, to his or her parent or guardian. Bill 81 does not define what is meant by "promptly", but it implies that this action is to be taken in a punctual fashion.

A student who is suspended is not considered to be engaged in school-related activities by virtue of using services, taking a course or participating in a program to assist suspended students.

Discretionary Suspensions

Section 307 of the *Education Act* permits a principal to suspend a student where the student engages in an activity for which suspension is discretionary. Under section 307(2), a student may be suspended either: from his or her school and from engaging in all school-related activities; or from one or more classes or one or more school-related activities or both.

The minimum duration of a discretionary suspension is as set out by the school board policy which authorizes the suspension; the maximum duration is 20 school days. The maximum duration may be varied by regulation, and different standards may be established for different circumstances or different classes of persons.

The principal may suspend a pupil who engages in an activity for which suspension is discretionary. Where a teacher observes a student engaging in an activity for which suspension is discretionary, the teacher may suspend the student or refer the matter to the principal. In circumstances where a teacher suspends a student, such suspension cannot be for a period longer than the minimum duration specified by school board policy (not to exceed one day). School boards may establish policies respecting which activities are deemed to warrant a discretionary suspension.

Preliminary Procedures

In reporting an incident which leads to a suspension, the following steps should be taken:

- The teacher or principal should seek detailed information from all staff involved in the incident.
- All staff involved with the suspension should make detailed notes of observations, conversations and decisions simultaneous with the event. Such notes may be used to "refresh memories" in a legal proceeding and will assist with the preparation of the report for a possible suspension review, appeal or expulsion hearing. Notes which are made well after the event are usually not helpful and can come under criticism in the course of a proceeding if a witness tries to use notes "made after the fact" to refresh his or her memory.
- All notes should be dated and should indicate the source of information and the name of the recorder.
- All notes should be stapled together and filed for future reference.[5]

Guidelines for Recording a Description of the Incident

In recording a description of the incident, the following guidelines should be kept in mind:

- Keep the language clear and use simple terms in sentence structure.

---

[5] Peterborough Victoria Northumberland and Clarington Catholic District School Board, "Report Writing: A Guide for Administrators" (Peterborough: October, 1998).

- Work with the data you have collected.
- Avoid mind reading and fortune-telling.
- Avoid opinions or wording which appear to make judgments; just state the facts.
- Use terms that the reader can picture, avoid "edubabble" or "jargon".
- Set out events in a chronological order.
- Proofread all statements and complete the description in a neat and professional manner.

Steps to be Taken

In suspending a student, the following steps should be taken:

- The teacher or principal must ensure that written notice of a mandatory or discretionary suspension is given promptly to the student and, if the student is a minor, the student's parent or guardian.
- The notification should include:
    - the name of the pupil who has been suspended;
    - the reason or reasons for the suspension (the stated reason must come within the grounds set out in the legislation and must give specific details of the act or omission giving rise to the suspension); and
    - the right of review of the suspension pursuant to school board policy.
- Where appropriate, the principal should discuss the suspension with the student's parent or guardian or the student, if an adult, before the student is readmitted to the school.
- Where appropriate, the principal should ensure that a board resource person, such as a guidance counsellor or social worker, reviews the circumstances of the suspension and develops an entry plan. The student and the student's parents should be informed of services which are available from the school board or elsewhere in the community to assist the student.[6]

Under section 306(10) of the *Education Act*, the pupil and, if the pupil is a minor, the pupil's parent or guardian must be given prompt written notice of the suspension. In circumstances where a parent or guardian is not available or is unwilling to come to the school, the suspension letter should either be hand-delivered or sent by mail.

Some lawyers who represent parents and students have requested a procedure whereby all documentation pertaining to the incident which led to the suspension would be distributed to parents or pupils at the time of suspension. Distribution of this type of documentation is not required by the legislation.

However, disciplinary consequences must be administered with due regard for procedural fairness.[7] This consideration requires that the student be told what rule

---

[6] *Ibid.*
[7] W. Freel, "Suspension and Expulsion Procedures" (Toronto District School Board, Student and Community Services, January 10, 2000), at p. 2.

has been broken and requires that the student be given an opportunity to be heard. In reviewing the case with the student, the principal should disclose the evidence which supports the principal's decision, based on a "balance of probabilities", to invoke disciplinary consequences. This disclosure need not involve the identification of sources, which could serve to compromise the best interests or safety of other students.

The question may arise as to whether a student can serve a mandatory or discretionary suspension in the school. The Act provides that a student who is suspended is not considered to be engaged in school-related activities by virtue of using services, taking a course or participating in a program to assist such students.[8]

What steps should the principal take if the parents refuse to accept their child's suspension and insist on returning the child to the school? The principal should inform the parents that the *Education Act* gives principals the legal authority to suspend a student from school for reasons which are specified in the Act.[9] In circumstances where parents oppose the suspension, they have the right to appeal the suspension. Parents should be aware, however, that an appeal against a suspension does not "stay" the suspension. The suspension will continue in effect notwithstanding the appeal.

If parents insist on having their child return to school while under suspension, they will be held accountable for causing their child to trespass on the school's property. In extreme circumstances, the principal, as "occupier" of the property, can request that the police remove the child and return the child to a parent. If the parent refuses to accept the child or is not available to receive the child, the police could take the child to a children's aid society for his or her safety.[10]

The question also arises as to whether a vice-principal can investigate an incident and suspend a student in the principal's absence.[11] Although only school principals have the statutory authority to invoke a suspension, vice-principals can investigate incidents and suspend a student in the principal's absence. Section 12(3) of Regulation 298[12] provides that:

> 12(3) In the absence of the principal of a school, a vice-principal, where a vice-principal has been appointed for the school, shall be in charge of the school and shall perform the duties of the principal.

In this regard, in the principal's absence, the vice-principal may sign the suspension letter on behalf of the principal.

---

[8] *Education Act*, s. 306(12).
[9] Freel, *op. cit.*, footnote 7, at p. 4.
[10] *Ibid.*
[11] *Ibid.*, at p. 7.
[12] *Operation of Schools – General*, R.R.O. 1990, Reg. 298.

Record-keeping of Violent Incidents

As indicated in Chapter 3, "Student Records and Confidentiality", certain provisions in the *Education Act* govern the establishment of the Ontario Student Record ("OSR"):

- Section 265(d) of the *Education Act* provides that it is the duty of a principal "in accordance with this Act, the regulations and the guidelines issued by the Minister, to collect information for inclusion in a record in respect of each pupil enrolled in the school and to establish, maintain, retain, transfer and dispose of the record".
- Section 266(2) states, in part, that a record is "privileged for the information and use of supervisory officers and the principal and teachers of the school for the improvement of instruction of the pupil".

The *Violence-Free Schools Policy*[13] (the "Policy"), published by the Ministry of Education and Training in 1994, provides that the information relating to serious violent incidents leading to reports to the police, as well as information relating to serious violent incidents leading to suspension or expulsion must be maintained in the OSR. This information is to be recorded on a violent incident form.

The Policy specifically deals with the requirement to insert information into the OSR. The Policy provides that the following information will be included in the OSR:

- a violent incident form containing a description of the serious violent incident leading to the suspension or expulsion or the call to the police, a reference to the call to the police or a reference to the school/board disciplinary response to the incident, if applicable; and
- a copy of the school board's letter(s) to the student and/or the student's parent or guardian regarding suspension or expulsion for violent behaviour.[14]

The Policy also deals with the removal of information from the OSR. It provides:

- The information relating to suspension for violent behaviour shall not be removed from the OSR unless three consecutives years have passed during which no further suspensions for serious violent incidents have taken place.
- The information relating to expulsion shall be removed five years after the date on which the school board expelled the student.
- Where an expelled student has been readmitted to school by a school board, and is expelled again, the information relating to the expulsions shall not be removed from the OSR until five consecutive years have passed without any further expulsion.
- Where the student has not been suspended or expelled, the Violent Incident Form shall be removed after three years if no further serious violent incident is reported to the police during that time.[15]

---

[13] Ontario Ministry of Education and Training, *Violence-Free Schools Policy* (Toronto: Ministry of Education and Training, 1994), at p. 23.
[14] *Ibid.*
[15] *Ibid.*, at p. 24.

In circumstances where a student transfers to another school, the information in the OSR relating to the serious violent incident which led to suspension or expulsion, as well as a report to the police, are required to be kept in the OSR unless removed pursuant to the preceding provisions.[16] The transfer will occur in accordance with section 6 of the *Ontario Student Record (OSR) Guideline, 2000.*[17]

Review of Suspension

Decisions to suspend a student are subject to a review and appeal procedure. However, the Act provides that a decision to suspend a student for one day or less cannot be reviewed or appealed.

Under section 308(1) of the *Education Act*, the following persons may request a review of the decision to suspend a student:

1. If the pupil is a minor, his or her parent or guardian.
2. If the pupil is not a minor, the pupil.
3. Such other persons as may be specified in a policy of the board.

The review is to be conducted in accordance with the requirements set out in the school board's policy and is to be conducted by the person specified in the board policy.

The Act also provides for an appeal process. After the review, the student, or his or her parent or guardian where the student is a minor, or such other person as is specified by board policy, may appeal the decision to suspend the pupil.[18] The Act provides that the school board must hear and determine the appeal. Under the Act, the board can delegate its powers and duties to a committee of the board who will hear the appeal.

This appeal must be conducted in accordance with the requirements established by school board policy. The school board will hear the appeal and make a determination. Section 308(6) of the *Education Act* specifically provides that the decisions of the school board are "final".

Bill 81 provides that an appeal of a suspension must be conducted in accordance with the requirements established by board policy. In general, to ensure procedural fairness, the appeal to be heard by the school board should comply with the provisions of the *Statutory Powers Procedure Act*[19] (the "*SPPA*").

The notice of the appeal hearing should be forwarded to the parent or guardian or adult student with a copy to the teacher and/or principal making the suspension. The notice of hearing should include the following:

- the time and place of the appeal;
- the purpose of the appeal;

---

[16] *Ibid.*
[17] Ministry of Education, *Ontario Student Record (OSR) Guideline, 2000* (Toronto: March, 2000).
[18] *Education Act*, s. 308(4).
[19] R.S.O. 1990, c. S.22.

- a specific statement that the appeal is held pursuant to provisions of the *Education Act*; and
- a statement that, if a party does not attend the appeal, the panel may proceed in the absence of the party and the party will not be entitled to any further notice of the proceeding.

The appeal of a suspension should be conducted in accordance with the requirements of the *SPPA*. These requirements include the following:

- A party to a proceeding is entitled to be represented by counsel or an agent.
- Any party may call and examine witnesses and present arguments and submissions.
- Any party may cross-examine witnesses.
- A record of the proceeding will be made.
- A statement of the final decision, including the reasons, if any have been given, will be issued to each party.

Board hearings regarding this matter are quasi-judicial legal proceedings. The burden of proof is based on a "balance of probabilities" rather than "beyond a reasonable doubt", which is the standard in criminal law proceedings.

In its determination, the school board or committee of the board will generally consider only two issues:

- whether the suspension should be removed, confirmed or modified; and
- whether it is appropriate that any record of the suspension should be expunged.[20]

Overall, the basis for a suspension appeal hearing lies in a person's right to be treated fairly when he or she is receiving sanctions or losing rights, such as the right to attend school. The procedural safeguards set out in the appeal process are based on the recognition that a person to be disciplined has a right to the principles of fundamental justice. These rules of procedural fairness are often referred to as "due process".

Purpose of a Suspension

The *Education Act* provides no indication of the purpose to be served in invoking a suspension. While there is probably some aspect of punishment implicit in a suspension, there may be little punitive effect in barring from school a child who, for example, already has persistent truancy problems. A suspension can, however, have several important purposes, including:

- A suspension operates as a deterrent by sending a strong signal to the pupil, the pupil's family and other pupils that the precipitating behaviour is inappropriate and unacceptable.

---

[20] E.M. Roher, "Everything You Always Wanted to Know (and Should Know) About Suspensions and Suspension Appeals", *Education Law News* (Fall, 1998) (Toronto: Borden & Elliot).

- Where two or more students have been involved in a violent incident, a suspension may serve as a period of reflection to prepare a climate for conflict resolution.
- A suspension leaves a record of the behaviour, which can be used to gain access to counselling and other support services.
- A suspension may encourage a pupil and a pupil's family to seek appropriate assistance themselves.
- A suspension alerts school personnel to the need for ongoing observation, support and intervention.[21]

In some circumstances, the use of a suspension is the only means by which to gain the serious attention of a student's parent or guardian in order to communicate that the child's behaviour has strayed unacceptably from established norms. An effective suspension process should encourage a possible meeting with the student's parent or guardian to discuss the student's behaviour and attitude. This meeting can provide an opportunity to review the student's past conduct and involve the parents in creating a plan for improving the student's behaviour to an acceptable level.[22]

THE EXPULSION PROCESS

Mandatory Expulsions

Bill 81 has created a new statutory regime to govern the expulsion of students. Section 309(1) of the *Education Act* provides that:

> 309(1) It is mandatory that a pupil be expelled if the pupil commits any of the following infractions while he or she is at school or is engaged in a school-related activity:
> 1. Possessing a weapon, including possessing a firearm.
> 2. Using a weapon to cause or to threaten bodily harm to another person.
> 3. Committing physical assault on another person that causes bodily harm requiring treatment by a medical practitioner.
> 4. Committing sexual assault.
> 5. Trafficking in weapons or in illegal drugs.
> 6. Committing robbery.
> 7. Giving alcohol to a minor.
> 8. Engaging in another activity that, under a policy of the board, is one for which expulsion is mandatory.

The principal is required to suspend a student whom the principal believes may have committed an infraction for which expulsion is mandatory. Where the principal suspends a student, the principal is required promptly to either:

---

[21] M.A. Zuker, "Violence and Schools: Student Rights and Discipline", in W.F. Foster, ed., *Education in Transition: Legal Issues in a Changing School Setting* (Chateauguay: Lisbro, 1996).

[22] H.M. Kelly, "Suspension and Expulsion" (paper presented to the Canadian Association for the Practical Study of Law in Education Conference, Toronto, April, 1999), at pp. 7 and 23.

- refer the matter to the school board; or
- conduct an inquiry to determine whether the student has committed an infraction for which expulsion is mandatory.

Conduct of Inquiry

In the event that the principal decides to conduct an inquiry, the inquiry must be conducted in accordance with the requirements established by a policy of the board. The powers and duties of the principal are specified by board policy.[23]

After the inquiry, where the principal is satisfied that the student committed an infraction for which expulsion is mandatory, the principal is required to either:

- impose a "limited expulsion" on the student; or
- refer the matter to the school board for its determination.[24]

Under section 309(8), the principal cannot expel a student if more than 20 school days have passed since the principal suspended the student, unless the parties to the inquiry agree upon a later deadline.

Hearing by Board

The matter may be referred to the school board by the principal and the board is required to hold an expulsion hearing. In this regard, the board has the powers and duties specified by board policy. Section 309(10) of the *Education Act* provides that the expulsion hearing is to be conducted in accordance with the requirements established by board policy.

After the expulsion hearing, where the board is satisfied that the student committed an infraction for which expulsion is mandatory, the board is required to impose either:

- a "limited expulsion"; or
- a "full expulsion".

The Bill 81 amendments provide a narrow time frame for the expulsion hearing by the board. The board cannot expel a student if more than 20 school days have expired since the principal suspended the student, unless the parties to the expulsion hearing agree upon a later deadline.[25]

Limited Expulsion

Section 309(14) of the *Education Act* sets out the requirements for a limited expulsion. It provides that:

> 309(14) A pupil who is subject to a limited expulsion is not entitled to attend the school the pupil was attending when he or she committed the infraction and is not entitled to engage in school-related activities at the school until the later of:

---

[23] *Education Act*, s. 309(6).
[24] *Education Act*, s. 309(7).
[25] *Education Act*, s. 309(12).

(a) the date specified by the principal or the board when expelling the pupil, which cannot be more than one year after the date on which the principal suspended the pupil under subsection (2); and
(b) the date on which the pupil meets such requirements as may be established by the board for returning to school after being expelled.

Section 309(15) provides that the provincial government could introduce a regulation to vary the time frame in section 309(14)(a) and may specify a different limit for different circumstances or different classes of persons.

Full Expulsion

Section 309(16) outlines the requirements for a full expulsion:

> 309(16) A pupil who is subject to a full expulsion is not entitled to attend any school in the province or to engage in school-related activities of any school in the province until he or she meets such requirements as may be established by regulation for returning to school after being expelled.

The minimum duration of a mandatory expulsion is 21 school days.[26] The period of a student's suspension is deemed to be a period of expulsion.

The Act provides that, when considering the type and duration of expulsion which may be appropriate in the circumstances, the principal or school board will consider the student's history, other factors which may be specified by regulation and other matters that the principal or school board considers appropriate.[27]

Discretionary Expulsions

Section 310 of the *Education Act* provides for discretionary expulsions. Under section 310, a student may be expelled if he or she engages in an activity that, under a policy of the board, is one for which expulsion is discretionary. Similar to the process under mandatory expulsions, where the principal suspends a student, the principal will promptly refer the matter to the school board or conduct an inquiry to determine whether the pupil has committed an infraction for which expulsion is discretionary.

Again, consistent with the procedure for mandatory expulsions, if after the inquiry the principal is satisfied that the student committed an infraction for which expulsion is discretionary, the principal will either impose a limited expulsion or refer the matter to the school board for a determination.

Appeal of Expulsion

Decisions to expel a pupil are subject to appeal under section 311 of the *Education Act*. The appeal must be conducted in accordance with the requirements established by board policy.

The appeal process provides for two types of appeals:

---

[26] *Education Act*, s. 309(18).
[27] *Education Act*, s. 309(19).

- appeals from the decision of the principal; and
- appeals from a decision of the board.

The school board is to hear and determine an appeal from the decision of a principal. With respect to an appeal from a decision of the board, a person or entity designated by regulation will hear and determine the appeal. The Act provides that these decisions on appeal are final.

PROCEDURAL FAIRNESS

In circumstances where an expulsion hearing or an appeal of a decision to expel is convened, the Act provides that such hearing or appeal must be conducted in accordance with the requirements established by board policy. Subject to the relevant board policy, in general, the procedures established in the *SPPA* will be followed in the case of both an expulsion hearing and an appeal proceeding.

As a party to the proceeding, the principal will receive notice of the relevant hearing. The notice must indicate the time and place of the hearing, the purpose of the proceeding, that the hearing is being held pursuant to the provisions of the *Education Act* and that the board may proceed with the hearing, without further notice, if a party fails to attend.

In advance of the hearing, the student or the student's parent or guardian has a right to sufficient disclosure to ensure that he or she is informed of the case to be met. Such disclosure forms part of the procedural fairness accorded a person whose rights are being determined by a public authority. In Ontario, the courts have considered the extent of pre-hearing disclosure which is appropriate in the case of an expulsion hearing.

The 1994 Ontario case of *Scarborough Board of Education v. G. (F.)*[28] involved an application to overturn a school board's expulsion decision. One of the issues raised by the student was insufficient disclosure in advance of the expulsion hearing. Prior to the expulsion hearing, counsel for the principal and supervisory officer provided to the applicants particulars in the form of a summary of the case and the evidence anticipated to be presented at the hearing. In addition, the student and his guardian were provided with information gathered by the vice-principals in the course of their investigation of the pupil, giving rise to the pupil's suspension and the recommendation for expulsion. They were also provided with the recommendation for expulsion by the principal and supervisory officer which described the essential facts in support of their recommendation. In addition, they received court material filed by the board with the court in a previous application in the same matter, including affidavits outlining the consequences of events giving rise to the expulsion recommendation.

The court determined that the student was entitled to procedural fairness in an expulsion hearing, but that the level of disclosure was not as high as that afforded

---

[28] (Unreported, September 19, 1994, Ont. Div. Ct.).

in a criminal or quasi-criminal proceeding. Rather, the content of procedural fairness is decided in the specific context of each case, taking into account various factors, including the nature of the decision being made, the effect of that decision on the individual's rights, the circumstances of the case and the governing statute. In this case, the court concluded that the student had been provided with "an adequate level of disclosure which ensured that they were fully informed of the case that had to be met. They were given every opportunity to make a meaningful response".[29]

The procedural rights under the *SPPA* applicable to suspension appeal hearings also apply to expulsion hearings. A party has a right to be represented by counsel, to call witnesses, to cross-examine witnesses, to a record of the proceeding and to receive a written statement of the reasons for the board's decision.

During the expulsion proceeding, the school will be called upon first to describe the reasons for the decision to expel. In this regard, the principal will be called upon to describe the reasons for the expulsion and for this purpose may make statements of fact based on his or her knowledge and, if the principal wishes, bring forward others to give similar information related to the expulsion. Relevant witnesses, such as a vice-principal, teacher or police officer, may be called to give evidence.

After each person has completed his or her statements, first the parent or student, then members of the school board may ask questions of those persons. The parent or student will then be called upon to set out their position. When the parent or student and their witnesses have completed their evidence, first the principal and then members of the school board may ask questions of those persons.

The principal will be given an opportunity to reply to the evidence introduced by the parent. After all the facts have been presented by both the principal and the parent, first the principal and then the parent will be entitled to present a summary of their respective positions. The school board or committee will retire to make a determination on the matter, and the parties will then be advised. All parties to the hearing will receive the decision in writing.[30]

At the expulsion hearing, there should be a procedure in place for determining if any of the trustees on the tribunal have a personal bias. Near the outset of the hearing, the trustees should be asked to declare if anyone should disqualify himself or herself in the interests of natural justice. Under the principles of natural justice, a duty is imposed on an individual called upon to make a determination in an adjudication to act in good faith and with an open mind.[31]

In the event that a trustee has been involved in the investigation leading up to the expulsion hearing and has received specific information relating to the case, a reasonable apprehension of bias may be raised. Where there is a reasonable

---

[29] See M. Fitzgibbon, "Expulsion Hearings: Procedural Requirements and Allegations of Bias", *Education Law News* (Winter, 1995) (Toronto: Borden & Elliot), at pp. 1-2.
[30] Roher, *op. cit.*, footnote 20, at p. 5.
[31] Freel, *op. cit.*, footnote 7, at p. 9.

apprehension of bias on the part of a trustee, he or she should disqualify himself or herself from taking part in the hearing.

PROGRAMS FOR SUSPENDED AND EXPELLED STUDENTS

Programs, courses and services for suspended and expelled pupils are authorized by section 312 of the *Education Act*. Under section 312(1), the Minister may require boards to establish and maintain specified programs, courses and services for students who are suspended. In addition, the Minister may impose different requirements for different circumstances, different locations or different classes of students.

Section 312(2) provides that the Minister may require boards to establish and maintain specified programs, courses and services for students who are expelled. The Minister can also authorize school boards to enter into agreements with other boards or to retain others to provide the programs, courses and services.

In addition, the Minister has the authority to establish one or more programs for expelled students to prepare them to return to school. Furthermore, the Minister may establish policies and guidelines both for a student's eligibility to participate in an expelled students' program and the criteria to be met for successful completion of the program.

PREVENTATIVE STEPS

In introducing the *Safe Schools Act, 2000* in the Ontario Legislature, the Minister of Education, Janet Ecker, said:

> Parents, students and teachers have told us they want their schools to be safe, respectful environments for learning and teaching . . . From the many letters and expressions of support I have received, it is clear that a vast majority of Ontarians support the measures being taken.[32]

It is evident that policies and procedures regarding suspensions and expulsions are important for students who persistently fail or refuse to follow the rules. However, in these circumstances, an old adage may also apply: "An ounce of prevention is worth a pound of cure." It is important to recognize that preventative steps can be taken by educators, on a proactive basis, to avoid circumstances which may lead to suspension and possibly expulsion. In this regard, the following guidelines are suggested:

- Students and parents should know in advance that failure to follow certain rules will result in suspension and/or expulsion. The standards of behaviour under

---

[32] "Legislature passes *Safe Schools Act*", News Release (Ministry of Education, June 14, 2000).

the *Safe Schools Act, 2000* must be clearly articulated in student assemblies and programs. Further, the school's code of conduct should clearly state that suspension and/or expulsion may be the consequence for certain misconduct.
- In circumstances where a suspension is not mandatory or required by school board policy, alternatives to formal school suspensions should be considered. For example, upon written request of the parent or guardian, a student may be temporarily excused from attendance at school by the principal.[33] In this regard, a parent may agree to keep the student home for a day or temporary period. This step should be used with caution in circumstances which warrant this type of response. Another alternative to suspension might be service to the school or the community.
- School administration should encourage and support early intervention strategies, such as conflict resolution, peer mediation, peacemakers and student crime stoppers, programs which demonstrate a proactive approach to preventing incidents of misconduct. Such programs will lead to improved communication skills, increased self-confidence and students taking responsibility for their own actions.
- Where there may be early warning signs of discipline problems or anti-social behaviour, a school official should contact the parents and discuss an appropriate course of action. The school administrator should consider possible resources, such as counselling, mentoring or peer assistance.
- Where appropriate, the school administration should exercise prudence before moving to a formal suspension. Factors to consider are the tone of the classroom, the need for a "cooling off" period and the effect the suspension will have on other students.[34]

---

[33] Regulation 298, s. 23(3).
[34] Roher, *op. cit.*, footnote 20, at p. 6.

SUMMARY OF PROCEDURE UNDER SAFE SCHOOLS ACT, 2000[35]

Suspensions

Mandatory Suspensions	Discretionary Suspensions
Behaviour violations: 1. Uttering a threat to inflict serious bodily harm on another person. 2. Possessing alcohol or illegal drugs. 3. Being under the influence of alcohol. 4. Swearing at a teacher or at another person in a position of authority. 5. Committing an act of vandalism that causes extensive damage to school property at the pupil's school or to property located on the premises of the pupil's school. 6. Engaging in another activity that, under a policy of the board, is one for which a suspension is mandatory.	Suspension in accordance with board policy from: 1. School and school-related activities. 2. One or more classes or one or more school-related activities.
• Teacher shall suspend the pupil (max. 1 day) or refer the matter to the principal with a possible recommendation for an extension of the suspension (max. 20 days). • Principal shall suspend the pupil unless the teacher has already suspended the pupil. • Principal shall consider factors that affect the duration of the suspension.	• Teacher may suspend the pupil (max. 1 day) or refer the matter to the principal for extension of the suspension (max. 20 days). • Principal may suspend the pupil (max. 20 days). • Principal shall consider factors that affect the duration of the suspension.

⇩ ⇩

Suspension Review

- At request of parent, adult student or other person specified by board policy.
- Conducted by person specified by board policy.
- The person specified by board policy to conduct the review has the powers and duties established by the board.

⇩ ⇩

Suspension Appeal

- At request of parent, adult student or other person specified by board policy.
- The board shall hear and determine an appeal and, for that purpose, the board has the powers and duties set out in its policy. The decisions of the board are final.
- The board may delegate its powers and duties to a committee of the board, and may impose conditions and restrictions on the committee.

---

[35] Handout prepared by W. Freel for the Toronto District School Board (Toronto: July, 2000). Reproduced with permission.

Expulsions

Mandatory Expulsions	Discretionary Expulsions
1. Possessing a weapon, including a firearm. 2. Using a weapon to cause or to threaten bodily harm to another person. 3. Committing physical assault on another person that causes bodily harm requiring treatment by a medical practitioner. 4. Committing sexual assault. 5. Trafficking in weapons or in illegal drugs. 6. Committing robbery. 7. Giving alcohol to a minor. 8. Engaging in another activity that, under a policy of the board, is one for which expulsion is mandatory.	A pupil may be expelled if the pupil engages in an activity that, under a policy of the board, is one for which expulsion is discretionary.
The principal shall suspend the pupil who the principal believes may have committed an infraction for which expulsion is mandatory unless mitigating factors exist as prescribed by regulation.	The principal may suspend the pupil if the principal believes that the pupil may have engaged in an activity for which expulsion is discretionary.

⇩   ⇩

The principal shall:
- Promptly notify the parent/guardian or the adult pupil.
- Conduct an inquiry in accordance with board policy or refer the matter to the board for a hearing.

⇩   ⇩

If, after the inquiry, the principal is satisfied that the pupil committed an infraction for which expulsion is mandatory or discretionary the principal shall:
- Impose a limited expulsion to a date specified by the principal (not to exceed 1 year from the date on which the principal suspended the pupil) or,
- Refer the matter to the board.

Note: The principal cannot expel a pupil if more than 20 school days have expired since the principal suspended the pupil unless the parties to the inquiry agree upon a later deadline.

⇩   ⇩

Expulsion Hearing
If, after the hearing, the board is satisfied that the pupil committed an infraction for which expulsion is either mandatory or discretionary, the board shall impose: • a limited expulsion to the later of either the date specified by the board (not to exceed 1 year from the date upon which the principal suspended the pupil) or the date on which the pupil meets such requirements as may be established by the board for returning to school, or • a full expulsion where the pupil is not entitled to attend any school in the province or to engage in school-related activities of any school in the province until he or she meets such requirements as may be established by regulation for returning to school. **Note:** The board cannot expel a pupil if more than 20 school days have expired since the principal suspended the pupil unless the parties to the hearing agree upon a later deadline.

⇩ ⇩

Expulsion Appeals	
• By parent, guardian, adult pupil or other persons as specified by board policy.	
Board Expulsion Appeals	**Principal Expulsion Appeals**
• A person or entity designated by regulation shall hear and determine an expulsion appeal. • The designated person or entity has the powers and duties set out in the regulations. • The decisions of the person or entity are final.	• The board shall exercise the powers and duties set out in its policy in hearing an appeal, or • The board may delegate its powers and duties for hearing an appeal to a committee of the board. • The board may impose conditions and restrictions on the delegated committee. • The decisions of the board are final.

10
Safe Schools

INTRODUCTION

The safety of Canadian schools is critically important to school principals and other school officials. In recent years, acts of violence in schools in various parts of North America have caused educators and politicians to take a closer look at anti-social behaviour in their own communities and school systems, and what is being done to prevent such behaviour. Violence, the use of weapons, intimidation and other threats to personal safety in a school setting are not new, but the severe consequences of violent incidents involving Canadian youth, often receiving widespread coverage in the media, have led to increased concerns for the safety of students and other members of the school community.

According to recent analysis, the rate of youth being charged in criminal incidents in Canada has been falling steadily. For example, between 1995 and 1999, the number of youths charged with *Criminal Code* offences dropped from 120,663 in 1995 to 99,746 in 1999.[1] However, trends such as an increase in the number of "level one" assaults (in which no weapon was used and no physical injury was sustained), greater levels of violence involving females aged 12 to 17 and increased gang activity among youth have created a sense of urgency in some Canadian communities. As a result, revisions have recently been made to the Ontario *Education Act*[2] and education policies dedicated to promoting safety in Canadian schools.

Over the course of the last 10 to 15 years, most school boards and schools have developed codes of conduct for schools, as well as policies and guidelines for dealing with serious incidents of anti-social behaviour, violence and/or threats of violence. Today, school staff are generally familiar with their board's policies regarding violent incidents. The goal of this chapter is to outline recently developed strategies for the prevention of violence and practical guidelines to properly respond to serious incidents. In addition, the chapter will review some

---

[1] Statistics Canada, "Youths and adults charged in criminal incidents, Criminal Code and federal statutes, by sex", online: http://www.statcan.ca/english/Pgdb/State/Justice/legal14.htm.
[2] R.S.O. 1990, c. E.2.

recent legislative changes which will affect how violent incidents are dealt with in a school setting.

At the outset, it is important to recognize that violence among youth is a community issue and not merely one involving schools. In November, 1999, the Task Force on Youth Violent Crime was formed in Toronto, shortly after the swarming and beating death of a 15-year-old student in a city park. An excerpt from the Executive Summary of the Task Force's Final Report indicates that the elements of youth violence reach far beyond school premises:

> The Task Force was directed to develop a strategy regarding swarmings. Members of the Task Force quickly realized that the problem of violence amongst youth was not simply an issue of school violence. Youth violence had its roots in the community in general; schools only provided a gathering place where violence could occur. The reality of youth violence was that it occurred throughout the community – in parks, shopping malls, subway stations, schools. With this viewpoint in mind the Task Force began its work of examining youth crime in general and youth violence in particular.[3]

Clearly, some school violence may be prevented through actions taken at the school level alone. However, prevailing strategies for addressing violence in schools involve the community at large.

It is recognized that students, staff and other community members have a right to a school environment which is safe and positive. Co-operation is expected between principals, teachers, staff, students, parents and guardians, police, emergency services personnel and social service agencies in order to develop strategies for preventing violence and responding to violent incidents.

Among other duties, the role of the principal is to maintain, in accordance with the requirements of relevant legislation and school board policies, a safe, orderly learning and working environment for students, staff and others on school property. As part of that role, the principal:

- acts *in loco parentis* to the students of the school;
- implements safe school and violence prevention policies and procedures; and
- communicates awareness of policies and procedures to staff, students, parents and school communities.[4]

WHAT IS VIOLENCE?

Violence encompasses much more than incidents involving physical contact or an assault. Violence can include any act which results in the victimization of a particular person or persons, irrespective of any physical contact. Violence, in a school context, has been defined as "anything that jeopardizes the climate for an

---

[3] Task Force on Youth Violent Crime, "Final Report" (Toronto: 2000), at p. 1.
[4] Toronto Police Service, Toronto District School Board and Toronto Catholic District School Board, "Police/School Protocol" (Toronto: June, 2000).

effective learning and working environment".[5] In the school setting, examples of violence may include:

- abusive language;
- taunting;
- intimidation;
- disruptive or aggressive behaviour in class;
- assaults;
- carrying and use of weapons;
- possession of illicit drugs;
- robbery;
- extortion;
- vandalism damaging school property;
- emotional and verbal abuse; and
- harassment.[6]

As a result, an understanding and awareness of violence in school communities should be broadly based. Students who find themselves being bullied, harassed or subject to acts of extortion are possible victims of violence. Also, in reviewing safe school strategies, it should be remembered that the perpetrators and victims of violence not only include students, but can include parents, teachers, staff, volunteers and visitors.

Identification of Threats to Safe Schools

Recent high-profile violent incidents involving youth, both on and off school premises, have resulted in an increased awareness of the warning signs of violence. School personnel and others who work with young people have sought information regarding the characteristics of potential victims of violence and the warning signs of people who may act out violently. As relevant research is communicated to members of the school community, educators will be in a better position to take preventative steps which may avoid incidents of violence.

For example, the Task Force on Youth Violent Crime was established in Toronto to provide statistics related to swarmings in that city. The Task Force defined swarmings as "any crime involving three or more suspects".[7] Its report reveals an association between student activities during and after school and occurrences of youth crime. The Task Force indicated that: assaults and robberies represent the greatest proportion of crime types; males were four times more likely than females to be the victim of a swarming; offender profiling for swarmings was

---

[5] E.M. Roher, *An Educator's Guide to Violence in Schools* (Aurora: Aurora Professional Press, 1997), at p. 1, citing S. Auty et al., "Violence in the Schools: A Dialogue on the Nature and Extent of the Problem" (Guest Speaker: S. Duggan), in W.G. West, ed., *ORBIT – Schooling in Violence*, Vol. 24, No. 1 (Toronto: Ontario Institute for Studies in Education, March, 1993).

[6] Roher, *ibid.*, at p. 1.

[7] Task Force on Youth Violent Crime, *op. cit.*, footnote 3, at pp. 4-5.

highest in the 15 to 17 age group; victimization for males was highest in 10-year-olds to 15-year-olds and for females in 10-year-olds to 13-year-olds; peak times for swarmings were from 12:00 p.m. to 1:00 p.m. and from 3:00 p.m. to 4:00 p.m.; and peak days were Fridays, Mondays and Thursdays.[8]

Following the shooting deaths of 12 students and one teacher at Columbine High School in Littleton, Colorado, in 1998, the National School Safety Center in the United States issued a list of characteristics that teachers and parents should watch for in students. While this list was distributed in the aftermath of a severe act of violence in a school setting, the characteristics it sets out are useful identifiers of students who may feel alienated and require support, even though they may not be capable of extreme violence. These include a student who:

- characteristically resorts to name-calling, cursing or abusive language;
- habitually makes violent threats when angry;
- has previously brought a weapon to school;
- has a background of serious disciplinary problems;
- has a background of drug, alcohol or other substance abuse or dependency;
- displays cruelty to animals;
- has witnessed or been a victim of neglect or abuse in the home;
- bullies or intimidates peers or younger children;
- tends to blame others for difficulties and problems;
- consistently prefers television shows, reading materials, movies or music expressing violent themes, rituals and abuse;
- reflects anger, frustration and the dark side of life in school writing projects;
- is involved with a gang or anti-social group on the fringe of peer acceptance;
- is often depressed and has significant mood swings;
- has threatened or attempted suicide; and
- has tantrums and uncontrollable angry outbursts.

YOUTH GANGS

They call themselves Looney Toons, Boys in Blue, Trife Kids, Vice Lords, the Tuxedo Boys and Mother Nature's Mistake. A recent article in *The Toronto Star* reported that there are more than 180 youth gangs carving out territories in the Greater Toronto Area.[9]

Not all of these youth are dangerous, some young people just band together, think up a name and try to act tough. But they are learning the art of power and

---

[8] *Ibid.*, at p. 5.
[9] M. Sheppard, "Teen gangs, Fear in our schools", *The Toronto Star* (October 24, 1998), p. A1.

intimidation and, in many cases, using it in our schools. There are at least 30 gangs in the Toronto area known by the police to carry firearms.[10]

Toronto police are being trained to look out for ritually branded members of two rival gangs, the Bloods and the Crips, which may be gaining a foothold in schools.[11] Several drug and weapons suspects arrested recently have worn the trademark red and black colours of the Bloods and the blue colours of the Crips, prompting fears that the gangs' presence in Ontario may be increasing. However, youth gangs are not just a Toronto phenomenon; police report that youth gangs are taking root in towns and cities across Canada.

It should also be noted that girls are the fastest growing group of violent offenders in the country. They constitute about 25% of the arrests in their age group, which is a significant increase over adult women, who are arrested for about 10% of adult violent crime.[12] Statistics Canada reports that in the past decade the rate of females aged 12 to 17 who were charged for violent offences in Canada increased by 179%. Police indicate that young females are increasingly involved in gang violence, accounting for 15% of all charges related to illegal gang activities. They are reportedly capable of being more violent than males.

The phenomenon of youth gangs is not limited to particular social, ethnic or class groups, but encompasses all socio-economic levels in Canadian society. According to police, school officials and social workers, some members of youth gangs in Ontario come from middle-class homes and become involved in gangs out of boredom and a desire for excitement.[13]

The Toronto District School Board, in a publication on recent trends and patterns of youth gang violence, reports that youth who join gangs do so in order to meet needs which are not being met by family, schools or community:

> The need for power and control, respect, enhanced popularity, protection and "wanting to belong", along with loss of faith in adults, especially their caregivers that are supposed to be their supports, are just a few of many reasons young people turn to gangs.[14]

The lure to join gangs is especially irresistible for younger, vulnerable, socially isolated youth whose need for protection and acceptance may be higher than for the average student.

To date, police do not have a clear picture of the problem of youth gang violence. They attribute this to low reporting statistics. In general, students are reluctant to come forward to report incidents of assault or intimidation due to fears

---

[10] *Ibid.*

[11] M. Sheppard, "Bloods and Crips: Gang ties spreading", *The Toronto Star* (October 26, 1998), p. B1.

[12] E. Roher, "Girls growing more violent, aggressive", *The Toronto Star* (April 7, 1998).

[13] Toronto District School Board – Safe Schools Advisory Committee, "Backgrounder: Recent Trends and Patterns of Youth Gang Violence" (Toronto: February 23, 2000), at p. 1.

[14] *Ibid.*, at p. 1.

of reprisal or retaliation. Students are also afraid of being stigmatized as "victims" and fear that, if they do file reports, no action will be taken.[15]

Prevention

There are a number of ways to discourage youth from joining gangs. The Toronto District School Board advises that educators should focus on "de-glamourizing" gangs and warning young people about the dangers and personal consequences associated with gang involvement.[16] Many school boards have developed programs to encourage students to report incidents of violence, to train staff to identify gang presence in the school and to keep the premises clean and well-maintained. The focus should be on empowering students and creating a culture in our schools that anti-social behaviour will not be tolerated.

It is advised that schools identify and intervene with isolated, vulnerable and at-risk youth. These individuals need to feel that they belong in their respective schools and that they are important and supported.

Parents, schools and community service organizations should find ways to assist young people to experience success and develop self-esteem. This could include a range of activities, such as after-school and evening sports programs, part-time employment, mentoring, skills development and community-focused work projects.[17]

Researchers have indicated that community protection from youth gangs must be balanced with proactive programs aimed at prevention. For example, early intervention strategies, such as conflict resolution, peer mediation, peacemaker programs and drama troupes which discuss anger management, demonstrate a proactive approach in attempting to prevent incidents of violence. It is also advised that training in the use of skills for non-violent conflict resolution become part of the curriculum for all children, particularly in the early and primary years.[18] Such training can provide children with alternative ways to express anger and help them defuse or avoid volatile situations.

What Can be Done?

Policies, programs and initiatives which may be taken to respond to the issue of violence in schools include the following:

- Educators could initiate programs to teach students about different cultures, races and lifestyles in an effort to increase acceptance and sensitivity towards others.
- School boards could develop special alternative programs for at-risk youth.

---

[15] *Ibid.*
[16] *Ibid.*, at p. 2.
[17] *Ibid.*
[18] Roher, *op. cit.*, footnote 5, at p. 211.

Safe Schools 199

- Educators should encourage greater parental involvement in young people's lives and the avoidance of harsh and inconsistent disciplinary practices.
- School boards could establish restorative justice programs for students who offend and wish to make amends to the people whom they have offended.
- Educators could work together with their community partners to provide social and recreational opportunities to attract youth into organized activities designed to teach social and interpersonal skills.
- School boards could utilize community outreach workers to provide liaison and intervention strategies with specific racial or ethnic communities.
- School boards could develop anti-violence programs, which may include an in-service program for teachers on how to respond to aggressive or violent students.[19]

Warning Signs of Gang Activity

Gang activity in a school is a common and serious threat to school safety. A general awareness of the signs of gang membership and the characteristics of persons vulnerable to gang recruitment should be fostered among all members of the school community. Gangs generally attract students who are not fitting into their surroundings. Some early warning signs of gangs in your school include the following:

- It can begin as early as elementary school, even for students seven to eight years of age.
- Students adopt a defiant attitude towards authority figures and can be disrespectful towards teachers.
- Students wear gang clothing or colours.
- Students use hand signals to communicate with other gang members.
- At school, the student will let everyone know of his or her new status.
- Students may fight to gain a reputations for being "bad".
- A student may have large sums of money or expensive items which cannot be explained.
- A student's grades may decline and truancy may increase.
- A student's friends may change.
- A student may experience increased alcohol or drug use.
- A student may begin to keep late hours.[20]

---

[19] Toronto District School Board – Safe Schools Advisory Committee, *op. cit.*, footnote 13, at p. 3.
[20] See "Gangs, Draw the Line: Gang Information Resource Guide for Parents & Teachers" (information compiled by R. Brock, Vice-Principal of Curtis Senior High, 1995), online: http://www.upsd.wednet.edu/UPSE/CHS/ganghand.html; "Parent Resource Guide" (S. Nawojczyk, 1997), online: http://www.gangwar.com/parent1.htm.

CLUB DRUGS

Rave and trance scenes have emerged lately in increasing numbers across the country, attracting teens and young adults from all walks of life. These events are night-long dances usually held in warehouses, abandoned buildings or after-hours nightclubs. Attendance may range from less than one hundred to several thousand. Raves are characterized by loud, fast-paced "techno" music, light shows and fog machines.[21] For some, club drugs are an integral part of the rave scene.

The Globe and Mail recently reported that the use of club drugs among Ontario students has jumped eightfold since 1993, and the use of hallucinogens has now matched or surpassed the levels of the 1970s.[22] Almost 5% of students in grades 7 to 13 report that they have used the drugs in the previous year. One in five adolescents say that over the past year they have been to a rave, where the use of ecstasy is fashionable. Recent research also indicates that 13.6% of junior-high and high-school students use the hallucinogenic drugs mescaline or psilocybin (magic mushrooms), up from 3.1% in 1993.[23] Increased drug use in general is reportedly related to: (i) decreased perception of risk; (ii) decreased moral disapproval; and (iii) increased availability.

The use of synthetic drugs has become a popular method of enhancing the club and rave experience. Users of drugs such as ecstasy, MDMA, rohypnol, GHB and ketamine report that the drugs heighten the user's perceptions, especially visual stimulation.[24]

These drugs are easily accessible, relatively inexpensive and provide an apparent increase in stamina and intensification of the trance-like experience. Club drugs have dramatically increased in popularity as many who are experimenting are under the false perception that these drugs are less harmful and less addictive than so-called mainstream hard drugs.

Rohypnol, GHB and ketamine are colourless, tasteless and odourless and may be slipped into beverages and ingested unknowingly. These "date rape" drugs act mainly as nervous system depressants and may be used to inhibit the victim's ability to resist sexual assault. Effects of the drugs, especially if mixed with alcohol or other depressants, include nausea, difficulty breathing, coma, increased risk of seizure and possibly death.

MDMA or "Adam", "ecstasy", "E" or "XTC", as they are known on the street, are psychoactive synthetics with hallucinogenic and amphetamine-like effects. Club scene users take the drugs to enable them to go long hours without the need to eat, drink or sleep. Psychological effects include confusion, severe anxiety and paranoia. Damage to critical areas of the brain involved in thought, memory and

---

[21] Drug Enforcement Administration, U.S. Department of Justice, "Drug Intelligence Brief" (February, 2000), at p. 10.

[22] A. Picard, "Huge Jump Reported in Use of Ecstasy by Ontario Students", *The Globe and Mail* (June 13, 2000), p. A6.

[23] *Ibid.*

[24] Drug Enforcement Administration, *op. cit.*, footnote 21, at p. 10.

pleasure has also been linked to the use of ecstasy. Physical effects of MDMA range from muscle tension, nausea and faintness to severe dehydration, increased heart rate and blood pressure, and severe hypothermia. Recent reports of ecstasy-related deaths showed body temperatures of users ranging from 107 to 109 degrees Fahrenheit.[25]

It is important that schools focus their efforts on education programs to inform students of the significant dangers in this type of drug activity. Schools should consider organizing assemblies or in-school presentations with guest speakers, such as former drug users, medical experts or police officers, to outline the serious risks involved with drug use. Examples of such programs include: encouraging students to report the trafficking of drugs; expanding student leadership; training staff to identify students who may be selling or using drugs; and empowering students to initiate a "say no to drugs" campaign.

POLICE INVESTIGATIONS ON SCHOOL PREMISES

As indicated earlier in this chapter, students, staff and other community members have a right to a school environment which is safe and positive. All serious incidents of anti-social behaviour, violence and/or threats of violence with a connection to the school should be reported to the police and should be investigated by the police promptly and thoroughly.[26]

It is the role of the police to prevent and solve problems related to both the safety and well-being of persons and the protection of property. This includes intervening in crises or emergencies and conducting investigations relating to alleged breaches of federal or provincial statutes.[27]

In a school context, this involves sharing with school boards and their employees the responsibilities for preserving the peace and preventing crime. As a result, it is essential that principals and local law enforcement agencies co-operate in their efforts. An agreement to co-operate in these instances, in the form of a protocol of procedures in the event that a police presence is required on school premises, may be of great assistance. Agreeing in advance on the steps each party should take to investigate an incident will foster a positive relationship between police and the school, and will assist in avoiding difficult delays and misunderstandings in a crisis. A police protocol should review the steps in a police investigation which may involve the school, from police conduct on entering a school, to interviewing students, to the ensuing judicial proceeding.

In June, 2000, the Toronto Police Service, Toronto District School Board and the Toronto Catholic District School Board entered into a "Police/School

---

[25] *Ibid.*, at p. 2.
[26] Toronto Police Service, Toronto District School Board and Toronto Catholic District School Board, *op. cit.*, footnote 4, at p. 2.
[27] *Ibid.*, at p. 3.

Protocol".[28] The protocol was designed, among other things, to encourage, enable and maintain a positive relationship between police officers, school administrators, staff, students, parents and members of the school community, and to establish guidelines for these various relationships.[29]

Under the terms of the protocol, when conducting an investigation, the police will make every effort to minimize disruption to school routines. Except in emergency situations, the police, upon entering a school, are expected to identify themselves to the main school office. This will allow the principal (or appropriate vice-principal) to greet the officer and facilitate the process.[30]

It is recognized that the norm is for interviews by the police to be conducted outside of the school. The protocol confirms that, in certain circumstances, it may be necessary to conduct police interviews on school premises during school hours. In such cases, interviews will be conducted in such a manner as to minimize disruption to school routines.

The protocol provides that, in cases where the police wish to interview, whether as a suspect or a witness, a student who is under the age of 18 years, on school premises during school hours, the principal, in fulfilling his or her *in loco parentis* role, will contact the student's parents or guardians promptly, unless prevented by urgent circumstances, to advise of the request for the interview and to invite the parents or guardians to be present. Where the principal is unable to contact a parent or guardian, the principal will record his or her attempts to make such contact.[31] Exceptions to this rule arise where the police have determined that the best interests of the student (*i.e.*, where the student is at personal risk) require that an interview take place without the prior knowledge and in the absence of the parents or guardians.

Under the terms of the protocol, the young person may consult with legal counsel or a parent or any other appropriate adult. In some cases, the young person may prefer to have a teacher or a principal present during a police interview or when making a statement. In any such case, the police will make all reasonable efforts to accommodate these rights of the student.[32]

With respect to arrest and restraint, the protocol provides that, whether or not the incident giving rise to the necessity to arrest is school-related, the police shall, in the interests of school safety and morale, consult with the principal and consider alternatives, to the extent possible, and effect the arrest at a location other than the school.[33]

---

[28] *Ibid.*, at p. 1.
[29] *Ibid.*
[30] *Ibid.*, at pp. 4-5.
[31] *Ibid.*, at p. 5.
[32] *Ibid.*, at p. 6.
[33] *Ibid.*, at pp. 6-7.

Investigations of Serious Incidents

The principal is responsible for conducting an investigation of a serious incident independent of the police. In appropriate circumstances, he or she is responsible for taking disciplinary action under the provisions of the *Education Act*. In undertaking an investigation, a principal should consider the following guidelines:

- Place each suspect, victim or witness in a separate room under supervision.
- Protect the scene as much as possible.
- Collect and secure any evidence which must be moved and retain custody until the evidence is turned over to the police or is no longer required.
- Have a staff member accompany any student or staff requiring medical treatment to the hospital.
- Obtain the name, address, telephone number or any other method of contact from a witness unable to remain at the scene.
- Notify the students' parents or guardians or the family of staff members.
- Have the witness and victim provide written statements independently.[34]

As always, documentation of serious incidents is vital. A principal may be required to give evidence at a suspension appeal, expulsion hearing or in a court of law. With the passage of time, immediate recall of the details of events becomes progressively more difficult. Details should be recorded as contemporaneously as possible with the events themselves. The notes should be kept in a file and should include dates, times, names of witnesses interviewed, any relevant observations and a summary of the action taken by school administration. Also, for violent incidents, a violent incident report should be completed as soon as possible.

Judicial Proceedings Affecting Schools

In prosecutions of students under the *Young Offenders Act*[35] and the *Criminal Code*,[36] courts may impose obligations upon the accused students which also affect the schools themselves. For example, a bail or probation order may require the student to attend school or prohibit the student from returning to school, or require that the student not come closer than some minimal distance from the alleged victim. At the same time as the court action is proceeding, the school may be in the process of suspending or expelling the student pursuant to the provisions of the *Education Act*.[37]

Unfortunately, courts may neglect to recognize this type of conflict and that the school may not be in a position to honour the obligation which has been imposed.

---

[34] Toronto District School Board, "Information Sheet: Investigations of Serious Incidents" (Toronto: February 23, 2000).
[35] R.S.C. 1985, c. Y-1.
[36] R.S.C. 1985, c. C-46.
[37] Toronto Police Service, Toronto District School Board and Toronto Catholic District School Board, *op. cit.*, footnote 4, at p. 10.

Even if the school had the lawful authority and the facilities to observe the condition, often there is no means available to advise a school of any such restriction or obligation.

In this regard, when charges are laid against a student, the police officers involved in the case should consult with school administrators before recommending release and/or probation conditions. Correspondingly, school administrators are encouraged to initiate discussions with the police regarding such conditions. In addition, police officers should alert the school and attempt to assist the school in its efforts to accommodate the bail or probation order while at the same time continuing to comply with its obligations under the *Education Act*.[38]

SEARCH AND SEIZURE IN SCHOOLS

From time to time, proper investigation of an incident at school may involve a search of a student or the student's property. A teacher may have reason to suspect that a student is carrying a concealed weapon. A student questioned with regard to a fight may blurt out that one of the antagonists sells drugs and keeps some in his locker. A student may report that her Walkman has been stolen and indicate that she believes it was taken by another student and may be found in his knapsack. What is the proper procedure to follow in circumstances such as these?

Section 8 of the *Canadian Charter of Rights and Freedoms* provides that: "Everyone has the right to be secure against unreasonable search or seizure." Also, section 10(b) of the Charter provides that everyone has the right on arrest or detention to retain and instruct legal counsel without delay and to be informed of that right.

In applying these provisions in a school context, Canadian courts have held that, in carrying out the duty to maintain order and discipline in the school, the principal may search a student. However, the courts have ruled that the school authority must have "reasonable grounds" to believe that there has been a breach of school regulations and that a search of a student would reveal evidence of that breach.

The courts have held that a warrant is not essential in order for a school authority to conduct a search of a student. The courts have recognized that school authorities are in the best position to assess information given to them and relate it to the situation existing in their school.

Random or arbitrary searches, or searches based on groundless suspicion, will likely be in contravention of the Charter. Even when investigating an incident on school premises, if it becomes apparent that a criminal offence may have been committed, the police should be contacted to conduct the search.

Generally, school searches can be divided into three categories, each with its own conditions and guidelines:

---

[38] *Ibid.*

- the personal search of an individual;
- the search of a locker or a desk search; and
- the sweep or dragnet search.

A personal search was the subject of a leading case on the educator's rights and responsibilities when investigating students. The case of *R. v. M. (M.R.)*,[39] decided in 1998, marked the first time that the Supreme Court of Canada had directly considered the scope of a student's constitutional right, within a school context, to be free from unreasonable search and, conversely, the school's interest in searching students.

The case arose out of the search of a 13-year-old student by a junior high school vice-principal in Nova Scotia. The search at issue in *R. v. M. (M.R.)* occurred during a school dance. The vice-principal was not only responsible for supervision at the dance, but was also responsible for enforcing school policies. The school had a policy that any student found in possession of drugs or alcohol would be suspended from school. The school policy also required the vice-principal to contact the Royal Canadian Mounted Police (the "RCMP") should he conclude that a criminal matter was involved.

The vice-principal had been told by several students that M.R.M. was selling drugs on school property. The vice-principal considered this information reliable because the student informants knew M.R.M. well and had previously given reliable information. On the day of the dance, the vice-principal had been told by one of the student informants that M.R.M. would be carrying drugs that evening.

When M.R.M. arrived, the vice-principal contacted the RCMP. The vice-principal approached M.R.M. and his friend and requested that they accompany him to his office. Once there, the vice-principal asked them if they had any illegal drugs in their possession and advised them that he was going to have to search them. The RCMP constable arrived and identified himself to the students. Although he remained for the interview, the constable did not say anything while the vice-principal spoke to the students.

At the request of the vice-principal, M.R.M. turned out his pockets and pulled up his pant leg. The vice-principal removed a bag of marijuana from the student's sock. He gave the bag to the RCMP constable who identified its contents as marijuana. The constable advised the student that he was under arrest for possession of a narcotic. The student was also advised of his right to counsel and his right to contact a parent.

At trial, counsel for the student argued that, because the search was conducted without a warrant and in the presence of the police, the search was unreasonable and the evidence should have been excluded from use against the student. Alternatively, counsel argued that the student had been detained and therefore had the right to consult a lawyer prior to giving any statement or submitting to any search.

---

[39] (1998), 129 C.C.C. (3d) 361, 166 D.L.R. (4th) 261 (S.C.C.), affg 7 C.R. (5th) 1, 159 N.S.R. (2d) 321 (C.A.).

The trial judge concluded that the evidence had been gathered in contravention of the student's Charter right to be free from unreasonable search and seizure. The trial judge found that the vice-principal was effectively acting as an agent of the police in conducting a criminal investigation. As the Crown had no other evidence on which to support a conviction, the possession charge against the student was dismissed. The Nova Scotia Court of Appeal overturned the ruling of the trial judge and the student brought a further appeal to the Supreme Court of Canada.

In determining when and in what circumstances a search by a school official should be considered unreasonable and therefore in violation of the student's rights under the Charter, Mr. Justice Cory, writing for the majority of the court, emphasized that the duties and obligations entrusted to schools are unique and important. At the same time, Mr. Justice Cory recognized that these duties and obligations cannot be separated from the practical responsibilities and challenges of running a school. The court affirmed that, in light of the contemporary challenges faced by school officials in teaching and caring for students, school officials must be provided with flexibility in addressing discipline problems. This flexibility, in the court's view, includes a broad right to search a student where that student is reasonably suspected of being in possession of a prohibited weapon or an illicit drug.

In asserting this right, the Supreme Court of Canada laid out some general principles:

(1) A warrant is not essential in order to conduct a search of a student by a school authority.

(2) The school authority must have reasonable grounds to believe that there has been a breach of school regulations or discipline and that a search of a student would reveal evidence of that breach.

(3) School authorities will be in the best position to assess information given to them and relate it to the situation existing in their school. Courts should recognize the preferred position of school authorities to determine if reasonable grounds existed for the search.

(4) The following may constitute reasonable grounds in this context: information received from one student considered to be credible, information received from more than one student, a teacher's or principal's own observations, or any combination of these pieces of information which the relevant authority considers to be credible. The compelling nature of the information and the credibility of these or other sources must be assessed by the school authority in the context of the circumstances existing at the particular school.[40]

The following would not likely provide an adequate foundation for "reasonable grounds" to believe:

- rumours, innuendoes or hunches;
- anonymous tips which are not corroborated in any way; or
- information which could not reasonably be considered to be credible.

---

[40] *Supra*, at pp. 384-5.

In *R. v. M. (M.R.)*, the vice-principal had received information from several students indicating that M.R.M. possessed marijuana and was trafficking it on the school grounds. He thought the information was reliable because the students knew M.R.M. well. One of the students had given him accurate information on a previous occasion. Mr. Justice Cory therefore concluded that the vice-principal had reasonable grounds to believe that M.R.M. was in breach of school rules.

Factors to Consider

Educators assessing whether to undertake a personal search of a student should consider the following:

- All serious incidents of anti-social behaviour, violence or threats of violence with a connection to a school should be reported to the police. Where there is a need to search a student personally and school authorities are not comfortable with conducting such a search, school authorities should contact the police.[41]
- Only principals or their designates should be permitted to conduct a search or to seize prohibited objects or substances, unless there is an immediate threat to the safety of a person or persons or the school premises.
- A search should only be conducted when there are reasonable grounds to believe that a student or visitor is in possession of an object or substance which is prohibited by school policies or regulations.
- Principals and their designates should exercise reason and judgment in determining the scope of any search. Searches should be conducted in a sensitive manner and be minimally intrusive. Due consideration should be given to the age and gender of the student and the gravity of the infraction.[42]
- All searches should be conducted in the presence of at least one adult witness. To be prudent, searches of a student's locker, desk or knapsack should be conducted in the presence of the relevant student.
- All personal searches of a student should be conducted in the privacy of the principal's office or another suitable room designated by the principal. Where the need for a personal search is indicated, the individual involved should be given the opportunity to produce the substance or object which he or she is suspected of possessing. School authorities are advised not to undertake a cross-gender search.
- When a search is conducted, a record of all pertinent information should be made. Information to be documented includes details of allegations, the names of relevant parties and possible witnesses, the time of the relevant incidents, the time and place of the investigation, the parties interviewed, the efforts made to

---

[41] R.A. Robertson, "Search and Seizure in a School Setting", in W.F. Foster and W.J. Smith, eds., *Focusing on the Future: Seeking Legal and Policy Solutions in Education* (Georgetown: Canadian Association for the Practical Study of Law in Education, 2000).

[42] R. Scott, "Search and Seizure in a School Setting: A Practical Legal Analysis" (paper presented at the Canadian Association for the Practical Study of Law in Education Conference, "Bridging the Millennium", Charlottetown, April, 2000).

contact parents, the discussions held to date, and the details of police involvement, if any. The principal should retain one copy of this documentation on file and should file a second copy with the appropriate supervisory officer. Access to, and disclosure of, such information is subject to the municipal freedom of information and protection of privacy legislation.

- When police are called in to an investigation involving a student, the police/school protocol should be followed. Except in emergency situations, police, upon entering a school, are expected to identify themselves to the main office. During a police investigation at school, it is primarily the responsibility of the police to explain to a young person his or her rights in a manner which enables him or her to understand them.
- In appropriate circumstances, where a prohibited substance or object is discovered as a result of a search, the principal or his or her designate should promptly contact the parents or guardians of a student under 18 years of age who is the subject of the investigation. The principal or his or her designate should maintain a record of the attempts made to contact the student's parents or guardians.
- Any prohibited substance or object discovered as the result of a search is to be confiscated and retained in a secure location. In all cases, a record should be kept of all seized substances or objects.

From time to time, searches of a student's locker may also be necessary. It is advised that a school board have appropriate policies or agreements with students which reduce a student's expectations of privacy in his or her locker. If the school "owns" the locker in question, it does not need anyone's permission to search it. To preserve the right to inspect lockers, even rented ones, without notice, schools should remind students when lockers are assigned, or on other occasions, that the lockers are school property, that the school will maintain a list of combinations or a master key, and that lockers will be inspected regularly. Students should also be notified that the school board reserves the right to remove locks, by force if necessary, to access a student's property where there are legitimate safety concerns.[43]

Policies and agreements should make it clear that the right to regulate access to lockers resides in the school board and its agents. The policy or contract should specify that the board could give any of its employees or agents access to the student's locker. Such policies should prohibit students from giving other students or third parties access to their lockers without the school's permission. If a school does not have such a policy or does not explicitly reserve the right to search lockers, it may still do so if it meets the legal test for any search. That is, the search is justified on reasonable grounds of suspicion and is reasonably related to the school official's duties.[44] In any case, when searching a locker, the student and another staff member should be present.

---

[43] *Ibid.*, at pp. 9-11; G. Dickinson, "Supreme Court Ruling Has Implications for School Locker Searches" (1995-96), 7 E.L.J. 279.

[44] Scott, *op. cit.*, footnote 42, at pp. 9-11.

Random searches are not likely to be reasonable in the eyes of a court. Unlike personal or locker searches which are aimed at a particular student or students, "dragnet" searches target a whole class or school. Under these circumstances, it is unlikely that a court would treat the search as reasonable, since it is intrusive and sweeping. Any evidence found in such a search may well be found inadmissible in court.[45]

DEALING WITH TRESPASSERS

Many acts of violence on school premises involve visitors or trespassers on the property, both as perpetrators and victims. Certain violent incidents could be avoided by removing such persons or preventing the entry of persons who might otherwise incite violence or become involved in anti-social behaviour on school premises. Persons presenting particular risks include members of gangs or students who have been suspended or expelled but have returned to school property.

It should be noted that schools are not public property. In Ontario, the right to use a school's facilities is determined by the *Education Act* and can also be permitted at the discretion of a school board for lawful purposes.[46] A person entering school property must have a valid and lawful reason for being there.[47]

Where a person does not have a lawful reason for being on school property and/or poses a threat to school safety, there are a number of ways for a school principal to protect the safety of others in the school. First, section 265(m) of the Ontario *Education Act* requires a school principal to refuse access to the school to certain persons:

> 265. It is the duty of a principal of a school, in addition to the principal's duties as a teacher,
>
> . . . . .
>
> (m) subject to an appeal to the board, to refuse to admit to the school or classroom a person whose presence in the school or classroom would in the principal's judgment be detrimental to the physical or mental well-being of the pupils;

This section provides the principal with a means to exclude persons who pose a risk to the safety of the school, including students properly in attendance at the school who are reasonably judged to be detrimental to the physical well-being of other students. However, such power should be used restrictively so as not to effectively suspend a student by other means.[48]

---

[45] Roher, *op. cit.*, footnote 5, at pp. 76-7.
[46] *Education Act*, s. 171, para. 24.
[47] Toronto District School Board – Safe Schools Advisory Committee, "Backgrounder: Trespass to Property Act" (Toronto: February 21, 2000).
[48] A.F. Brown and M.A. Zuker, *Education Law*, 2nd ed. (Toronto: Carswell, 1997), at pp. 42-3.

Provisions of the *Education Act* enacted by the *Safe Schools Act, 2000*[49] (Bill 81) permit a school principal to direct persons prohibited by regulation or board policy from being on school premises to leave such premises. Section 305(2) of the *Education Act* provides that no person shall enter or remain on school premises unless he or she is authorized by regulation to be there on that day or at that time. Under section 305(3), a person shall not enter or remain on school premises if he or she is prohibited under a board policy from being there. Section 305(5) provides that every person who contravenes subsection (2) is guilty of an offence.

On September 1, 2000, the regulation governing access to schools came into force.[50] Section 2(1) of the regulation expressly permits the following persons to be on school premises:

1. A person enrolled as a pupil in the school.
2. A parent or guardian of such a pupil.
3. A person employed or retained by the board.
4. A person who is otherwise on the premises for a lawful purpose.

As well, persons who are invited onto school premises for an event, a class or a meeting are permitted to be on school premises for that purpose as are other individuals invited by the principal, vice principal or another person authorized by the policy of a school board.[51]

The regulation makes it clear that persons who are permitted to be on school premises are not necessarily entitled to be on those premises. In other words, the regulation does not limit the ability of a principal to restrict access to the school even for individuals who are permitted by the regulation to be on school premises. Thus, the operation of the *Trespass to Property Act*[52] and a principal's authority to issue trespass notices pursuant to that statute are not encumbered by the regulation.

The regulation provides the principal with a parallel ability to limit access to the school premises. Section 3(1) of the regulation provides that a person is not permitted to remain on school premises if, in the judgment of the principal or vice-principal, his or her presence is detrimental to the safety or well-being of another person on the premises. Section 3(2) of the regulation also provides that a person is not permitted to remain on school premises if a school board policy requires that person to report his or her presence and the person fails to do so.

By virtue of the *Safe Schools Act, 2000*, no persons other than those set out in the regulation are permitted to enter or remain on school property. Every person who contravenes this provision is guilty of an offence and, pursuant to the *Provincial Offences Act*,[53] is subject to a fine of not more than $5,000.

As noted, the Ontario *Trespass to Property Act* also applies to school premises and permits a school principal to take action in order to meet his or her duty under the *Education Act*. School boards are expressly recognized as "occupiers" under

---

[49] S.O. 2000, c. 12.
[50] *Access to School Premises*, O. Reg. 474/00.
[51] O. Reg. 474/00, s. 2(2) and (3).
[52] R.S.O. 1990, c. T.21.
[53] R.S.O. 1990, c. P.33, s. 61.

the *Trespass to Property Act*, having all the rights and duties of an occupier with respect to school premises.[54] Therefore school principals, as representatives of the board, can exercise the rights of an occupier. Trespassing is an offence under the Act and can result in a fine of up to $2,000. Actions which constitute an offence under the *Trespass to Property Act* include:

- entering the premises when entry is prohibited under the Act (*i.e.*, when entry is prohibited by a notice to that effect or by a deemed prohibition under section 3);
- engaging in an activity on the premises when the activity is prohibited under the Act; and
- failing to leave the premises immediately after being directed to do so by the occupier of the premises or a person authorized by the occupier.[55]

Valid notice under the *Trespass to Property Act* can be given orally, in writing, by posted signs or by means of a marking system.[56] Where possible, it is preferable to provide written notice. Where a student is suspended or expelled, the student should be provided with written notice that he or she will be charged with trespassing if found on school property. Written notice can also be provided on a regular or annual basis to students who have become habitual trespassers.[57] This notice should indicate that the students will be charged with trespassing should they enter school property, and should refer to the *Trespass to Property Act* specifically. The letter should also be copied to the proper board official as well as the local police so that no confusion arises as to whether notice was provided to the student.[58]

Once it is established that a person is trespassing on school premises, the *Trespass to Property Act* permits an occupier of the premises, or a person authorized by the occupier, to arrest the person he or she believes on reasonable and probable grounds to be on the premises and committing the offence of trespass.[59] However, for the safety of the persons involved, and to avoid the acquittal of a trespasser due to an improper arrest, it is best to call the police to carry out the arrest. It should be noted that section 41 of the *Criminal Code* permits an occupier of premises to remove a trespasser provided that he or she uses no more force than is necessary.

In taking preventative steps to deal with trespassers on school property, principals should consider the following:

- Unknown visitors should be required to proceed to the main office and sign their name in a visitors' book.

---

[54] *Trespass to Property Act*, s. 1(2).
[55] *Trespass to Property Act*, s. 2(1). See also Roher, *op. cit.*, footnote 5, at p. 79.
[56] *Trespass to Property Act*, s. 5(1).
[57] Toronto District School Board – Safe Schools Advisory Committee, *op. cit.*, footnote 47.
[58] Roher, *op. cit.*, footnote 5, at pp. 80-81.
[59] *Trespass to Property Act*, s. 9(1).

- Unknown visitors should be required to produce proper identification upon request.
- The principal has a duty to refuse admission to anyone whose presence in the school or classroom would be detrimental to the physical or mental well-being of the pupils.
- A person identified as a trespasser should be warned by an appointed person acting as an "authorized occupier" of the premises.
- Upon discovering a trespasser, the principal may wish to conspicuously take the person's photograph in order to encourage the trespasser to stop any criminal or violent conduct or to cause the trespasser to leave the premises. At a later date, the photograph may also provide useful evidence of the person's identity and presence in the school.
- If a school official becomes aware of a person who has entered the premises where entry is prohibited, or is engaging in prohibited activity or fails to leave the premises immediately after being directed to do so, the principal may:
    - if possible, confront the trespasser and verbally request that the trespasser leave and not return;
    - ask the trespasser to identify himself or herself and give the reason for his or her presence on school premises;
    - send the trespasser a written notice, by registered mail, with a copy of the letter sent to the proper board official, the board lawyer and the police; and
    - if unable to identify the person for the purpose of sending a letter, the principal should record the incident and that the trespasser received a verbal warning.
- Once a trespasser has been warned, if the school official becomes aware of the return of that person, the official should contact the police immediately and then monitor the situation pending the arrival of the police.
- Where there is an element of danger with respect to any trespass situation, the police should be contacted immediately in accordance with established protocol.[60]

REPORTING CHILD ABUSE

In most Canadian jurisdictions there is legislation placing a general duty on people to report the abuse and neglect of children to the appropriate authorities. This general duty correspondingly applies in the school context. However, many child protection statutes also place a greater duty on educators to make reports where they gain information regarding abuse. In Ontario, legislative changes effective March 31, 2000,[61] have expanded the duty to report which was

---

[60] Roher, *op. cit.*, footnote 5, at p. 81.
[61] Contained in the *Child and Family Services Amendment Act (Child Welfare Reform), 1999*, S.O. 1999, c. 2.

previously reserved for persons performing professional or official duties with respect to children to all members of the public. Failure to make proper reports as required by the *Child and Family Services Act*[62] can lead to penalties which may include fines or imprisonment.[63]

Section 72 of the *Child and Family Services Act* sets out the duties of *all* members of the public to report to a children's aid society if they have reasonable grounds to suspect that one of a list of circumstances exist and those circumstances can be attributed to the care (or lack thereof) of the person responsible for the child, or the direct actions of that person. A "child" is generally defined in the legislation as a person actually or apparently under the age of 16. The obligation to report a "reasonable suspicion" formerly applied only to professionals with duties relating to children but has now been extended to all persons.[64]

The report must be made by the person who actually has the duty to make the report and that duty cannot be delegated. Also, a report must be made despite the confidential nature of some of the information which may be communicated, including information contained in the Ontario Student Record. The statute protects a person coming forward with a report of abuse by preventing a lawsuit against that person unless the person acted maliciously or without reasonable grounds for the suspicion.[65]

For all persons subject to the *Child and Family Services Act*, the requirement of reporting must be carried out "forthwith". The timely reporting of abuse serves to protect the child and, in some cases, may prevent the contamination of a child's evidence.

Where a principal receives allegations of abuse from a child, a record of relevant information should be created, including:

- where the information is received from an informant, the informant's name, relationship with the child and where the informant may be contacted;
- the name, address, age and sex of the child and any other information which might be helpful to the person receiving the report (*e.g.*, whether the child has special needs);
- details of communication, if any, with social services or police prior to reporting;
- how the matter came to the informant's attention, including dates and places;
- in objective and factual language, an accurate report of what the child stated or how the informant came to believe or suspect abuse (if possible the description should include the alleged offender(s) and their relationship to the child, when and where the incident(s) occurred and the names of any other children who may be involved);

---

[62] R.S.O. 1990, c. C.11.
[63] In Ontario, the failure to report is punishable by a fine of up to $1,000.
[64] T. Murphy, "Recent Amendments to the Child and Family Services Act", *Education Law Alert* (Summer, 2000) (Toronto: Borden Ladner Gervais LLP).
[65] *Child and Family Services Act*, s. 72(7); Brown and Zuker, *op. cit.*, footnote 48.

- a simple drawing showing the parts of the body allegedly touched;
- any preliminary action taken with respect to the child or alleged abuser, including any suspensions, parental contact or student interviews;
- the name of the agency to which the report of abuse was made and the name of the contact person as well as a follow-up to ensure that the agency took action; and
- a space for the informant's signature and date of making the report.[66]

In all cases, a trusted person should remain with the child until the police or society worker arrives at the school. Reference should also be made to board protocols which may be in place. Procedures may vary according to the age of the alleged victim and perpetrator. Where the alleged victim is not a "child" within the meaning of the legislation, school authorities may still wish to respond.

Section 37 of the *Child and Family Services Act* sets out possible grounds for finding that a child is in need of protection, permitting intervention to take place. Though the legislation should be consulted, prior to the amendments of March 31, 2000, three of these grounds required a finding of a "substantial" risk of harm to the child. This was thought to create too high a threshold. Accordingly, these grounds now require the mere risk that the child is likely to suffer the itemized harm to support a finding that the child is in need of protection. Delayed development has been added to the list of means demonstrating emotional harm and the threshold of "severe" anxiety, depression, withdrawal or self-destructive or aggressive behaviour has been lowered to "serious" incidences of that nature. Also, a "pattern of neglect" has been added as one of the ways in which the conduct of a child's parent or guardian can be connected to the physical harm, emotional harm, or risk thereof, suffered by the child, in the context of determining whether the child is in need of protection.[67]

ONTARIO SAFE SCHOOLS ACT, 2000

As discussed earlier, the Ontario provincial government has responded to public concerns regarding safety in schools by enacting the *Safe Schools Act, 2000*, which amends the *Education Act* and other statutes. These amendments contain two major initiatives to promote safety in schools. The first is to establish mandatory consequences for seriously unacceptable conduct on school premises. The second is to take steps towards implementing province-wide standards for conduct in Ontario schools.

While the vast majority of schools and school boards already have codes of conduct for student behaviour in place, the Ontario government felt that a consistent code of conduct across the province was required. In her statement to

---

[66] "The Duty to Report Child Abuse", *Education Law Reporter* (Calgary: Edulaw, May, 1998); Toronto District School Board, "Administrative Procedures – Policy on Abuse and Neglect of Students" (October 6, 1999).

[67] Murphy, *op. cit.*, footnote 64.

the Ontario Legislature to introduce the *Safe Schools Act, 2000*, Education Minister Janet Ecker noted that:

> Many school boards have varying codes and rules for safety. But this legislation will ensure that there are clear, province-wide standards, especially for the most serious infractions, like bringing weapons to school.[68]

The legislation permits the Minister of Education to establish a code of conduct governing the behaviour of all person in schools. The purposes of the code of conduct are as follows:

1. To ensure that all members of the school community, especially people in positions of authority, are treated with respect and dignity.
2. To promote responsible citizenship by encouraging appropriate participation in the civic life of the school community.
3. To maintain an environment where conflict and difference can be addressed in a manner characterized by respect and civility.
4. To encourage the use of non-violent means to resolve conflict.
5. To promote the safety of people in the schools.
6. To discourage the use of alcohol and illegal drugs.[69]

The *Ontario Schools Code of Conduct*[70] (the "Code") was released by the Ministry of Education on April, 26, 2000. It is required that the Code be communicated to all members of school communities in Ontario. Specifically, the *Education Act* provides:

> 301(3) Every board *shall* take such steps as the Minister directs to bring the code of conduct to the attention of pupils, parents and guardians of pupils and others who may be present in schools under the jurisdiction of the board.

(Emphasis added.) The Code is not a regulation under the *Education Act*. Rather, it is a policy of the Minister.[71] In addition to the Code, the *Education Act* provides that the Minister of Education may establish additional policies and guidelines regarding safe schools to be implemented at the board level.

School boards are also empowered to establish certain policies and guidelines to promote school safety. These policies and guidelines will allow school boards to establish their own procedures for certain infractions. In most cases, this will involve revisions, if necessary, to existing codes of conduct in order to comply with the province-wide standards. Specifically, section 302 of the *Education Act* provides:

> 302(1) Every board shall establish policies and guidelines with respect to the conduct of persons in schools within the board's jurisdiction and the policies and guidelines must address such matters and include such requirements as the Minister may specify.

---

[68] "Statement by the Honourable Janet Ecker: Introduction of the proposed *Safe Schools Act, 2000*", News Release (Ministry of Education, May 31, 2000).

[69] *Education Act*, s. 301(1).

[70] Ontario Ministry of Education, *Ontario Schools Code of Conduct* (Toronto: Queen's Printer, 2000).

[71] *Education Act,* s. 301(4).

(3) If required to do so by the Minister, a board shall establish policies and guidelines to promote the safety of pupils, and the policies and guidelines must be consistent with those established by the Minister under section 301 and must address such matters and include such requirements as the Minister may specify.

(4) A board may establish policies and guidelines governing access to school premises, and the policies and guidelines must be consistent with the regulations made under section 305 and must address such matters and include such requirements as the Minister may specify.

In recognition of the need to involve the school community in violence prevention, the legislation provides that, when establishing policies and guidelines under this section, a school board shall consider the views of school councils with respect to the contents of the policies and guidelines. In addition, the school board is required to, in periodically reviewing its policies and guidelines, solicit the views of pupils, teachers, staff, volunteers working in the schools, parents and guardians, school councils and the public.[72]

School principals can expect to participate in this process. As leaders of the school community, and through their involvement with the school council, the principal is likely to play a consultative and active role in preparing the school's policies and guidelines.

The amendments under the *Safe Schools Act, 2000* also permit the board, or the Ministry of Education, to direct the principal of a school to establish a "local code of conduct" for an individual school. Such a code of conduct will deal with school-specific requirements. Any such policy designed and implemented by a principal must comply with the province-wide Code. Section 303 of the *Education Act* provides:

> 303(1) A board may direct the principal of a school to establish a local code of conduct governing the behaviour of all persons in the school, and the local code of conduct must be consistent with the provincial code established under subsection 301(1) and must address such matters and include such requirements as the board may specify.
>
> (2) A board shall direct a principal to establish a local code of conduct if the board is required to do so by the Minister, and the local code must address such matters and include such requirements as the Minister may specify.
>
> (3) When establishing or reviewing a local code of conduct, the principal shall consider the views of the school council with respect to its contents.

Ontario Schools Code of Conduct

In addition to the mandatory discipline provisions of the *Safe Schools Act, 2000*, the Code represents the Ontario government's specific response to what it perceives as an increase in serious incidents of violence in its schools. The Code sets out provincial standards of behaviour and specifies mandatory consequences for student actions which do not comply with these standards. The Code sets out

---

[72] *Education Act*, s. 302(9) and (10).

the roles and responsibilities of members of the school community, including school boards, principals, teachers, school staff, students, parents, police and community members. The Ministry of Education envisions that the principal will have the following role:

> *Principals*, under the direction of their school board, take a leadership role in the daily operation of a school. They provide this leadership by:
> - demonstrating care and commitment to academic excellence and a safe teaching and learning environment;
> - holding everyone, under their authority, accountable for their behaviour and actions;
> - communicating regularly and meaningfully with all members of their school community.[73]

Through the Code, as well as other provisions set out in the *Safe Schools Act, 2000*, the Ministry of Education clearly expects the principal to take a leadership role in developing, communicating and enforcing standards of behaviour in the school community. The principal has been provided with new powers to enforce statutorily required rules of behaviour. The challenge for the principal will be to effectively take provincial standards and implement them at the school level, accounting for the unique characteristics of the school, in a fair and equitable manner.

CREATING A PROBLEM-SOLVING SCHOOL CULTURE

Whether it is in the context of safe schools, negligence and liability issues, rights of non-custodial parents, dealing with problem individuals, managing medication or responding to changing government policy, the role of the principal has become increasingly complex. Principals are balancing competing sets of demands. School boundaries have become more and more transparent.

In addition, the lives of educators are running faster than ever before. If one quality appears to define our modern age, it is "acceleration". In the context of education, there are a plethora of access points. Principals, in their daily work, are bombarded with e-mail, faxes and telephone calls from a range of sources, including students, parents, senior school board personnel and trustees. In a school setting, educators are being overwhelmed by demands regarding new curriculum, new safe schools policies, new instructional time provisions and new Ministry requirements.

In a recent book, entitled *Faster: The Acceleration of Just about Everything*,[74] James Gleick explores the human condition at the turn of the millennium. He examines time-related facets of life in what he calls the "epoch of the nanosecond" and observes that "a compression of time" characterizes life in this new century.

---

[73] *Ontario Schools Code of Conduct, op. cit.*, footnote 70.
[74] J. Gleick, *Faster: The Acceleration of Just about Everything* (New York: Pantheon Books, 1999).

He notes that we have become a quick-reflexed, multi-tasking, channel-flipping, fast-forward species.

And what is the effect of all of this rapid technological change? Gleick asserts that, as a society, we get dizzy. He says that knowledge is changing so fast that we need to "re-skill" ourselves constantly in order to keep a job. Communication theorist Marshall McLuhan said that, in the information age, individuals will not earn a living, but in fact "learn a living". In this regard, it is more important than ever that educators re-skill themselves to keep up in this changing environment.

Principals must endeavour to stay informed and constantly upgrade their knowledge regarding policies, procedures and the law. They should be in contact with their colleagues with respect to their school practices, attend in-service programs on new and emerging education law issues and constantly peruse articles, newsletters and texts pertaining to the *Education Act*, Ministry of Education memoranda, and school board policies, regulations and procedures.[75] In creating a culture of improvement in their respective schools, principals should promote staff development, leading to student achievement, and recognize and foster leadership among staff.

In this age characterized by "acceleration", principals may be involved, from time to time, in "firefighting". This involves rushing from task to task, not completing one before another interrupts them. At best, this may lead to situations where minor problems are ignored. At worst, chronic firefighting can consume a school's resources. Efficiency will suffer. Managing becomes a constant juggling act of deciding where to allocate overworked people and which crisis to ignore for the moment.[76]

Roger Bohn, a business professor at the University of California, states that firefighting is one of the most serious problems facing many managers of complex, change-driven organizations.[77] He says that firefighting is characterized as a collection of symptoms, including situations where solutions may be incomplete, problems can recur and cascade and ongoing problem-solving efforts are repeatedly interrupted.

Professor Bohn advises that, to avoid firefighting, organizations should develop a strong problem-solving culture. He says that, in tackling a problem, an organization should understand its root cause and find valid solutions. He notes that, in today's highly dynamic environment, the key tasks for people in charge are innovating, improving and dealing with the unexpected.[78]

In creating a problem-solving school culture, principals should consider the following:

---

[75] "The Catholic School Principal in the Dufferin-Peel Roman Catholic Separate School Board" (Mississauga: Dufferin-Peel Roman Catholic Separate School Board, 1999), at p. 24.
[76] R. Bohn, "Stop Fighting Fires", *Harvard Business Review* (July/August, 2000), p. 83.
[77] *Ibid.*, at p. 84.
[78] *Ibid.*, at p. 91.

- *Enthusiasm for change* – Educators need to have passion about excellence in education and instructional leadership. Tom Peters, a management expert, states that to be innovative an organization requires passion.[79] He says that the greatest innovation is to provide great service to one's customers. In a school context, principals should encourage staff to think from the perspective of students and parents. A school should focus on being responsive to its community. The principal should attempt to build strong bonds and connections with school staff, students and parents. They should share ideas and inspiration. People who trust one another will be more open to innovation and more accepting of new ideas.
- *Creating front porches* – Effective leaders are able to get things done on the "front porch" in places which enable them to reflect upon what they are doing. Robert Lengel, Associate Dean of the College of Business at the University at San Antonio, recommends that leaders "create front porches – places where people can slow down and reflect on what's happening around them".[80] He suggests that conversations with people at different levels and in different departments are a tool which will allow people to self-organize.[81] In a school setting, collaboration with staff, students and parents will assist in building a sense of belonging. By spending time listening to people's ideas, a principal will build trust, respect and commitment.[82] By letting school staff and students have a say in decisions which affect their goals and how they do their work, a principal will increase flexibility and responsibility. And by listening to their concerns, a principal may learn what to do to keep morale high.
- *Obsession with learning* – In an article for *Atlantic Monthly*, author Charles Trueheart recently commented on the rise of community service in the United States. He said: "What brings people to their gift of service is a desire to do something ... that matters."[83] Learning is at the core of the education enterprise. It is critical to the growth, development and future of our community. In a school context, staff should understand that what they do matters. The principal should attempt to maximize commitment to the school's goals and strategy. The principal can motivate people by making clear to them how their work fits into the larger vision of the organization.[84] In giving performance feedback, one criterion may be whether or not the performance furthers the vision. In addition, a principal may set out a vision of the objectives of the school, but give staff leeway to devise their own means.[85] In this regard, school staff may be given freedom to innovate, experiment and take calculated risks.

---

[79] T. Peters, *The Circle of Innovation* (New York: Vintage Books, 1999), at p. 479.
[80] R. Balu, "Leaders, Learners and Searchers", *Fast Company* (April, 2000), p. 50.
[81] *Ibid.*, at p. 52.
[82] D. Goleman, "Leadership that Gets Results", *Harvard Business Review* (March/April, 2000), p. 87.
[83] C. Trueheart, "Welcome to the Next Church", *Altantic Monthly* (August, 1996), p. 56.
[84] Goleman, *op. cit.*, footnote 82, at p. 83.
[85] *Ibid.*, at p. 84.

- *Building trust* – The challenge of leadership is often to provide the "glue" to bring together the independent units in an organization where there is a range of different interests and personalities.[86] One element which has been identified as powerful enough to overcome these diverse forces is trust. James O'Toole, author of the book *Leading Change*,[87] attempted to identify the factors which create trust in a leader. He said: "What creates trust, in the end, is the leader's manifest respect for the followers."[88] In a school, a principal should consider the importance of appreciation and respect for members of the school community. It is suggested that positive feedback provides a sense of recognition and reward for work well done. Such feedback has a special potency in the workplace because it is often rare. Outside of an annual review, most people receive no feedback on their day-to-day efforts – or only negative feedback.[89] Recognition of people's efforts may build a sense of belonging and commitment, and perhaps enhance trust within the school community.
- *Prioritizing tasks* – Business professors advise that bringing about deep-seated cultural change in a large organization is an enormous long-term challenge. They suggest that the better approach is to break the problem up into smaller, more manageable pieces, rather than tackle it all at once. Leaders can experiment with these smaller efforts to unearth resources, allies and potential sources of resistance.[90] In a school context, in a job which changes every day, principals should prioritize tasks. Focus on two or three objectives and allocate resources to accomplish them. Seeking "small wins" can be an important strategy in reducing large problems to ones which are easier to manage. A string of small wins is usually more palatable to an organization than is an attempt at wholesale change.[91]
- *Developing people* – Researchers have indicated that learning in most organizations is not attributable to formal structures or programs. They indicate that most learning occurs through word of mouth in communities of practice, most often in the workplace.[92] Writer Alan Webber has observed that it "all depends on the quality of the conversations".[93] For example, an organization may have the perfect e-mail system but it may not result in information being shared among employees. In a school setting, principals should focus on the quality of their conversations, particularly in preparing professional development plans for their staff. They should assist employees in identifying

---

[86] Peters, *op. cit.*, footnote 79, at p. 142.
[87] J. O'Toole, *Leading Change: Overcoming the Ideology of Comfort and the Tyranny of Custom* (San Francisco: Jossey-Bass Publishers, 1995), at p. xiii.
[88] *Ibid.*, at p. 56.
[89] Goleman, *op. cit.*, footnote 82, at p. 84.
[90] D. Meyerson, "Practical Radicals", *Fast Company* (September, 2000), p. 162.
[91] *Ibid.*, at p. 168.
[92] E. Wenger, "Communities of Practice: Where Learning Happens", *Benchmark* (Fall, 1991), p. 8.
[93] A.M. Webber, "What's so New About the New Economy", *Harvard Business Review* (January/February, 1993), p. 24.

their strengths and weaknesses and tie them to their personal and career aspirations.[94] They should encourage staff to establish long-term goals and help them conceptualize a plan for attaining these goals. Efforts should be made to assist employees in understanding their role and responsibilities and to give them instruction and feedback. In this regard, the principal will help an employee improve performance and develop long-term strengths.

School principals have a fundamental role in the education enterprise. They are a critical link between senior school board personnel, teachers, students and parents. They are on the front line in dealing with and responding to complaints and concerns from members of the school community. Principals are both leaders and managers in their respective schools. It should be recognized that, among other things, an understanding of education law is essential to the effective management and operation of their schools.

Every action taken by a school board, school administrator, principal or teacher is founded upon a law which either permits those actions or limits them in some way. As we have discussed, school principals have unique common law and statutory powers and responsibilities in relation to their staff and students. Of great relevance in their daily work are issues such as negligence and liability, student records, harassment, rights of non-custodial parents, medication, student discipline and violence. An awareness of education law and an ability to recognize that an issue has legal aspects is critical in properly responding to events and preventing problems from arising in the future.

Strong leadership is key to generating positive change in the education community. In this regard, we encourage school boards to develop thorough training and in-service programs for new principals and vice-principals. In addition, we suggest that boards support peer coaching and mentoring and focus on the development of leadership strategies and skills.

Overall, it is essential to recognize and foster leadership among principals and vice-principals. They set the tone, provide the direction and articulate the vision in their respective schools. In developing a collaborative school culture, creating school goals and objectives, promoting staff morale, listening to members of the school community and encouraging staff development and professional growth, a principal and vice-principal can play a critical role in creating and shaping a positive, productive and safe school environment.

---

[94] Goleman, *op. cit.*, footnote 82, at p. 87.

Index

Allergies, 153-4, 166-70
    food, 167-9
    insect bites, 169
Attendance, 143-51
Bill 74, 3, 8-11
    class size and, 9
    co-instructional activities and, 9-10
    investigation of school boards and, 10-11
    secondary school teaching time and, 8-9
Bill 81, 3-4, 11-13, 173
    access to school premises, 118
    expulsions and, 182-3
    suspensions and, 174-5
    trespassers and, 210
Bill 104, 3-5
Bill 160, 3-8, 13-15
    class size and, 6
    collective bargaining and, 6-8
    school councils and, 6
    school funding and, 5-6
    teachers and, 6-8
Canadian Charter of Rights and Freedoms
    disclosure of records and criminal proceedings, 93
    freedom of association and Bill 160, 7-8
    search and seizure, 204-207
Careful or Prudent Parent. *See* Negligence, standard of care
Change of Name Act
    student names, 139-40
Child Abuse
    reporting, 212-14
Child and Family Services Act
    duty to report abuse, 213-14

Children's Law Reform Act
    access to Ontario Student Record, 79-80
    rights of access parent, 132
Class Size, 9
Code of Conduct. *See* Ontario Schools Code of Conduct
Collective Bargaining
    exclusion of principals from, 7-8
Confidentiality
    communications in school, 90-95
    court proceedings and, 91-3
        criminal proceedings, 92-3
    Ontario Student Record, 79, 82
    professional ethics and, 94
Court Proceedings
    attendance in court, 85-6
    conflict with school policies, 203-204
    disclosure of Ontario Student Record for, 82-4
        civil proceedings, 83
        criminal proceedings, 83-4
        criminal proceedings and confidentiality, 92-3
    preparation of witnesses, 84-5
    release of confidential information, 91-3
Criminal Code
    criminal harassment, 127-30
    disclosure of confidential records and, 92-3
    removal of trespassers, 211
    statistics on violent offences, 193
Custody and Access. *See* Parents, rights of non-custodial parents
Defamation
    of educators, 121-7
Defences
    contributory negligence, 51-2
    limitation periods, 49-51
    statutory limitation, 51
    voluntary assumption of risk, 52, 70
Diabetes, 164-6
Discipline
    Bill 81 and, 12-13
    principal's duty to maintain, 16, 203
Disease. *See* Health Protection and Promotion Act
Divorce Act
    access to Ontario Student Record, 80
    rights of access parent, 132, 134

Drugs
    club drugs, 200-201
    search for, 204-206
    suspension for possession of, 174
Duty of Care. *See* Negligence
Education Accountability Act, 2000. *See* Bill 74
Education Act
    Nova Scotia —
        health of students, 155
    Ontario —
        attendance, 144-51
        codes of conduct, 215-16
        discretionary suspensions, 176
        duties of principal, 16-18
            controlling admission to school or classroom, 118
            health and comfort of pupils, 155
            keep school safe and in good repair, 68-9
            mandatory expulsions, 182
            mandatory suspensions, 175
            teacher evaluation, 99-100
        duties of teachers, 20-21, 23-5
        duty of care and, 42-3
        expulsions —
            appeal of, 184-5
            discretionary, 184
            full, 184
            hearing, 183
            limited, 183-4
            mandatory, 182
            programs for expelled students, 187
        maintenance of student records, 77
        Ontario Student Record, 79-80
            access to, 79-80
            correction of, 80-81
            recording violent incidents, 179
            use in legal proceedings, 82-3
        parental harassment and, 114
        recent amendments to, 3-15
        school councils and, 27, 29-30
        suspensions —
            appeal of, 180
            mandatory, 175
            notice of, 177
            programs for suspended students, 187
            review of, 180

Education Act — *continued*
    Ontario — *continued*
        suspensions — *continued*
            vice-principal, by, 178
        trespassers, 209-210
    Saskatchewan —
        limitation of liability, 51
Education Improvement Commission, 5
Education Quality and Accountability Office, 5
Education Quality Improvement Act, 1997. *See* Bill 160
Educational Malpractice, 71-3
Emergencies
    allergy-based, 169-70
    standard of care, 160-62
Expulsions
    appeal of, 184-5
    discretionary, 184
    full, 184
    hearing, 183
    inquiry, 182-3
    limited, 183-4
    mandatory, 182-3
    procedure, 189-91
    programs for expelled students, 187
Fewer School Boards Act, 1997. *See* Bill 104
Field Trips, 64-5
    medication and, 161-2
    permission forms and, 65-8
Foreseeability
    of injury, 46-7
Freedom of Information. *See* Municipal Freedom of Information and Protection of Privacy Act
Gangs
    female gangs, 197
    identification, 196-8
    prevention, 198
    warning signs, 199
Health Protection and Promotion Act
    communicable diseases and admission to schools, 19
    reporting communicable diseases, 73-4
Hours of Instruction, 24-5
Human Rights Code, 36-7
    teacher evaluation and, 108
Incident Reports
    suspension of student, 176-7

Index 227

Labour Relations Act, 1995
    collective bargaining and principals, 7
    Ontario Labour Relations Board, 31-2
Leadership
    principals and, 2-3, 217-21
Liability
(*See also* Negligence)
    educational malpractice, 71-3
    managing medication, 159-62
    occupiers' liability, 69-71
    off school property, 61-2
    outside school hours, 58-61
    prevention, 74-5
    school excursions, 64-5
Limitations Act, 50
Medication
    assignment to administer, 162-4
    duty of care, 154-5
    factors to consider, 157-9
    policy and procedure, 155-7
    risks in managing, 159-60
Minister of Education, 10, 27, 187, 215
Municipal Freedom of Information and Protection of Privacy Act
    access to school records, 87-8
    job interviews and, 88-9
    personal information and, 88-9
Negligence
    confidentiality and, 95
    contributory negligence, 51-2
    damages, 47-8
    definition of, 41
    duty of care, 41-4
        common law duty of care, 43-4
        in emergencies, 160-62
        off school property, 61-2
        outside school hours, 59
        school excursions, 65
        statutory duty of care, 42-3
    foreseeability, 46-7
    physical education and sports, 56-7
    school excursions, 64-5
    standard of care, 44-6
        breach of, 46
        in emergencies, 160-62

Negligence — *continued*
    supervision of students, 52-61
    transportation of students, 62-4
Negligence Act
    contributory negligence, 51
Nuisance
    parental harassment and, 126-7
Occupiers' Liability Act
    liability under, 69-72
Ontario College of Teachers Act, 1996, 22-3, 72
Ontario Schools Code of Conduct
    Bill 81, 4, 11-12
    establishment of policies, 215-16
    suspension and, 173-4
    violence and, 216-17
Ontario Student Record
    confidentiality of, 79, 82
    contents of, 78-9
    correction of, 81-2
    removal of information from, 81-2
    transfer of, 80-81
    use in legal proceedings, 82-4
    violent incidents and, 179-80
Ontario Teachers' Federation, 21
Parental Harassment, 114
    appropriate response, 115-18
    criminal harassment, 126-9
    defamation, 123-4
    nuisance, 126
    parent protocol, 129-30
    restraining order, 119-20
Parents
    child's attendance, duty to ensure, 145
        prosecution of parent, 147-8
    complaints regarding teacher performance, 104-105
    harassment. *See* Parental Harassment
    medical information from, 155-6
    permission forms, 65-8
    rights of non-custodial parents, 134-8
    suspension of student and, 178
Peanut Allergies, 168-9
Personal Information
    criminal proceedings and, 93
    Municipal Freedom of Information and Protection of Privacy Act, 88-9

Physical Education
    liability and. *See* Negligence
Police
    investigations on school premises, 200-201
    police/school protocol, 200-201
Policies
    attendance, 146-7
    liability prevention, 74-5
    managing diabetes, 162-4
    managing medication, 156-7
    parent protocol, 129-30
    permission forms, 66-7
    police/school protocol, 200-201
    response to parental harassment, 115-18
    school excursions, 65
    search and seizure, 208
    severe allergic reaction, 170
    supervision of schoolyard, 58
    supervision of students, 54
    suspension and expulsion, 189-91
    teacher evaluation, 103-12
    violence-free schools policy, 179-80
Prevention
    attendance problems, 150-51
    severe allergic reactions, 167-9
    suspension and expulsion, 187-8
    trespassers, 211-12
Principals
    changing role of, 13-15
    duties of —
        attendance, 145-6
        class content, 72
        discipline, 203
        expulsion of students, 182
        general, 15-19
        keep school safe and in good repair, 68-71
        maintenance of student record, 77
        medication, 155
        reporting child abuse, 213-14
        reporting communicable diseases, 73-4
        supervision, 52-64
        suspension of students, 175
        teacher evaluation, 99-103
    investigation of serious incidents, 203
    leadership and, 2-3, 217-21

Principals — *continued*
    managing medication, 157-9, 162-4
    Ontario Student Record and, 82
    parental harassment and, 114-18
    professional associations, 15
    school councils and, 29-30
    school relationships and, 140-41
    unfair labour practices and, 31-2
Procedural Fairness
    appeal of suspension, 181
    suspensions and expulsions, 185-7
Provincial Offences Act
    prosecution for non-attendance, 147-9
    trespassers, 210
Public Authorities Protection Act
    limitation periods, 49-51
Records. *See* Ontario Student Record; Student Records
Restraining Order, 120-21
Safe Schools
(*See also* Violence)
    generally, 193-4
    identification of threats to, 195-6
    recent legislation, 3-4, 214-16
Safe Schools Act, 2000, 3-4, 11-13, 187, 214-16
(*See also* Bill 81)
    suspension and expulsion procedure under, 189-91
School Act
    Alberta —
        health of students, 155
    Prince Edward Island —
        health of students, 155
School Attendance Counsellor, 146
    prosecution for non-attendance, 147-9
School Boards
    amalgamation of, 4
    expulsion hearing, 183
    investigation of affairs of, 10-11
    liability of, 48-9
        occupiers' liability, 69-72
        transportation of students, 62-4
        use of board property, 60-61
School Councils
    establishment of, 27-8
    members of, 28
    parental harassment and, 115

School Councils — *continued*
    role of, 6, 28-9
    role of principal and, 28-9
School Day, 23
School Hours
    liability outside of, 58-61
School Trustees
    reduction in number of, 5
    role of, 5
School Year, 23
Search and Seizure, 204-209
    Canadian Charter of Rights and Freedoms and, 204-207
    locker search, 208
    personal search, 205-208
        factors to consider, 207-208
    random searches, 209
Sports
    liability and. *See* Negligence
Statutory Powers Procedure Act
    appeal of suspension, 180-81
    procedural fairness, 185-6
Student Names, 138-40
Student Records
(*See also* Ontario Student Record)
    access to, 87-8
    court proceedings and, 91-3
Supervision. *See* Principals, duties of
Suspensions
    Bill 81 and, 12-13, 174-5
    discretionary, 176
    mandatory, 175
    procedure, 177-8, 189-91
    programs for suspended students, 187
    purposes of, 181-2
    vice-principal, by, 178
Task Force on Youth Violent Crime, 194-6
Teachers
    administering medication, 162-4
    defamation by, 125-6
    duties of, 20-27
        implied, 162-4
        reporting child abuse, 213-14
        suspension of students, 175-6
        voluntary and required duties of, 25-7
    evaluation of, 97-112

Teachers — *continued*
    right to strike and, 33-6
    secondary school teaching time, 8-9
    standards of practice, 22-3
    transport of students, 64
Teaching Profession Act
    Alberta —
        confidentiality and, 94
    Ontario —
        confidentiality and, 94
        duties of teachers, 21-2
Toronto District School Board
    police/school protocol, 200-201
    publication on youth gangs, 197-9
Tort. *See* Negligence
Transportation of Students, 62-4
Trespass to Property Act
    dealing with a problem parent, 114, 118-19
    trespassers on school property, 210-11
Trespassers, 209-212
    preventing, 211-12
Vicarious Liability. *See* School Boards, liability of
Vice-principal
    delegation of duties to, 18
    investigation of incident and suspensions by, 178
Violence
(*See also* Child Abuse; Gangs)
    definition of, 194-5
    identification of potentially violent students, 196
    Ontario Schools Code of Conduct and, 216-17
    recording violent incidents, 179-80
    statistics, 193, 195-7
Violence-Free Schools Policy, 179-80
Young Offenders Act, 203
Youth Gangs. *See* Gangs